ACTIVIST FEMINIST GEOGRAPHIES

Edited by
Kate Boyer, LaToya E. Eaves, and Jennifer Fluri

First published in Great Britain in 2025 by

Bristol University Press
University of Bristol
1-9 Old Park Hill
Bristol
BS2 8BB
UK
t: +44 (0)117 374 6645
e: bup-info@bristol.ac.uk

Details of international sales and distribution partners are available at bristoluniversitypress.co.uk

© Bristol University Press 2025

British Library Cataloguing in Publication Data
A catalogue record for this book is available from the British Library

ISBN 978-1-5292-2509-9 hardcover
ISBN 978-1-5292-2510-5 paperback
ISBN 978-1-5292-2511-2 ePub
ISBN 978-1-5292-2512-9 ePdf

The right of Kate Boyer, LaToya E. Eaves, and Jennifer Fluri to be identified as editors of this work has been asserted by them in accordance with the Copyright, Designs and Patents Act 1988.

All rights reserved: no part of this publication may be reproduced, stored in a retrieval system, or transmitted in any form or by any means, electronic, mechanical, photocopying, recording, or otherwise without the prior permission of Bristol University Press.

Every reasonable effort has been made to obtain permission to reproduce copyrighted material. If, however, anyone knows of an oversight, please contact the publisher.

The statements and opinions contained within this publication are solely those of the editors and contributors and not of the University of Bristol or Bristol University Press. The University of Bristol and Bristol University Press disclaim responsibility for any injury to persons or property resulting from any material published in this publication.

Bristol University Press works to counter discrimination on grounds of gender, race, disability, age and sexuality.

Cover design: Hayes Design and Advertising
Front cover image: stocksy/ Alicia Bock

Contents

List of Figures		v
Notes on Contributors		vi
Acknowledgements		xi
Introduction		1
Kate Boyer, LaToya E. Eaves, and Jennifer Fluri		
1	Evacuation Lost: Activism and Scholarship in a Time of Geopolitical Crisis	15
	Jennifer Fluri	
2	Women Weaving Critical Geographies	31
	GeoBrujas-Comunidad de Geógrafas: Frida Itzel Rivera Juárez, Gabriela Mariana Fenner-Sánchez, Karla Helena Guzmán Velázquez, Valeria Ysunza, Tlazol Tlemoyotl, Esperanza González Hernández, and Karina Flores Cruz	
3	Critical Geography Collective of Ecuador as Feminist Geography Collective Praxis	55
	Sofia Zaragocín, Soledad Álvarez Velasco, Guglielmina Falanga, Amanda Yépez, and Gabriela Ruales	
4	Legacies of Black Feminist Activism in the US South	73
	LaToya E. Eaves	
5	LGBT+ Activism and Morality Politics in Central and Eastern Europe: Understanding the Dynamic Equilibrium in Czechia from a Broader Transnational Perspective	94
	Michal Pitoňák	
6	Sexual Harassment and Claiming the Right to Everyday Life	120
	Kate Boyer	
7	Giving Birth in a 'Hostile Environment'	145
	Maria Fannin	

8   Respectful Relationalities: Researching with Those Who   161
     Contest or Have Concerns about Changes in Sexual and
     Gender Legislation and Cultures
     Kath Browne and Catherine Nash

Conclusion   178
Kate Boyer, LaToya E. Eaves, and Jennifer Fluri

Index   184

List of Figures

4.1	Billboard facing Church Street, Murfreesboro, Tennessee	84
4.2	Screenshot from Healthy and Free Tennessee's #SMAy campaign (2022)	86
4.3	Excerpt from the SMA Toolkit for The People's First 100 Days (2021)	88
5.1	Share of population that reported knowing someone who is LGBTQ+	115

Notes on Contributors

Editors

Kate Boyer is Reader in Human Geography in the School of Geography and Planning at Cardiff University in the UK. She has been researching and publishing in feminist geography since receiving her PhD from McGill University in 2000. Over this time she has explored activist feminist geographies in the context of motherhood, breastfeeding outside the home, cultural activism in the city, and efforts to combat sexual harassment.

LaToya E. Eaves is a North Carolina native. Her Southern upbringing informs her research, which centres questions of power and place, asking where, how, and why social and political processes impact communities and individuals unequally and to understand how geographic tools might be employed as strategies for understanding inequalities better. Her work is situated in Black geographies, queer geographies, feminist geography, Black feminisms, and Southern studies. Eaves is a faculty member in the Department of Geography and Sustainability at the University of Tennessee.

Jennifer Fluri is Professor and Chair of the Department of Geography at the University of Colorado-Boulder. She is a feminist political geographer whose work focuses on gender, geopolitics, international aid and development, in Afghanistan. Her current project examines the experiences of Afghans evacuated from Afghanistan, and the status of women's leadership in the diaspora and under the Taliban regime in Afghanistan. In Colorado, she co-directs the CU-Boulder Affordable Housing Research Initiative (www.colorado.edu/bahri), a community-based service-research project that provides information for individuals and organizations seeking, living in, or caring about affordable housing.

Contributors

Soledad Álvarez Velasco is a social anthropologist and human geographer whose research analyses the interrelationship between mobility, control, and spatial transformations across the Americas. She investigates the intersection between undocumented global south-north and global south-south transit migration, border regimes, the formation of migratory corridors across the Americas and the migrant struggle across these transnational spaces, particularly that of migrant women and migrant children. She works as an Assistant Professor of the Departments of Anthropology and Latin American and Latino Studies at the University of Illinois, Chicago and she is member of the Colectivo de Geografía Crítica del Ecuador.

Kath Browne is Professor of Geography at University College Dublin. She currently leads the Beyond Opposition research, an European Research Council consolidator project that seeks to investigate the experiences of people who are concerned about socio-legal changes in sexualities and genders in the 21st century and explore new ways of engaging difference, differently. Her research has focused on social justice and inequalities, specifically around gender and sexualities. She has worked with those marginalized because of their sexual and gender identities, exploring how lives can be ameliorated in ways that take place seriously. She has also worked on those who are opposed to sexual and gender equalities, with Catherine Nash and Andrew Gorman-Murray, developing the concept of heteroactivism.

Guglielmina Falanga has a PhD in Social Sciences with a mention in Andean Studies (FLACSO Ecuador). Her work specializes on subjectivity, gender, bodies, and sexuality from critical theory and feminist geography. In addition, she is a cultural mediator and psychological first aid operator. She is a member of the Critical Geography Collective of Ecuador.

Maria Fannin is Professor of Human Geography and leads the Gender Research Group at the University of Bristol. Her research focuses on gendered notions of risk and responsibility in the healthcare sector and gender-sensitive approaches to economic agency. She is an experienced collaborator in multidisciplinary projects exploring women's health and is Trustee of the Feminist Archive South.

Gabriela Mariana Fenner-Sánchez, born in southern Mexico, is a geographer from the Universidad Autónoma Metropolitana – Iztapalapa and the Centro de Investigaciones de Geografía Ambiental, Universidad Nacional Autónoma de México. She has participated and coordinated research projects related to environmental issues, from a social point of view, as well as with the development of critical and participatory cartography methodologies. She also works with urban issues in small and medium cities, such as touristification. In addition, as part of GeoBrujas, she has addressed issues of gender and feminist cartography. Since 2013 she has participated in the research group ESTEPA (Espacio, Tecnología, y Participación), at the National University of Colombia. She is currently part of the Digital Historical Atlas of Chiapas project.

Karina Flores Cruz is a native of the Jñatrjo people in the state of Mexico, and a human geographer, who studied Environment and Water Resources at Universidad Autónoma Metropolitiana – Iztapalapa. She has worked in universities and NGOs carrying out technical assistance projects, and as a teacher in the fields of Agronomy Engineering and Environmental Engineering. She has collaborated with communities in Ciudad de México and throughout the nation of México, carrying out community work, workshops, and tours with an environmental education approach. She currently works in Tlachinollan, Centro de Derechos Humanos de la Montaña and is part of GeoBrujas.

Esperanza González Hernández, a native of Mexico City with coastal roots, is an activist, cartographer, agroecologist, environmentalist, and entrepreneur. She holds a degree in human geography from Universidad Autónoma Metropolitiana – Iztapalapa and a master's degree in regional rural development sciences from Universidad Autónoma de Chihuahua. She has accompanied land defence processes in Veracruz and has participated in activities related to strengthening the organizational capacities of collectives in Mexico City and peasant communities in the Oaxacan coast. For the last eight years she has been part of GeoBrujas. She currently works as Advisor in Sustainability and Territorial Processes in the municipality of Santiago Pinotepa Nacional.

Karla Helena Guzmán Velázquez is an activist geographer and feminist popular educator, and an independent researcher of territory-body and territory-earth. As an independent workshop leader, she shares courses on body mapping, and popular education through artistic expressions ranging from ecology to feminism, and counter-cartographies. She is a member of a support network for the Zapatista movement 'Mujeres y la Sexta', 'Las Grietas en el Muro', and cooperative spaces of alternative economies in Mexico City. She earned a master's degree in Agroecology, Territory and Food Sovereignty at the Centro de Estudios para el Desarrollo Rural. She also holds a diploma in Social Studies on Body and Emotions and studied in certificate courses for Humanist Dance Therapy, Transitional Justice,

Feminisms from Latin America, Peasant and Popular Feminisms, and Community Feminisms.

Catherine Nash is Adjunct Professor in the Department of Geography, Queen's University and Professor Emerita, Brock University, Ontario. Her research interests include sexualities/queer/feminist geographies, as well as mobilities and digital sexualities. She is currently working with Kath Browne examining transnational oppositions to LGBTQ rights in Canada, the UK and Ireland, and with Andrew Gorman-Murray on new mobilities, digital life and the transformations in LGBT and queer neighbourhoods in Sydney, Australia, and Toronto, Canada. She has published in a wide range of national and international journals, has authored numerous book chapters and is co-editor of several books and compendia.

Michal Pitoňák received his PhD in human geography at Charles University in Prague by defending the first dissertation focused on geographies of sexualities in Czechia. He widely employs queer and feminist thought to inform his transdisciplinary work about societal heteronormativity and its effects on LGBT+ peoples' lives. Dr Pitoňák works as a researcher at the National Institute of Mental Health, Klecany, Czechia, where he also pioneered research in local LGBTQ+ psychology. To promote the fields of geographies of sexualities and LGBTQ+ psychology, he founded an NGO, Queer Geography, through which he aims to advocate for the improvement of the societal standing of LGBT+ people.

Frida Itzel Rivera Juárez, is originally from the State of Hidalgo, Mexico. Activist woman, mountain lover, geographer graduated from UAM-Iztapalapa, she has collaborated in action-research projects focused on territorial management and patrimonial valuation of the landscape through the development of participatory methodologies for the critical mapping of the territory and social history. She is a member of GeoBrujas, of the La Sexta Hidalgo collective and the group Cícloris – Rodada por la vida y la libertad de las mujeres, as well as a member of the Colegiado de Investigación y Cultura Hidalguense. She is currently studying for a master's degree in geography at CIGA-UNAM.

Gabriela Ruales has a master's in sociology with a mention in gender and development from FLACSO Ecuador. She is currently a PhD student in regional rural development at the Chapingo Autonomous University in Mexico. She has organizational and research experience on feminisms, gender, feminist critical geography, and political ecology, mainly on issues of extractivism in the Ecuadorian Amazon. She has publications on feminist political ecology, gender-based violence, and feminist geography. She is member of the Critical Geography Collective of Ecuador, the Critical Views of the Territory from Feminism Collective and part of the Consejo Latinoamericano de Ciencias Sociales Working Group on Territorial Bodies and Feminisms.

Tlazol Tlemoyotl is an artist, a community educator, dancer, and folk herbalist. She was born in Oklahoma and has lived and learned in Mexico for the last 18 years. She is a weaver of worlds and is lucky to participate in amazing projects such as Bordando Abya Yala with Red Latinoamericana Feminista and the Feminarias and Fanzines with Mujeres y la Sexta. Anytime she is able to create and share with the GeoBrujas, she considers it as truly an honour to experience such magic. These collaborations are what give fire to her faith and inspire her to continue her path respecting the earth and all life.

Amanda Yépez is a geographical engineer, with a Master's degree in Rural Territorial Development (FLACSO Ecuador) She is a feminist activist linked to social, peasant, and indigenous organizations. Founder of the Collective of Critical Geography of Ecuador and contributes to territorial defence and monitoring processes, mainly in the Ecuadorian Amazon, through technical support and creating geographic analyses of inequalities in contexts extractives. She is currently working on monitoring activities mining in the province of Napo.

Valeria Ysunza is a geographer, traveller, social and corporal cartographer, teacher at Universidad Nacional Autónoma de México (UNAM), as well as a Mexican dancer and activist. She studied for a degree in geography at UNAM and obtained her master's in geography at Universidade Federal Fluminense (Brazil). She is currently finishing her PhD in social sciences at UAM-X (Mexico). She is a member of GeoBrujas, of the Instituto de Geografía para la Paz, as well as Hanin, a Mexican dance collective of Middle Eastern cultures, and of the organizing committee of the 9 Congreso Internacional de Geografías Críticas in October 2023, in Mexico City.

Sofia Zaragocín is a decolonial feminist geographer based at the Universidad San Francisco de Quito (USFQ), Ecuador. Her research focuses on developing Latin American decolonial feminist geography thought and praxis as well as connecting Latinx and Latin American geographies across the Americas. She is co-director of the Institute of Advanced Studies on Inequalities at USFQ and part of the Critical Geography Collective of Ecuador.

Acknowledgements

First, we want to heartily thank all the chapter authors for their time and intellectual contributions to this work. We also want thank all the research participants whose generous time and sharing contributed to the different chapters of this book, as well as our families and friends for their support. We would like to thank our feminist geography teachers, mentors, and friends as well as our many feminist fore-mothers and compatriots across different time periods and cultural contexts outside academia for their inspiration. In addition, LaToya Eaves would like to thank Nikki Luke for the collaborations and conversations on the state of feminist activism. She would also like to thank the students from the University of Tennessee Fall 2022 Feminist Geographies course for feedback on the volume. Finally, to Zenaida, for her love, patience, and support. Jennifer Fluri would like to thank Rachel Lehr for her amazing insights, collaborations, and commitment to our Afghan colleagues and friends, and Samantha, Jessica, Lily, and Jeffrey for their love and support. And Kate Boyer would like to thank her colleagues Cardiff for their intellectual support, as well as Michael and Jake for their love and support. Finally we would like to thank Emily Watt, Anna Richardson and the design and editing team at Bristol University Press for all their help, knowledge, patience and faith in this project, as well as our respective academic institutions for the time and resources needed to support our work.

Introduction

Kate Boyer, LaToya E. Eaves, and Jennifer Fluri

This book was borne in a period of history that has felt particularly alive with activism. From global protest movements around human rights; racial justice; women's rights; climate change/climate justice and more, the second decade of the new millennium looks to be a time marked by mass social activism in the struggles for rights, respect, and representation. Enabled in part by social media and responsive organizing, this activity has drawn in a wide range of citizens from young people to seniors, for some of whom this was their first taste of activism. At the same time this activity has shown the power of activism to produce concrete and significant social change, from Black Lives Matter to the rise of the Climate Justice movement, and the 2022 women-led revolution in Iran ignited in response to the murder of Jina Masha Amini in police custody after being arrested by the morality police or allegedly wearing her hijab improperly. As scholars and citizens, we have been inspired by the scale, power, and urgency of this work, and hope this edition might serve to further these goals.

Based on feminism's longstanding insistence on the need for praxis as well as theory, the purpose of this book is to explore what it means to *enact* feminist geography in this political moment. Feminist geography has seen a groundswell of scholarship in recent years engaging with questions of social justice activism and collaborative research with activists and activist movements. This work has ranged widely by topic and cultural context, engaging themes of abolitionism, reflexivity, anti-immigration policies, and the power of social media. *Activist Feminist Geographies* is a sampler of some of the most exciting work in this field, drawing this scholarship together in one place so that students and scholars draw out cross-cutting themes. It will be an agenda-setting work for the sub-discipline as well as a means of tracing feminist activism through cutting-edge research. It explores research in contemporary feminist geography on social justice and activism broadly conceived, across a range of research foci, methodological approaches, and theoretical frameworks.

Our aim is to not only to showcase the strength and vibrancy of activist-engaged scholarship taking place within contemporary feminist geography, but also to serve as a call to action: hopefully serving to inspire budding (as well as seasoned) academics to explore how their work might advance gender justice, including through collaborations between scholars and broader publics. It features high-calibre, original scholarship that engages different types of activisms across a range of cultural contexts, showing both the vibrancy of feminist geography and how this sub-discipline serves as a natural home for scholar activism within the discipline as a whole. It highlights the empirical and methodological range of this work as well as its conceptual sophistication. At the same time, it does not remain exclusively in the realm of high theory, but rather expresses the work of feminist geography in different spatial contexts; in, through, and alongside real-world struggles for social justice. Much of feminist academic research occurs through intensive and extensive engagements and collaborations with local communities. As such, this edition both sets out an agenda for furthering this type of collaborative work and shows how feminist geography remains a home for scholar activism within the larger discipline.

Thematically, this volume explores questions of intersectionality; the dynamic and culturally situated nature of activism; and the benefits (and challenges) of working across academic and non-academic spaces. After laying out the scholarship on which this book builds in this introduction, eight substantive chapters will explore feminist geographic engagements with activism in contemporary and historical contexts across seven cultural contexts (the US, Canada, Afghanistan, Latin America, Ireland, Eastern Europe, and the UK). Through these works, the book will engage questions of: Black feminist organizing in the American South; the opportunities and challenges of attempting feminist activism within and beyond government and academic institutions; the politics and potentials of creating dialogue with groups opposed to sexual and gender rights; feminist geography collectives in Latin America; LGBTQ activisms in Eastern Europe; and activism against both sexual harassment on the one hand and the withdraw of maternity services for immigrants in the UK on the other.

The work also explores cross-cutting themes of authorship and expertise; reflections on our own subject positions as researchers and educators, how we want to enact change through life experiences, and ideas about the politics and conceptions of what will make the world a better place. The collection of essays in this book seeks to continue conversations and start new ones in and beyond geography about the ways we do research and how to best serve the communities we work within. Finally, the book is also conceived as a commentary on the divergent approaches to feminist geography and activist scholarship currently in circulation, together with a reflection on the commonalities and shared vision of research that seeks to transgress and transform our world.

The aim of this work is to bring together new research and thinking within feminist geography scholarship that is focused on and engaged with different forms of social justice activism, and is aimed at undergraduate and post-graduate human geography students and scholars. This project came out of a desire to explore the role feminist geography is playing (and might play) within contemporary programs of social activism following a number of inspirational sessions at the 2019 meeting of the Association of American Geographers in Washington, DC. We were particularly inspired by the session entitled 'enough!', organized by Natalie Oswin, that focused on scholar activism and included LaToya Eaves as one of the presenters. Building on the spirit and aims of that session (which focused on activist-engaged research across the discipline as a whole) we wanted to produce a more targeted exploration of activist-focused feminist geography scholarship. Specifically, this book provides an opportunity to more fully appreciate this exciting body of work and reflect on the role of feminist geographers and feminist geography scholarship on social justice activism.

In developing this project, it was very important to us that it reflect the values and practices of inclusive and intersectional feminism, and, as much as possible, the diversity which characterizes contemporary feminist geography. To achieve this, we sought to 'build diversity in' from the outset, approaching scholars whose work concentrates on efforts to resist oppression across a range of different fronts including outside Anglophone and global north contexts, and to explore the effects of multiple forms of intersectional oppression. We are proud that the final work covers a wide range of activist work, including: postcolonial activisms; global south activisms; battles for racial and gender justice; LGBTQ+ rights; and economic justice. It was also important to us that the authorship of the book represent scholars across different social locations including by race, ethnicity, gender, and sexual orientation in order to both highlight the important role this scholarship plays in feminist geography and challenge historical patterns of exclusion and erasure within (and beyond) the discipline.

While we view its diversity as a key strength of this collection, we also note that working across difference is not always easy. Working across different cultural contexts with non-academics and/or with participants from substantially diverse backgrounds (as a number of the studies herein do) can mean bringing together people who may have significantly divergent kinds of life experiences and understandings of the world to one's own. As a result, research participants have different conceptualizations about what is important, 'what the problem is' and how it should be addressed. For some of the work in this collection, these encounters highlighted for authors the need to confront their positionality in terms of their privileges (especially by race and class) and how those privileges may have shaped the contours of what they do (and do not) know. At the same time, in other chapters authors instead found themselves reflecting on what it meant to do 'insider' or 'partial insider' research. We suggest that all of these constitute productive challenges which together open a space for deeper understanding across difference; a richer and more complex set of knowledges that address the diverse experiences of people in distinct spaces and places, along with a fuller appreciation of the power dynamics endemic to identify a person or place as 'different'. This attention to diversity includes acknowledging and incorporating into our research and writing how the experiences and struggles of historically marginalized peoples have been, and in many instances remain, obscured.

Broadly speaking, we conceptualize 'activism' as the work of resisting systems of oppression against marginalized peoples together with the work of seeking redress for historical injustices. However, the authors herein do not all approach the concept of activism in exactly the same way. While some may find this frustrating, we argue that it is both a natural function of engaging with activism across distinct contexts, and in fact that this constitutes a strength of this book. Activism itself is a dynamic, complex concept, and – echoing the point just made about intersectionality – we suggest that reading this concept across the different chapters herein can lead to a richer understanding of how this concept is constituted differently across distinct spaces, cultural contexts, and historical moments.

This book brings something new to the existing docket of monographs in feminist geography. It adds to and complements titles published in feminist geography with different topical foci such as Moss and Donovan's *Writing Intimacy into Feminist Geography* (2017) and Little's *Gender and Rural Geography* (2017); while likewise adding depth to works that are much broader in scope offering overviews of the sub-discipline as a whole, such as the *Routledge Handbook of Feminist Geography* (Datta Johnson and Hopkins, 2020), which constitutes the most recent (and broadest ever) works of its kind. The two works which relate most closely to our volume are Peake and Rieker's *Rethinking Feminist Interventions in the Urban* (2013) and Oberhauser et al's *Feminist Spaces: Gender and Geography in a Global Context* (2017). While we share Peake's concern with activism, we offer an updated and more-than-urban take on this concern, and while we share Oberhauser et al a central concern about the importance of intersectionality in feminist geography scholarship, we differ in our focus on engagements with activism.

Legacies on which this book builds

In order to help readers who may be new to feminist geography or outside academia's engagements with this work, we would like to take a moment to trace out the intellectual and political objectives from which this book is built by framing it with an overview of feminist geography's history of building solidarities with activists. Feminist geographic scholarship has continually produced research focused on the perspectives of individuals and groups operating on the margins of social, economic, and political power, while highlighting the everyday, local, and so-called mundane as important sites of analysis. Action and activism among feminist geographers have included various approaches to fieldwork, writing, and disseminating knowledge, as well as addressing geography's historical association with colonialism and the dominance of white male scholars, particularly in Europe and North America. Thus, the history of feminist geographic action and activism can be summarized into three broad categories: 1) Activism within the discipline and academy; 2) Collaboration, mentoring, and methodologies; and 2) Scholar activism.

Beginning in the late 1980s, feminist scholarship in geography began by identifying the lack of women as scholars within the discipline (Oberhauser et al, 2017). As more women joined the ranks of geographic scholars and feminist geography began to grow as a sub-discipline, feminist scholars began to call further attention to the negative and marginalizing experiences of non-white, non-heterosexual, and non-male identifying scholars (Kobayashi, 1994; Kobayashi and Peake, 1994). In 2002 there were a series of articles focusing on the continued dominance of white male scholars within the discipline, along with the need to conduct research that is more useful to the communities studied rather than the academy or academic researchers (Gilmore, 2002; Nagar, 2002; Peake and Kobayashi, 2002; Pulido, 2002).

Gilmore (2002) called for geographers to develop research agendas that examined 'race as a condition of existence and as a category of analysis, because the territoriality of power is key to understanding racism' (Gilmore, 2002, p 22). Therefore, race and gender were identified more than 20 years ago as areas that required additional attention by geographers both within the discipline and through the research praxis of geographers. Feminist contributions to Black geographies exemplified the need for additional academic attention on race, gender, and bodies. These researchers further address the need to work across categories of social and identity politics as well as addressing power relations through intersectional frameworks (McKittrick, 2006; Mollett and Faria, 2018; Hawthorne, 2019). De Leeuw and Hunt (2018) further addressed the shortfalls of decolonization within the discipline of geography by amplifying critical scholarship and knowledges produced by indigenous scholars.

In addition to race, ethnicity, indigeneity, and gender, feminist geographers have expanded research trajectories that incorporate class, caste, and sexuality, which has helped to transform the types of questions asked by feminist geographers along with methodological approaches to both research and activism within and outside the academy (Pulido 2000; Gilmore, 2002;

Mahtani 2004; Mollet 2006; McKittrick 2011; Finney, 2014; Faria and Mollett, 2016; Eaves, 2017; Jibrin, 2017; Hunt, 2018; Mollett and Faria, 2018; Raghuram, 2019). However, many of these scholars also point out that while the discipline has made minor improvements, geography still has 'a long way to go' to be a fully inclusive discipline (Doan, 2010, 2017; Eaves, 2017, 2019; Faria et al, 2019; Al-Saleh and Noterman, 2020; Faria and Mollett, 2020). In response to negative treatment within various geography departments, several feminist geographers have been forced out or chosen to leave the discipline for friendlier departments in gender studies, ethnic or cultural studies, while others have left academia all together. Thus, while feminist geography *in action* includes disciplinary reflexivity towards improving the diversity of ideas, persons, and research agendas, critical analyses within the discipline remain an ongoing process that needs more attention and support across academic hierarchies throughout the discipline.

Feminist geographers, in addition to calling attention to disciplinary exclusions, have incorporated a variety of research practices and methodologies that focus on critical self-reflexivity and positionality along with research ethics and *working with* rather than conducting research on socially, politically, and economically marginalized populations. Field-based research that includes qualitative and ethnographic methods is a common (but not exclusive) research method among feminist geographers. Activist scholars have adopted Participatory Action Research (PAR) as a key methodological framework for both working with and researching progressive and activist organizations or communities (Cahill, 2007; Davies and Dwyer, 2008; Schurr and Segebart, 2012) and addressing power relations and vulnerability while collecting qualitative data (Parker, 2017; Fertaly and Fluri, 2019; Elwood and Martin, 2000).

Many feminist geographers view collaboration (both among scholars and with research populations) as another method of scholar activism and progressive politics while addressing the difficulties and challenges associated with this type of work and scholarship, particularly within universities operating within a neoliberal economic framework (Monk et al, 2003; Kohl and McCutcheon, 2015; Mountz et al, 2015; Singh and Mathews, 2019).

In this vein, Richa Nagar's analyses of feminist research methodologies, scholar activism, and collaborations have been particularly influential. Her collaborative approach to scholar activism includes two key concepts that have been taken up by other feminist geographers: situated solidarities and radical vulnerability. Nagar's collaborative project with the Sangtin Writers (2006) illustrates the multiple complications, contradictions, and conceptions of caste and class across the lives of these authors. Nagar (2014) reflects upon her work with the Sangtin Writers through the concepts of situated solitaries and radical vulnerability. Situated solidarities draws from a number of feminist scholars and activists that attend to 'the specificities of geographical, socioeconomic, and institutional locations of those who enter into intellectual and political partnerships, and to the particular combination of processes, events, and struggles underway in those locations' (Nagar, 2014, p 5).

Radical vulnerability arises from journeys

> enabled by trust and with the ever-present possibility of distrust and epistemic violence; journeys of hope that must continuously recognize hopelessness and fears; and journeys that insist on crossing borders even as each person on the journey learns of borders that they cannot cross – either because it is impossible to cross them, or because it does not make sense to invest dreams and sweat in those border crossings. (Nagar, 2014, pp 5–6)

Nagar (2019) further argues for a shared *hunger* among researchers and research participants for transformative entanglements that inspire political and scholarly disturbances toward re-making how we understand, locate and represent ourselves and others.

Drawing on Nagar's work, geographers have discussed the various opportunities, challenges, frustrations, achievements, failures, and entanglements that arise from their involvement in activist scholarship (Derickson and Routledge, 2015; Routledge and Derickson, 2015; Reynolds et al, 2018). Torres (2019) further reminds us that activist scholarship does not need to occur elsewhere, but can also arise from our everyday encounters with individuals and organizations that 'provides an opening for reciprocity and reducing power differentials inherent in researcher-subject relationships' (Torres, 2019, p 165). Building upon these foundations of activisms within the discipline and through scholarship along with mentoring and collaboration, this book provides an extensive view of the diverse ways in which activism and feminist geography intermingle.

Book layout

Activist Feminist Geographies showcases a selection of some of the exciting work taking place in contemporary feminist geography, gathering together some of the best contemporary work on activism across a range of cultural contexts. We offer this collection as a resource for students and scholars in the field. Each chapter engages issues of current political and social relevance through the lens of cutting-edge conceptual work. The book is comprised of eight substantive chapters, some of which began life as papers at the (planned for but cancelled) 2020 American Association of Geographers Annual Meeting in a special themed session organized by Boyer, and others were solicited between 2020 and 2022 by Eaves, Fluri, and Boyer.

The book begins with the theme of feminist collectives and collective action across different cultural contexts (Chapters 1–3). The book then turns to explore intersectionality in different ways, first in the US context through frames of race and class (Chapter 4) then in Chapters 5–6 through LGBTQ activisms within different cultural contexts. Chapters 7–8 explore efforts to fight against state-sponsored misogyny, xenophobia, and street harassment in the UK, and the concluding Chapter 9 summarizes the major themes and types of activism discussed in this book, and suggestions for future research and activism collaborations. In more detail, each chapter covers the following themes:

Chapter 1: Evacuation Lost: Activism and Scholarship in a Time of Geopolitical Crisis, by Jennifer Fluri. Fluri reflects on her research in Afghanistan and attempts to assist Afghan colleagues and friends to evacuate and resettle after the Taliban resurgence and US withdrawal in August 2021. This chapter highlights the connections and relationships that qualitative researches develop with research associates and participants over time. Fluri discusses the challenges researchers face when they do not have the power or influence provide assistance. Activist research often includes attempts to shape political or public policy, or offer a counternarrative that complicates simplistic and prejudicial representations or places and people. This chapter also engages with capitalist-based hierarchies of assistance, the limitations of researcher privilege, her limited ability to assist others when faced with layers bureaucratic blockades, limited financial resources, and the intractability of hierarchal power. The chapter concludes by requesting additional discussion and dialogue regarding which tools can and should researchers use to disseminate knowledge that challenges inequalities and injustices.

Chapter 2: Women Weaving Critical Geographies, by the GeoBrujas Feminist Geography Collective, Mexico. The collective actions of organized women in Mexico and Latin America have become a guide and seedbed for the development of a feminist approach in Latin American geographic thought. In this chapter, the GeoBrujas Feminist Geography Collective share the theoretical-methodological production that has germinated from their space, in the collective work of a community of geographers in Mexico, GeoBrujas; where collaborative mapping, popular education, the arts and critical geographies have led them to seek ways to subvert cartographies to weave with various social organizations and communities, new narratives about dispossession, violence, pain, and hopes that inhabit their territories, landscapes and bodies.

Chapter 3: Critical Geography Collective of Ecuador as Feminist Geography Collective Praxis, by Sofia Zaragocin, Soledad Álvarez Velasco, Guglielmina Falanga, Amanda Yépez, and Gabriela Ruales. Leading off the preceding chapter, this chapter explores how, in Latin America, feminist geography collectives have become part of larger critical geography praxis. As Zaragocin et.al discuss, the surge of feminist geography collectives as autonomous groups of feminist geographical praxis coincides with the predominance of decolonial feminisms in the region. These feminist geography collectives have published manuals, fanzines, and pamphlets emphasizing method and methodology in the construction of decolonial feminist geographic knowledge. As part of the Critical Geography Collective of Ecuador, the authors explore the potentials of collective feminist geographic praxis in the Americas. In particular, they respond to the following question: what happens to feminist geographical praxis when it is done from autonomous collective feminist decolonial spaces? In Latin America where research-activism is encouraged among progressive academic circles, there are important alliances between an institutionalized feminist geography and autonomous feminist geography collectives. Herein the authors examine this fruitful relationship based on their own experiences of belonging to collective spaces in Latin America and an elite conservative university in Ecuador. They draw on recent webinars, discussions, and interviews with feminist geography collectives in Latin America and established Latin American feminist geographers based in universities in the region.

Chapter 4: Legacies of Black Feminist Activism in the US South, by LaToya. E. Eaves. Black women's presence in the US South dates back over four centuries, originating with their forced migration under European colonialism and chattel slavery. In spite of their longstanding presence in the region, Black women as producers of spatial knowledges continue to be peripheral in geography, including in feminist geography. Black women in the South have long been engaged in movement and liberation work, emphasizing racial, economic, gender, social and sexual justice. In the chapter, Eaves uses first-hand accounts from Black women's lives and work, including from slave narratives from the Federal Writers' Project, oral histories, and autobiographies to articulate foundational tenets of Southern Black feminist activism. Then, the chapter highlights the range of contemporary activist work in the South by examining three organizations that demonstrate the roots of Black feminist activism. In the chapter, Eaves demonstrates the ways in which Black women's multi-issue activism has involved advocating in defence of their own lives and has prioritized coalition work, denaturalizing the geographic imagination about Black women in the South.

Chapter 5: LGBT+ activism and morality politics in Central and Eastern Europe: Understanding the dynamic equilibrium in Czechia from a broader transnational perspective, by Michal Pitoňák. In this chapter, Pitoňák aims to understand the current condition and challenges of the LGBT+ movement in Czechia as well within the wider region of Central and Eastern Europe (CEE). He begins by briefly describing the current local context to show that it is embedded in an often overlooked longer historical development, and then describes the current situation in Czechia as a stalemate of activism and political opposition. He then turns to explore how LGBT+ activism and opposition that has mobilized against LGBT+ presence in public space or various pro-LGBT+ agendas can be manipulated by populist politicians. Finally, in resonance with Browne and Nash (this volume), he considers the nascent oppositional movements and illiberal mobilizations, which not only pose novel challenges but also represent a vast set of overlooked problems. He argues that scholars pursuing sexuality and feminist research in the CEE are not shielded from populism, and that a backlash against LGBT+ together with the specific conditions in which academic work is evaluated may find itself in potentially conflicting situations which may not be easy to reconcile for scholars who care for their community but at the same time need to sustain their living.

Chapter 6: Sexual Harassment and Claiming the Right to Everyday Life, by Kate Boyer. Freedom from harassment is a basic human right and precondition to mental and physical health. While sexual harassment has become a higher-profile issue in recent years across a range of cultural contexts, including through the global rise of the *#MeToo* movement and the *Everyday Sexism* project, this issue has also attracted the attention of policy makers at the highest levels, leading, in the UK, to a Parliamentary Inquiry in 2018 on sexual harassment in public places, and a briefing paper on sexual harassment in higher education from the House of Commons in 2018. All of this highlights the urgent need for both deeper understanding – and cultural change – on this issue. Meanwhile sexual harassment constitutes an important area of academic inquiry across a wide range of scholarly fields including psychology, sociology, women's studies, criminology, law and social policy, as well as geography. This chapter critically reviews key trends in scholarship on sexual harassment in public. It focuses on the spatial contexts of the street, the night-time economy, and higher education institutions. A fundamental question of spatial justice, I argue that sexual harassment can be approached through three conceptual lenses: the relational emergence of bodies; the politics of everyday spatial practice; and the ways affects and the atmospheres they generate shape spatial experience. I argue that geographers have a vital role to play in working with activists on this issue, and conclude by outlining a research agenda tracing out lines along which this work might unfold.

Chapter 7: Giving Birth in a 'Hostile Environment', by Maria Fannin. In 2012, the UK government's Home Office, under the leadership of then Home Office Secretary Theresa May, outlined a series of policies aimed, in May's words, at creating a 'really hostile environment for illegal migration'. Formalized in subsequent pieces of legislation on immigration in 2014 and 2016, these policies sought to implement a range of practices aimed at reducing the number of migrants living in the UK who had not been granted legal right to remain. The policy also created new procedures aimed at identifying those without legal right to remain. Measures were put in place to restrict migrants' ability to access education, rental accommodation, driving licenses, bank accounts, and healthcare. Although healthcare during pregnancy is defined by the UK government as 'immediately necessary' and therefore should never be withheld even if a woman has no means of payment, fear of being asked for payment upfront has meant women without legal right to remain may delay or avoid accessing needed healthcare. This chapter explores activist responses to the hostile environment policies related to maternal care. It focuses on a local project aimed at resisting the Hostile Environment policy and the vulnerability faced by pregnant and birthing women navigating 'hostile healthcare' by accompanying women through their pregnancies and births. Linking the disciplining of pregnant bodies to broader anxieties over migration and citizenship, it explores the connections between the work of the midwives, doulas, birth companions, and activists involved in this project to the theological and radical social justice roots of accompaniment as political practice.

Chapter 8: Respectful Relationalities: Researching Those Opposed to Sexual and Gender Rights and Equalities, by Kath Browne and Catherine Nash. Feminist geographies have long been engaged in thinking about the power relations that constitute gendered spatialities. This has often focused on the spatialized experiences of those who are marginalized and oppressed by unequal power relations related to gender (and sexuality). This chapter takes a different focus and explores the possibilities and limitations of doing feminist geography with those who are opposed to sexual and gender rights and equalities. Our chapter begins by describing, and critically reflecting on, our methodologies as researchers on a project expressly examining the experiences of those so opposed as well and thinking about methodologies that seek to complicate simple binaries of for/against through a 'post-oppositional' approach. Adopting this stance involves numerous risks. In the second part of our chapter, we therefore consider the (im)possibilities of orienting ourselves as researchers in 'post-oppositional' ways. As such, we point to the complications and incoherences of engaging in this way with people who are opposed to gender and sexuality rights and equalities in Canada, the UK, and Ireland. We argue that this work is difficult, but necessary. Thus, the chapter contends that feminist (and sexualities) geographies need to continue the central work of engaging with those who are marginalized and oppressed, and also consider resistances to progress around sexual and gender equalities. But, we argue, this work needs to be done with a significant degree of caution, an advanced feminist ethics of care, and a keen attentiveness to the complicated ways in which privilege and marginality are enacted between researcher and researched. Finally, a conclusion will tie the work together, teasing out main themes, take-away messages and challenges; and suggest directions for future work.

References

Al-Saleh, Danya and Elsa Noterman (2020). 'Organizing for Collective Feminist Killjoy Geographies in a US University'. *Gender, Place & Culture*, 17 February: 1–22.

Cahill, Caitlin (2007). 'The Personal Is Political: Developing New Subjectivities through Participatory Action Research'. *Gender, Place & Culture* 14(3): 267–92.

Datta, A., P. Hopkins, L. Johnston, E. Olson, and J.M. Silva (eds) (2020). *Routledge Handbook of Gender and Feminist Geographies*. London: Routledge.

Davies, Gail and Claire Dwyer (2008). 'Progress Reports'. *Progress in Human Geography* 32(3): 399–406.

De Leeuw, Sarah and Sarah Hunt (2018). 'Unsettling Decolonizing Geographies'. *Geography Compass* 12(7): e12376.

Derickson, Kate Driscoll and Paul Routledge (2015). 'Resourcing Scholar-Activism: Collaboration, Transformation, and the Production of Knowledge'. *The Professional Geographer* 67(1): 1–7.

Doan, Petra L. (2010). 'The Tyranny of Gendered Spaces – Reflections from beyond the Gender Dichotomy'. *Gender, Place & Culture* 17(5): 635–54.

Doan, Petra (2017). 'Coming Out of Darkness and into Activism'. *Gender, Place & Culture* 24(5): 741–6.

Eaves, LaToya E. (2019). 'The Imperative of Struggle: Feminist and Gender Geographies in the United States'. *Gender, Place & Culture* 26(7–9): 1314–21.

Eaves, LaToya E. (2020). 'Fear of an Other Geography'. *Dialogues in Human Geography* 10(1): 34–6.

Elwood, Sarah A. and Deborah G. Martin (2000). ' "Placing" Interviews: Location and Scales of Power in Qualitative Research'. *The Professional Geographer* 52(4): 649–57.

Faria, Caroline and Sharlene Mollett (2016). 'Critical Feminist Reflexivity and the Politics of Whiteness in the "Field."' *Gender, Place & Culture* 23(1): 79–93.

Faria, Caroline and Sharlene Mollett (2020). ' "We Didn't Have Time to Sit Still and Be Scared": A Postcolonial Feminist Geographic Reading of "An Other Geography."' *Dialogues in Human Geography* 10(1): 23–9.

Faria, Caroline, Bisola Falola, Jane Henderson, and Rebecca Maria Torres (2019). 'A Long Way to Go: Collective Paths to Racial Justice in Geography'. *The Professional Geographer* 71(2): 364–76.

Fertaly, Kaitlin and Jennifer L. Fluri (2019). 'Research Associates and the Production of Knowledge in the Field'. *The Professional Geographer* 71(1): 75–82.

Finney, Carolyn (2014). *Black Faces, White Spaces: Reimagining the Relationship of African Americans to the Great Outdoors*. Chapel Hill: University of North Carolina Press.

Gilmore, Ruth Wilson (2002). 'Fatal Couplings of Power and Difference: Notes on Racism and Geography'. *The Professional Geographer* 54(1): 15–24.

Hawthorne, C. (2019). 'Black Matters Are Spatial Matters: Black Geographies for the Twenty-First Century'. *Geography Compass* 13: e12468.

Hunt, Sarah (2018). 'Researching within Relations of Violence: Witnessing as Methodology'. In Deborah McGregor, Jean-Paul Restoule, and Rochelle Johnston (eds) *Indigenous Research: Theories, Practices, and Relationships*. Toronto: Canadian Scholars, pp 282–95.

Jibrin, Rekia (2017). '"Ain't I a Feminist?": The Politics of Gender Violence, Anti-Violence, and Education in Oakland, CA'. *Gender, Place & Culture* 24(4): 545–62.

Kobayashi, A. (1994). 'Coloring the Field: Gender, "Race," and the Politics of Fieldwork'. *The Professional Geographer* 46(1): 73–80.

Kohl, Ellen and Priscilla McCutcheon (2015). 'Kitchen Table Reflexivity: Negotiating Positionality through Everyday Talk'. *Gender, Place & Culture* 22(6): 747–63.

Little, J. (2017). *Gender and Rural Geography*. London: Routledge.

Mahtani, Minelle (2004). 'Mapping Race and Gender in the Academy: The Experiences of Women of Colour Faculty and Graduate Students in Britain, the US and Canada'. *Journal of Geography in Higher Education* 28(1): 91–9.

Mollett, Sharlene and Caroline Faria (2018). 'The Spatialities of Intersectional Thinking: Fashioning Feminist Geographic Futures'. *Gender, Place & Culture* 25(4): 565–77.

Monk, Janice, Patricia Manning, and Catalina Denman (2003). 'Working Together: Feminist Perspectives on Collaborative Research and Action'. *ACME: An International Journal for Critical Geographies* 2(1): 91–106.

Moss, P. and C. Donovan (eds) (2017). *Writing Intimacy into Feminist Geography*. London: Routledge.

Mountz, Alison, Anne Bonds, Becky Mansfield, Jenna Loyd, Jennifer Hyndman, Margaret Walton-Roberts et al (2015). 'For Slow Scholarship: A Feminist Politics of Resistance through Collective Action in the Neoliberal University'. *ACME: An International Journal for Critical Geographies*, 14(4): 1235–59.

Nagar, Richa (2002). 'Footloose Researchers, "Traveling" Theories, and the Politics of Transnational Feminist Praxis'. *Gender, Place & Culture* 9(2): 179–86.

Nagar, Richa (2006). *Playing with Fire: Feminist Thought and Activism through Seven Lives in India*. Minnesota: University of Minnesota Press.

Nagar, Richa (2014). *Muddying the Waters: Coauthoring Feminisms across Scholarship and Activism*. Chicago: University of Illinois Press.

Nagar, Richa (2019). *Hungry Translations: Relearning the World through Radical Vulnerability*. Chicago: University of Illinois Press.

Oberhauser, A. M., Fluri, J. L., Whitson, R., and Mollett, S. (2017). *Feminist Spaces: Gender and Geography in a Global Context*. New York: Routledge.

Pain, Rachel (2004). 'Social Geography: Participatory Research'. *Progress in Human Geography* 28(5): 652–63.

Parker, Brenda (2017). 'The Feminist Geographer as Killjoy: Excavating Gendered Urban Power Relations'. *The Professional Geographer* 69(2): 321–8.

Peake, Linda and Audrey Kobayashi (2002). 'Policies and Practices for an Antiracist Geography at the Millennium'. *The Professional Geographer* 54(1): 50–61.

Peake, L. and M. Rieker (eds) (2013). *Rethinking Feminist Interventions into the Urban*. London: Routledge.

Pulido, Laura (2000). 'Rethinking Environmental Racism: White Privilege and Urban Development in Southern California'. *Annals of the Association of American Geographers* 90(1): 12–40.

Pulido, Laura (2006). 'Reflections on a White Discipline'. *The Professional Geographer* 54(1): 42–9.

Raghuram, Parvati (2019). 'Race and Feminist Care Ethics: Intersectionality as Method'. *Gender, Place & Culture* 26(5): 613–37.

Reynolds, Kristin, Daniel Block, and Katharine Bradley (2018). 'Food Justice Scholar-Activism and Activist- Scholarship: Working Beyond Dichotomies to Deepen Social Justice Praxis'. *ACME: An International Journal for Critical Geographies* 17(4): 988–98.

Rosenberg, Rae and Natalie Oswin (2015). 'Trans Embodiment in Carceral Space: Hypermasculinity and the US Prison Industrial Complex'. *Gender, Place & Culture* 22(9): 1269–86.

Routledge, Paul and Kate Driscoll Derickson (2006). 'Situated Solidarities and the Practice of Scholar-Activism'. *Environment and Planning D: Society and Space* 33(3): 391–407.

Schurr, C. and D. Segebart (2012). 'Engaging with Feminist Postcolonial Concerns through Participatory Action Research and Intersectionality'. *Geographica Helvetica* 67(3): 147–54.

Singh, Taveeshi and Tayler J. Mathews (2019). 'Facilitating Queer of Color Feminist Co-Mentorship: Reflections on an Online Archive of Scholar-Activism'. *Gender, Place & Culture* 26(12): 1701–20.

Torres, Rebecca Maria (2019). 'Everyday Encounters with Activist Scholarship'. *The Professional Geographer* 71(1): 161–6.

Trauger, Amy and Jennifer Fluri (2014). 'Getting Beyond the "God Trick": Toward Service Research'. *The Professional Geographer* 66(1): 32–40.

Wright, Melissa W. (2010). 'Geography and Gender: Feminism and a Feeling of Justice'. *Progress in Human Geography* 34(6): 818–27.

Zaragocin, Sofia (2019). 'Feminist Geography in Ecuador'. *Gender, Place & Culture* 26(7–9): 1032–8.

1

Evacuation Lost: Activism and Scholarship in a Time of Geopolitical Crisis

Jennifer Fluri

Introduction

This chapter provides an overview of my research and experiences in Afghanistan as a reflective foundation for my research team's attempts to assist our Afghan colleagues and friends evacuate from in August 2021 (due to the resurgence of the Taliban regime and United States (US) military withdrawal from the country). I focus on this situation in an effort to draw out some of the challenges associated with academic fieldwork and feminist activism. This chapter does not examine a specific social movement or form of feminist activism. Rather I reflect on my relationships with fellow academics, and the individuals and communities that facilitated our research. I consider the opportunities and difficulties associated with challenging prevailing public discourse about people and places through teaching, public talks, and our attempts to influence political action and policy. Additionally, through a brief overview of my 20 years of research on/in Afghanistan, I discuss the limitations of academic privilege and limited ability to assist Afghans and effectively navigate through the multiple layers and intricacies of international geopolitics and state bureaucracy.

I begin this chapter with an historical overview of geopolitical conflict in contemporary Afghanistan, followed by a discussion of research and activism. The final section of this chapter focuses my attempts to help Afghan friend and colleagues evacuate along with a few volunteers, and my long-term research collaborator, Dr Rachel Lehr (who worked with me as a postdoctoral researcher on two separate projects and with whom I have co-authored a book on Afghanistan and several articles). I am not including the names of the other volunteers upon request. The chapter concludes with my reflections and analyses of these events.

Historical overview of conflict in Afghanistan

Afghanistan has experienced several waves of international economic, political, and military interventions throughout the 20th century and first two decades of the 21st century. The government of Afghanistan has changed several times since the early 1970s. The regularity of government transitions in Afghanistan have become a punch line of an often repeated joke: 'In Afghanistan you go to bed, and wake up to a new regime' (for more information on Afghan humour see Fluri, 2019, and Shrestha and Fluri, 2021).

For much of the 20th century, Afghanistan's government was a constitutional monarchy with Mohmmad Zahir Shah as the head of state. In 1973, Zahir Shah's cousin and former Prime Minister, Mohammad Daud, instigated a coup when Zahir Shah was out of the country seeking medical attention in Italy. This bloodless coup led to the formation of the Republic of Afghanistan with Daud as its president (Crews, 2015). The 1970s were also filled with new forms of intellectualism and political activism in the country. Women's rights organizations formed, such as the Revolutionary Association of the Women of Afghanistan (RAWA), a left leaning political feminist organization, founded by a 20-year-old student, Meena (Fluri, 2008).

Other leftist organizations challenged the authority of both the monarchy and Daud's republic. A leading political group, the People's Democratic Party of Afghanistan (PDPA), included a women's auxiliary organization the Democratic Women's Organization of Afghanistan. The PDPA split into two factions, Parcham (banner) and Khalq (masses/people). These factions were divided along ideological lines, but eventually came together to instigate a coup against Daud's government in April of 1978, known as the Saur Revolution. This bloody coup, which killed Daud and several members of his family, ushered in a socialist government under the careful watch of the Soviet Union. The Soviet Union bordered Afghanistan to the north (currently the states of Turkmenistan, Uzbekistan, and Tajikistan), providing geostrategic territorial advantage to the Soviet Union (Crews, 2015).

The PDPA's government was beset upon by infighting among the leadership and pushback against this government's attempts to impose new policies. Government policies focused on land tenure reform and women's roles in society were met with intensive resistance from various communities throughout Afghanistan. The Soviet Union, seeking to 'assist' the Afghanistan government initiated a military invasion in December 1979, attempting to violently crush the growing opposition to the PDPA government. The US used this invasion as an opportunity to challenge Soviet territorial expansion by first covertly and later overtly funding and suppling weapons to several disparate resistance factions known collectively as the mujahideen.

The Soviet Union militarily occupied Afghanistan until 1989, while the disparate mujahideen factions resisted this occupation. The US and the Soviet Union were fighting a proxy war against each other on Afghan soil, while this conflict led to continued divisions between different political factions within the country, and killed over a million Afghans while displacing and injuring millions more. Many Afghans fled to neighbouring countries, particularly Iran and Pakistan. Refugee life was also politicized in Pakistan, as different mujahideen groups recruited men to fight among the refugees and required families to register their affiliation with a particular group. Additionally, various organizations focused on women's rights, such as the Afghan Women's Network (AWN), were formed within these refugee camps.

The Soviet Union, after its military withdrawal from Afghanistan in 1989, continued to back the central government in Kabul, under the leadership of President Najibullah. Once the Soviet government fell in 1991, their backing of the Najibullah's government ceased. In response the disparate and divided mujahideen groups all sought to take over the central government in the capital city Kabul, which devolved into a bloody civil war from 1992–1996. This led to another wave of deaths, injuries, and displacements. During this time, the Taliban was being formed by recruiting boys and young men from refugee camps in Pakistan, with significant influence from Pakistan Inter-Services Intelligence (ISI). The Taliban began to make military and political inroads into Afghanistan in 1994, and by 1996 controlled of the majority of the country including the capital city.

Initially, the Taliban received both domestic and international support as this regime was viewed as a positive antidote to the violent atrocities that occurred during the civil war. However, once the Taliban firmly took hold of power, they instituted draconian methods of control over the population such as public corporeal punishments (that is, floggings and amputations) and executions. The Taliban imposed strict restrictions on women, such as preventing women from working outside the home, attending school, or being treated by a male physician. If women needed to leave their home, they could only do so by wearing the *chadri* (burqa) and being accompanied by a male *mahram* (close male relative). Additionally, music, television, and similar forms of entertainment were banned.

The Taliban remained in power until the United States (US)-led invasion of Afghanistan on 7 October 2001, in response to the attacks against the US on 11 September 2001. While none of the 9/11/2001 hijackers were Afghans, the US targeted Afghanistan because the Taliban had provided a 'safe haven' for Osama bin Laden, the leader of Al Qaeda, the person and organization identified as responsible for the attacks against the US. Within a month of the US-led invasion, criticism of the US handling of the war began to grow, and in response the Bush Administration's political discourse shifted from the 'hunt for Bin Laden' to 'saving' Afghan women from the Taliban. This discourse worked, and garnered additional support within the US by co-opting Afghan women's rights for the geopolitical purposes of the US (Hirschkind and Mahmood, 2002; Hunt, 2002; Abu Lughod, 2013). Thus, the realities of Afghan women's lives, diverse needs, activism, and ideas for change were largely ignored or minimally included in US military, humanitarian, or economic development assistance efforts in Afghanistan over the subsequent two decades (Fluri and Lehr, 2017).

While this historical overview details major events, I want to also emphasize the extensive amount of war related violence, displacement, infrastructural destruction, and associated trauma experienced by Afghans. In what follows I briefly review the research and activism associated with my research team, culminating in our attempts to assist research associates, colleagues, and friends in Afghanistan to evacuate during the chaotic weeks following the Taliban resurgence and US withdrawal from Afghanistan in August 2021 up to the time of this writing (April 2022).

Research on gender, geopolitics, and economic development

I began my dissertation research on feminist activism in Afghanistan in August 2001. After the attacks against the US on 9/11/01 and subsequent US-led invasion of Afghanistan on 10/7/01, I focused my research on the activism of the RAWA, including their international supporters' network and effective use of the internet as a tool for garnering support and sharing information about both civil war mujahideen and Taliban atrocities, along with critiques of the US-led military actions in Afghanistan (Fluri, 2006, 2008, 2009a). As part of this research, I volunteered as one of RAWA's international supporters, including fundraising, and assisting with their supporters' network in the US.

This was followed by a research project (2006–2012) on the international humanitarian aid and economic development efforts in Afghanistan with a focus on the capital city, Kabul. This research also examined gender-based programming and the mismatch between donor-driven approaches and the diverse experiences, needs, and ideas of Afghan women (Fluri, 2009a, 2009b, 2009c, 2011a, 2011b, 2012, 2014, 2017; Fluri and Lehr, 2017). As part of this research, I also met and began to collaborate with Rachel Lehr. In 2007 we began to work with the New Hampshire Humanities Council to provide public library talks on Afghanistan in an effort to counter prevailing notions and Orientalist assumptions about Afghan people.

This research was also shared with various organizations in the US in an attempt to shape policy such as United States Agency for International Development (USAID), US Military (that is, a presentation at Fort Leavenworth and meetings with US military analysts), United States Institute for Peace (USIP), and the Department of State (DOS). Dr Lehr developed a curriculum and provided pre-deployment training for USAID employees starting in 2011, and I assisted with a few of these trainings. However, these efforts along with those of the US government's own Special Inspector General for Afghanistan Reconstruction (SIGAR), John Sopko, went largely ignored by the US government (Sopko, 2014a, 2014b).

USIP continued to work in Afghanistan and funded a study we developed on Afghan Women's roles in peace building in Afghanistan (2014–2016), which culminated in a comprehensive report to USIP and several publications (Fluri, 2019; Fluri and Lehr, 2019; Fluri and Bagheri, 2019; Lehr and Fluri, 2019; Shrestha and Fluri, 2021). This led to a US-National Science Foundation funded project on Security, Gender, and Development (Award Number 1759701) with a focus on Afghan women's leadership across disparate places in Afghanistan and at different scales (that is, home, community, provincial, national) (Fluri and Lehr, forthcoming). This research is ongoing and has shifted to include interviews with Afghan women leaders, both those who evacuated and remained in the country.

Additionally, there has been extensive war profiteering and capitalization and commodification of Afghan women's oppression and liberation as part of aid and development missions to assist the women of Afghanistan. Many Afghan women benefited from internationally funded projects and programs focused on education, job skills training, and health care (2002–2021). Also, Afghan women's participation in politics since 2002 was partially due to quotas (influenced by the US), which included positions for women in both the upper and lower houses of parliament (Reynolds, 2006). Afghan women were elected to political offices and served as provincial governors and district/city mayors, along with being chosen by different presidents as ministers or holding cabinet positions. With the fall of the US-backed Afghanistan government in 2021, these positions along with those held by many Afghan men have been radically altered or eliminated. Therefore, focusing on women and the changes to their lives during the Taliban regime remains an important discussion, but should include extensive criticism of US-led international military, humanitarian aid, and economic development assistance.

During the successive waves of increasing women's participation in politics, education, and economic opportunities, along with improving women's health over two decades; the reach and sustainability of these programs and projects remains in question. This was evident from our research on international aid and development interventions, which included surveys and interviews with individuals (both Afghans and internationals) working within various local and international governmental and non-governmental organizations (Fluri and Lehr, 2017).

The reach of programs targeting women's lives has been limited geographically and by existing socioeconomic hierarchies. Women with English language competency and connections to US and other internationals donor countries and organizations were undoubtedly more successful in garnering financial and political support from these organizations. However, the effectiveness of Afghan women's organizations was limited by several factors. The following is a brief overview of the five major factors that caused these limitations.

Factor 1: Subcontracting

Most of the economic development projects and programs funded by USAID were subcontracted to implementing partners, which are pejoratively referred to as the 'beltway bandits'. These are mostly for-profit companies geographically located in the beltway around Washington DC, who compete for USAID and DOS contracts to implement projects and programs in various countries including Afghanistan (Roberts 2014). Once in Afghanistan, these companies used US government allocated funds to pay international staff six figure salaries, rent office and housing space for exorbitant prices, pay private security firms and logistic companies for protection and assistance (also at exorbitant prices). After funds are spent on these expenses, the 'implementing partners' use the leftover funds to hire local Afghan-run NGOs. These organizations are then tasked with the difficult and dangerous work of fulfilling a particular project or program mandate, which has generally been conceptualized by individuals living outside Afghanistan with little to no cultural knowledge or understanding of the complexities of daily life for Afghans. The Afghan-run NGOs operate on much less funding than their international counterparts, which led to extensive and rampant turnover within both international and Afghan organizations.

Factor 2: Internal brain-drain

Due to the massive pay disparities between international and local organizations, many Afghan organizations had difficulty maintaining staff and institutional knowledge within their own organizations. The majority of organizational leaders – my research team and I interviewed – complained about investing time and energy into training young Afghan women to work within their organizations, only to have them leave, once they had enough skills to work for an international organization. While they did not blame these individuals for wanting to increase their salaries and provide for their families, this situation calls attention to income disparities, which made the process of creating sustainable and long-lasting programs for Afghan-led organizations difficult if not impossible.

Factor 3: Ignore rather than listen

Many programs funded by USAID and their implementing partners, were as mentioned, conceptualized by internationals rather than Afghan partners. This donor-driven approach has been critiqued by most development scholars as a flawed system due to the lack of community support and therefore inability of the projects to continue over the long-term. For example, when interviewing international workers for the UN and USAID, I asked why they were not designing projects based on Afghan women's ideas or needs, and the regular response was 'because I don't think they have good ideas'. While these international workers may not have agreed with Afghan women, their criticism was from the perspective of their own social, economic, and political contexts (Daulatzai, 2006). Additionally, their experiences were from the geographic location of their own 'home-country', not Afghanistan. They did not consider the complexities, complications, and at times contradictions of Afghan women's activism nor the diverse social, cultural, economic, and political contexts within which they live.

Factor 4: Diversity of women's experiences

Afghanistan is a multi-lingual and multi-ethnic country that is predominantly Muslim but with diverse belief systems based on different religious sects, teachings, and interpretations of Islam. It is also stratified based on socioeconomic class, and education levels, along with cultural diversity, and differential access to resources based on several factors. Therefore, a one-size-fits-all approach to assistance programs or advocating for women's rights was a flawed endeavour from the start. Afghan women are not a singular identity, rather they have a diverse set of ideologies and beliefs. This diversity should be celebrated and attended to with all its complexities rather than attempting to push projects and programs that reflected the values and beliefs of US-based organizations. In addition to these issues many international workers had limited access to Afghan communities due to strict security protocols, which prevented them from engaging with Afghans in their homes and with their families and communities.

Factor 5: Security

Afghan women's rights and women-led NGOs and Civil Society Organizations regularly identified security, followed by lack of funding, as the main barriers for implementing projects. Insecurity was the primary reason for disrupting or halting existing projects and programs. Lack of sustained funding made it difficult for these organizations to retain legitimacy from the community members and leadership in the places where these NGOS/CSOs were implementing projects or programs. However, security was viewed as the responsibility of the community and therefore did not disrupt the legitimacy of these organizations.

Security in Afghanistan over the past 20 years (2001–2021) included US and other international players combined into the International Security Assistance Force (ISAF). ISAF officially closed its operations in Afghanistan in 2014, and security was transferred to Afghan forces, with US special forces and other US military support remaining until the withdrawal in August 2021. The Afghan forces were stymied by corruption and mismanagement, such as the lack of effective ground support and intermittent or non-existent payments for soldiers.

This was further buttressed by the Trump administration's legitimization of the Taliban by way of its so-called 'peace talks' in Doha, Qatar. These talks side-lined the Afghanistan government and included women leaders, as part of a performance of women's participation. Several women we interviewed after their participation in the 'peace talks' in 2019 discussed their distrust of the Taliban and the lack of effective listening or engagement with women leaders. Additionally, while the 'peace talks' were occurring in Qatar, many places in Afghanistan were besieged by Taliban violence such as suicide bombings and extra-judicial murders.

Due to various failures as briefly discussed here, this assistance was neither sustainable nor self-supporting. It would be easy to place the blame on Afghans. Certainly there were entrenched and extensive problems across various branches of government throughout the country, such as corruption and cronyism. Yet, it is vitally necessary to also critique the role of the US in ongoing and unrelenting conflict and uncertainty in Afghanistan. Without a robust and continued critical reflection on the failures and successes of US-led interventions in Afghanistan, the US government is doomed to repeat its mistakes. I say this with confidence because they have made these mistakes before. The US did not begin intervening in Afghanistan in 2001. US entanglements with Afghanistan began after WWII when the US engaged in massive infrastructural development projects in the country, competing with the Soviet Union for political influence. The US also intervened in the 1980s during the Soviet occupation of Afghanistan, when the US funded and supplied the radically religious and disparate mujahedeen groups to violently resist the Soviet Union. Osama bin Laden was one of many foreign fighters allied with the US at that time, and later one of the many who turned against the US. Interestingly, each of successive government from the PDPA to the Taliban and their international backers/occupiers weaponized gender through discursive promises to protect or save Afghan women. In the 1980s the Soviets were 'saving' Afghan women, and the US-backed mujahideen were 'saving' Afghan women from the Soviet-backed government and military occupation; in the 1990s the Taliban were 'saving' Afghan women from the gendered violence during the civil war, and in the 2000s US-led international military and economic interventions were 'saving' Afghan women from the Taliban. But none of these power brokers effectively engaged women leaders, or incorporated the complex demographics and diverse needs, beliefs, and experiences of Afghan women.

After the US withdrawal, Afghans who were able to evacuate left their homes, families, and everything behind to face the arduous process of refugee resettlement, others remain in Afghanistan and faced the hardships of economic collapse, and uncertain future, some remain in hiding due to fears or threats of Taliban violence. Fighting wars and providing assistance under the banner of 'saving women' is a false and flawed narrative that is used to garner political support and far too quickly and easily abandoned for geopolitical expediency. However, the US continues to make the same policy and political errors, while expecting a positive result that never truly materializes.

I included this overview of my research to highlight the failures and missteps of US-led interventions in Afghanistan. Furthermore, and most importantly absolutely none of this research would have been possible without the extensive assistance, facilitation, and insights I have received from Afghan research associates. This includes individuals who provided housing and transportation during my field research trips along with those who assisted with the collection of data, language translations, logistics assistance, fixers, and care for me and other research associates when we fell ill (see Fertaly and Fluri, 2019). Most individuals – with whom I have worked – sought to evacuate from Afghanistan in August 2022 based on legitimate fears that the Taliban would retaliate against them and their families due to their relationship with me (a US citizen) and other international workers and organizations.

Evacuation lost – Plan A to Plan ...?

My phone filled with calls and text messages when the Taliban took control of the capital city, Kabul on 15 August 2021. These calls and messages expressed worry, sadness, grief, and requests for evacuation assistance.

The ensuing panic included questions such as: How do we get onto the evacuation planes? Can you help us get on the right list? Can you help us evacuate to America? While the process for submitting names for the Special Immigrant Visas program, or the Priority 1 and Priority 2 (P1 and P2) Refugee Referral program was identified by the Department of State and several other agencies; the actual process for processing these requests remains murky.

I reached out to various friends and colleagues with experience working in Afghanistan in an attempt to help those who were trying to evacuate. These connections mainly led to dead-ends, or opportunities that did not materialize. While several amazing people both in Afghanistan and the US attempted to provide aid, the logistical ability to do so was limited. It became increasingly impossible to evacuate individuals without sanctioned and significant support within the Biden Administration or individuals with the Department of State directly involved in the evacuations. We were offered smuggling options by some; however, my collaborator Dr Lehr and I chose not to take this path due to the risks involved.

The process of attempting to secure evacuations for Afghan colleagues began with a tremendous amount of hope. On 16 August 2021, I was contacted by the National Science Foundation's (NSF) international division. My current NSF grant had been flagged by the DOS. This meant that individuals that worked directly with me as part of the research funded by this grant could be included on a list for Priority 2 (P2) refugee referrals, which would be submitted by NSF to the DOS.

Over the next days and weeks, our team put together a series of spreadsheets for NSF to submit to the DOS. The information requested for these lists and spreadsheets changed several times. While placing names of colleagues and their families on these lists offered a window of opportunity and modicum of hope, the window began to close as the days crept closer to the US final evacuation date of 31 August 2021. We worked continuously each day to update the lists, ensuring the information was correct. Checking and cross referencing. Speaking and texting with our Afghan colleagues to confirm information.

These days were also filled with calls, emails, and texts to various colleagues, friends, and associates also working to help Afghans evacuate. Gathering information from several colleagues was difficult. In several cases information was unavailable or inconsistent. Some documents were difficult to read or did not have consistent or complete information. Several of our Afghan colleagues did not have passports or they were expired, or their passports were awaiting processing at the passport office. Other families did not have passports or travel documents to cross borders. Others had already submitted requests for refugee referral or Special Immigrant Visas with the US Embassy in Kabul, only to have their passports shredded by the US Embassy employees before they departed to prevent the Taliban from finding them.

The chaotic scenes at the Kabul airport were communicated to us by Afghans on the ground. Many feared going to the airport because of violence and threats of violence. Air travel, from Kabul airport became more precarious when a bomb was detonated on 26 August 2021, killing

170 Afghan civilians and 13 US military personnel, and damaging the air traffic control equipment, making international flights impossible for weeks. There were continual stories and rumours of flights from Mazar-e-Sharif (a city in northern Afghanistan) to Doha, Qatar, where a US military base was set up to process refugees. Getting on the planes to Qatar seemed to be the best option for securing a flight out of Afghanistan at the expense of the US.

However, there was no clear information about how to get on the lists that allowed one entry onto these flights. Additional leads suggested helping Afghans to travel to another country to await paperwork processing. The US required all Afghans seeking resettlement in the US to first travel to a third county (meaning a country other than the US or Afghanistan) and then register at a US Embassy or consulate office to begin the one-to-two-year (or longer) process waiting for their paperwork to be reviewed and administered prior to being resettled in the US. Additionally, they also needed to pay for their own travel, lodging, and other expenses, as the US provided no financial support for Afghans to live in another country while awaiting refugee referral processing.

I began attending meetings organized by the American Association of Land Grant Universities, focused on academics trying to help colleagues in Afghanistan evacuate and resettle in the US. Through these meetings, we were provided another opportunity. If we could help our colleagues evacuate to Albania, the Albanian government would allow temporary resettlement while Afghans awaited processing. However, this quickly became unfeasible for our group. The Albanian government required official institutional (that is, university) funding agreements for room, board, and incidentals for Afghans awaiting processing in Albania. Neither I nor anyone among the small group of volunteers working on assisting our efforts had the funding, influence, or connections to orchestrate such an evacuation, or secure room and board for one to two years while they wait for approval. Our team was able to raise nearly $60K to assist our Afghan colleagues, the estimated costs for evacuation and temporary resettlement for our 30 colleagues and their families was $1.8 million.

As weeks turned to months, after the US military withdrawal, it became clear that additional evacuations with the assistance of the US government would not be forthcoming. A few of my colleagues in Afghanistan (and the diaspora in the US, Canada, and UK) were able to help family members leave. As we continued to work on helping colleagues leave Afghanistan, the hierarchy of acceptability for evacuations became abundantly clear.

First, several who were able to get onto the evacuation planes were able to do so by the use of brute force. Mostly young men were able to push their way onto the planes, including those who did not work with international organizations and were not allied with the US. Second, high-profile members of the government, including women's rights advocates and activists, were evacuated due to their own existing connections with highly influential individuals in the United States (that is, Hilary Clinton, famous feminists, and so on). Third, individuals with connections to US organizations and universities with influence and funding to pay for chartered flights and room and board in a third country (approved by the US) for temporary housing while their paperwork and screenings were processed by US embassies or consulates in those countries. Fourth, several other countries with extensive development programs in Afghanistan evacuated some of their Afghan colleagues and staff to their respective locations (that is, Canada, UK, several EU countries).

Unfortunately, nearly all of those who worked with me in Afghanistan were firmly entrenched in the fifth hierarchical category, namely Afghans working as support staff for international organizations, support staff for high-profile Afghans who evacuated, or Afghans working with low-profile internationals such as myself and my research team. Additionally, neither I nor anyone working with our US-based volunteers had the influence, funds, or connections necessary to orchestrate an evacuation plan.

The NSF's emails and acceptance of my list of Afghan colleagues provided hope, this hope dwindled by the end of August and became a dead-end by December 2021. Initially NSF international officers who worked closely with DOS were extremely supportive and helpful. They answered my various questions and met with me several times via zoom to review the process and provide moral support. However, by November 2021 it was difficult to garner information from them or get a sense of the process and whether the lists I provided had been submitted or processed. By the end of December 2021, NSF stopped answering my emails and calls. It became clear that the window of opportunity and hope provided by NSF had completely closed.

While working with NSF, we also sought other avenues, including reaching out to immigration lawyers, and further connecting with existing networks of individuals from government employees to US military personnel, and private organizations offering extraction for a fee. Similar to the work with NSF, all of these potential avenues began with a significant amount of hope and possibility but ended with no clear path for safely evacuating anyone. For example, we were poised to spend a significant amount of funding to pay an immigration law firm to process Humanitarian Parole applications for several colleagues, only to find out that US government was arbitrarily rejecting these requests, and that the burden of proof for this program had been increased (that is, requiring confirmation of a specific threat by an independent agency, rather than accepting the resurgence of the Taliban as a threat to Afghans allied with the US). As time went on, less and less information was forthcoming through official channels without any clear pathway or navigation for how to help people our colleagues and friends evacuate.

Most of the individuals on our list had large families, and some with very young children (including newborns). Some considered leaving without their families but continued to struggle with the possibility of being separated from their children for years. Others remained haunted by previous refugee experiences in the 1980s, 1990s, or early 2000s and were reluctant to once again face the hardships, uncertainty, and abuse that are endemic to these displacements.

The best assistance we received was the amazing generosity of colleagues and friends who donated to the fund we created to assist with refugee resettlement. We are currently using these funds to provide financial assistance to our Afghan colleagues and friends who remain in Afghanistan (many still in hiding) without much hope for repatriation to the US or another country. This financial assistance has made a significant difference in their daily lives, as prices for food and other essentials have soared, and unemployment continues to increase, particularly for those who worked for US and other international organizations.

Media and public presentations, and academic action/influence/activism?

I was able to contribute (in a local and small way) to the extensive media attention toward Afghanistan in August 2021 and over the next few months. I was interviewed by several local media outlets and asked to give public talks including at a few universities in the US. The TEDx Mile High organization in Colorado reached out to me to prepare and deliver a talk about Afghan women, which I did in October 2021.

My interest in doing these public events was focused on attempting to keep the media attention on Afghanistan, to increase pressure on the US government to provide more funding and assistance for those remaining in Afghanistan, and for those seeking refuge in the US. This work included connecting with various organizations that sought assistance from within the US government such as the Afghanistan Adjustment Act, which if it is passes, would provide a fast track for permanent residency (within one year) for Afghan refugees in the United States. At the time of this writing (fall 2022), this Act has been introduced in the US Senate and will be voted on in early 2023.

As a scholar and educator, I am committed to sharing knowledge and information. However, I think it is also important to underscore the difficulty of navigating this terrain. It is an honour to be asked to weigh in on contemporary geopolitical events such as this. However, this also comes with little or no hope of influencing policy or political action. This also creates new ethical challenges within an obstacle course of questions beginning with 'how best to proceed?'

Remaining silent is not a solution. While speaking out has the potential of being viewed (by myself and others) as self-serving. Thus, our roles as researchers and our ethical, moral, and human-to-human responsibility for those who assist with our research requires more thought, thoughtful engagement, discussion, and dialogue, particularly among feminist academic activists. For example, is it appropriate to promote your research in the service of others or in attempt to draw attention to injustice, even when those injustices are not remedied?

Summary and conclusion

Afghans with connections to US government officials, individuals, or groups with extensive funding and influence were more likely to be evacuated and assisted than those without those associations. Wealth (social, economic, or political) were necessary precursors for individuals to enter the US and access resources needed for daily survival. It cannot be understated that most Afghan who were able to evacuate, were educated, accomplished, and 'connected' individuals. While the support staff and assistants to the elite are without influence within their own country and many remain in hiding for fear of Taliban reprisals.

Strong-man masculinity was also a winner in the evacuation process. Men who could push their way through the crowds and onto planes at Kabul airport. While some women were part of the evacuation they were not well represented and among the families of my Afghan colleagues, most did not want to risk injury or death of their family members. The rumours and risks of going to the airport also pushed many to wait. They were also filled, as I was, by the misguided hope that the US would continue evacuations until every Afghan affiliated with the US was safely out of the country. This did not happen!

Despite the loss of evacuation hopes for many of our colleges and the subsequent disheartening and depressing heaviness of the ongoing crisis in Afghanistan, our small team remains committed to assisting our colleagues and friends, monetarily and continuing to advocate on their behalf toward eventual asylum in the US and other states. This experience continues to lay bare the limitations of academic privilege and ability to assist others when faced with mountainous bureaucratic barriers, along with falling financially short, and being continually stymied by structural violence, endemic inequalities, and the intractability of the mountainous hierarchies of economic and political power.

References

Abu-Lughod, L. (2013). *Do Muslim Women Need Saving?* Boston, MA: Harvard University Press.

Crews, R.D. (2015). *Afghan Modern: The History of a Global Nation*. Boston, MA: Belknap Press of Harvard University Press.

Daulatzai, A. (2006). 'Acknowledging Afghanistan: Notes and Queries on an Occupation'. *Cultural Dynamics* 18(3): 293–311.

Fertaly, K. and Fluri, J.L. (2019). 'Research Associates and the Production of Knowledge in the Field'. *The Professional Geographer* 71(1): 75–82.

Fluri, J.L. (2008). 'Feminist-nation Building in Afghanistan: An Examination of the Revolutionary Association of the Women of Afghanistan (RAWA)'. *Feminist Review* 89(1): 34–54.

Fluri, J.L. (2009a). '"Foreign Passports Only": Geographies of (Post) Conflict Work in Kabul, Afghanistan'. *Annals of the Association of American Geographers* 99(5): 986–94.

Fluri, J.L. (2009b). 'The Beautiful "Other": A Critical Examination of "Western" Representations of Afghan Feminine Corporeal Modernity'. *Gender, Place & Culture* 16(3): 241–57.

Fluri, J.L. (2009c). 'Geopolitics of Violence form Below' *Political Geography* 28: 256–65.

Fluri, J.L. (2011a). 'Armored Peacocks and Proxy Bodies: Gender Geopolitics in Aid/Development Spaces of Afghanistan'. *Gender, Place & Culture* 18(4): 519–36.

Fluri, J.L. (2011b). 'Bodies, Bombs and Barricades: Geographies of Conflict and Civilian (In)security'. *Transactions of the Institute of British Geographers* 36(2): 280–96.

Fluri, J.L. (2012). 'Capitalizing on Bare Life: Sovereignty, Exception, and Gender Politics'. *Antipode* 44(1): 31–50.

Fluri, J.L. (2014). 'States of (in)security: Corporeal geographies and the elsewhere war'. *Environment and Planning D: Society and Space* 32: 795–814.

Fluri, J.L. (2019). 'What's so Funny in Afghanistan? Jocular Geopolitics and the Everyday Use of Humor in Spaces of Protracted Precarity'. *Political Geography* 68: 125–30.

Fluri, J.L. and Bagheri, N. (2019). 'Gendered Circular Migrations of Afghans: Fleeing Conflict and Seeking Opportunity', in K. Mitchell, R. Jones and J.L. Fluri (eds) *Handbook of Critical Geographies of Migration*. Cheltenham: Edward Elgar Publishing.

Fluri, J.L. and Lehr, R. (2017). *The Carpetbaggers of Kabul and Other American-Afghan Entanglements: Intimate Development and the Currency of Gender and Grief*. Athens, GA: University of Georgia Press.

Fluri, J.L. and Lehr, R. (2019). '"We Are Farkhunda": Geographies of Violence, Protest, and Performance'. *Signs: Journal of Women in Culture and Society* 45(1): 149–73.

Hirschkind, C. and Mahmood, S. (2002). 'Feminism, the Taliban, and Politics of Counter-insurgency'. *Anthropological Quarterly* 75(2): 339–54.

Hunt, K. (2002). 'The Strategic Co-optation of Women's Rights'. *International Feminist Journal of Politics* 4(1): 116–21.

Reynolds, A. (2006). 'The Curious Case of Afghanistan'. *Journal of Democracy* 17(2): 104–17.

Roberts, S.M. (2014). 'Development Capital: USAID and the Rise of Development Contractors'. *Annals of the Association of American Geographers* 104(5): 1030–51.

Shrestha, R. and Fluri, J.L. (2021). 'Geopolitics of Humour and Development in Nepal and Afghanistan,' in E. Vanderheiden and C.H. Mayer (eds) *After You Have Been through Hell*: Cultural and *Positive Psychology Perspectives on Humour – The Palgrave Handbook of Humour Research*. Cham: Palgrave Macmillian, pp 189–204.

Sopko, J.F. (2014a). 'Afghan Women: Comprehensive Assessments Needed to Determine and Measure DOD, State, and USAID Progress'. Special Inspector General for Afghanistan Reconstruction (SIGAR), 15–24 Audit Report (December), 1–44.

Sopko, J.F. (2014b). 'SIGAR 15–24 Audit Report: Afghan Women: Comprehensive Assessments Needed to Determine and Measure DOD, State, and USAID Progress'. *Office of the Special Inspector General for Afghanistan Reconstruction (SIGAR)*, 1–44.

2

Women Weaving Critical Geographies

*GeoBrujas-Comunidad de Geógrafas: Frida Itzel Rivera Juárez,
Gabriela Mariana Fenner-Sánchez, Karla Helena Guzmán Velázquez,
Valeria Ysunza, Tlazol Tlemoyotl,
Esperanza González Hernández, and Karina Flores Cruz*

Assembling the warp: introduction

We are a collective of eight women geographers that strives to create community among women geographers from diverse latitudes. We began this project in September 2014, rooting ourselves in the march on Mexico City after the forced disappearance of the 43 students of Ayotzinapa.[1] GeoBrujas, Community of Women Geographers, arises as a political necessity against the violent context of the state, the extreme violence against women in Mexico, and the lack of spaces for women geographers within and outside of academia. We align with the creation of other geographies through political and social relationships.

Our impulse and continuous work are the development of a community stemming from self-generated, radical, and alternative geographies that do not adhere to the rhythms of hegemonic systems or the hierarchical relations within any field or level. Our aim is to integrate the rhythms of each *compañera* (comrade) to collectively amplify our perspectives.

As a collective, GeoBrujas positions ourselves alongside other collaborative networks which centre projects, organizations, movements, and people looking towards autonomy as a common horizon, those that include self-critique between that which is personal as well as political. We perform this collective labour to construct 'geografías otras'[2] among all of us and for all of us with our activism and our academic, political, and personal work in our day-to-day activities.

Among us, we use diverse methodological perspectives and foci to create critical cartographies, counter-cartographies, and mapping from a multileveled analysis. We use tools based in the arts, therapeutic techniques, popular education, social cartography, participatory systems of geographic information, and other foci. We share common concerns, interests, and learning processes through workshops and talks. Through this, we continue working towards learning about self-care, the strengthening of and the emotional health of our *territorio-cuerpo-tierra* (territory-body-earth)[3] in different contexts of dispossession.

The body, as the first level of our work, has regained recent importance in militant activism and academic investigation. In this sense, our work emphasizes mapping the body as territory and as feminist cartography, though this mapping is not over-generalized across communities. The foci and the experiences of each integrant are distinct, thus enriching and challenging us to amplify each individual standpoint impacting the multiple geographies and perspectives that cross our bodies.

The objective of this chapter is to share our lessons and constructed experiences during seven years of collective adventures, and to recall some of the workshops that have been the most significant for us. We reflect upon two grand thematic areas that have called us to different spaces: environmental issues and gender violences.

More than just thematic subjects or conceptual axis theories, we define these tools or techniques as 'threads' because we use them to weave epistemological, methodological, pedagogical, and experiential tapestries among diverse groups of people brought together within the space created through our workshops. Our community has mainly conducted the workshops in university settings, or in self-managed and community centres with the duration of the workshops ranging from two to four hours as we have attempted to hold space in our collective encounter with trust and reflection about the topic which has brought us together. In the majority of cases, these workshops are solicited by a group, organization or centre of investigation, and we adapt our methodologies to the context and the specific people involved. This disposition has allowed us to amplify our own creativity, while at the same time implying challenges that we must face collectively and while valuing our individual experiences and wisdom. The context of the COVID-19 pandemic, for example, led us to transform our dynamics and to create new ones based on both the possibilities and the limitations that virtuality offers. It was important for us to continue to fulfil our mission of creating spaces of empathy, trust, and, above all, *apapacho* (loving care). Since 2020, we have dared to weave ourselves into the virtual space, often very intangible and distant, but always real.

Our goal of becoming more acquainted with and utilizing new visual tools as ways to denounce the violence against women led us to express some of the feelings and the experiences that we had when we called for and organized the collective. We launched the photographic exhibition: *Altermiradas viajeras* (Traveling Other-views) in which we reclaimed our perspectives and the practice of travelling as women.

We share two 'threads', both demonstrating the manners in which we have understood these subjects. We offer the rationale by which we propose developing our multi-scalar approach through critical thinking and knowledgeable dialogue, interaction between art and popular education, and the importance of an approach from the *cuerpo-territorio* (body-territory) that we take along on our path. We close with a third section by intertwining both threads, from an auto-critical analysis, leaving some obvious 'loose threads' which leads us to realize that what we share here is only a fragment of our journey. This tapestry, this weaving, delves into the relationship that exists among the topics shared within our proposal for a critical, Latin American, feminist, antipatriarchal, anticolonial, anticapitalist, and antiracist geography.

The first thread: environmental perceptions through emotions

How do we approach 'environment'? Why are the GeoBrujas interested in thinking and acting with *otrxs* (others) regarding environmental topics? We considered our path and we recognized the coming-together of three large fields of thought and ways of seeing the world: political ecologies, humanist geography, and anticolonial thought.

Through political ecologies, we have developed a view that looks for and recognizes the underlying structural relationships of power beneath all the environmental problems that we are confronting today in the world. Many of these underlying structures result in conditions of social inequality and injustice concerning the use and enjoyment of, and the interweaving and experience with 'the second nature' (Santos, 2000; O'Connor, 2001; Smith, 2008). When they are not totally opposing, the clashes and disputes between thought paradigms and divergent cosmovisions are brought to light like the contrasts between the extractivist model that promotes private property and the exploitation of resources for the benefit of a small percentage of the population, and the collective manners of belonging to a whole in which human beings as well as non-humans offer mutual care.

In this sense, anticolonial thought allows us to understand that the inequalities and the injustices mentioned stem from a social, political, and legal (dis)order established during the colonial-modernity period, and from which colonialist power and being having been deployed.[4] This (dis)order has transformed into a deviating power, one of political practices and gestation in environmental and cultural terms. Upon examining and questioning the relationships of power that are woven into our societies by way of the environment, we cannot leave out the reflections made by Rita Segato, in which the category of 'race' is one of historic creation that spoils and arranges corporality in a hierarchical model:

> it is a sign, a trace of history in the subject, that marks a position and signals the inheritance of a dispossession ... race is not necessarily a sign of a constituted people, of an ethnic group, of an other culture, rather it is a trace like a footprint in the body of the passages of an 'otherfied' history that constructed 'race' to create 'Europe' as an epistemic, economic, technological and a 'moral jurisdiction' idea that distributes value and meaning to our world. (Segato, 2007, p 23)

This delineation of dispossession, in addition to being applied to the corporealities, is also superimposed upon territories in the form of environmental racism. The displacement and the violence caused by the Nation-States of the global north have organized a 'new international division of work' characterized by the globalization and the neoliberal phase of capitalism, which include distinct forms of manipulating the sexual division of this 'new capitalist ideology'. Within traditional, ecological, and political perspectives, the analytical tiers and the subjects studied are represented in the macro scale. For example, studies are done concerning the manner of organization between the macroeconomy of Latin American countries and other 'global south' countries, taking into account the roles of the state, the market, and the community regarding activities such as mega-mining and industrial monoculture.

On the other hand, political feminist ecologies question these dynamics on a global measure but weave in the analysis with more local and daily elements. They include reflections about the way macroeconomy is sustained by the microeconomy of a place, how they are based on work as well as the exploitation of communities, and how, in reality, they are not considered consistent. From these perspectives, the corporeal effects of these economic activities are questioned:

> feminist political ecology comes in with a feminist perspective and a critique that demands its own epistemiology and methodologies. From there, many systematic projects have been generated by diverse investigators that deconstruct the nature/culture relationship and the relationship of gender in order to position other perspectives and visions having to do with power processes that cut through the production of knowledge and social practices. (Ulloa, 2020, p 75)

The need to encounter intrinsic epistemologies and methodologies is a rallying point for political, ecological feminists, and anticolonial thought.

Both proposals question the relationship of power concerning the production of knowledge and the validation of the same. This epistemic node has allowed us to imagine and creatively develop the workshops that we offer. It has also helped us to recognize, position, and question our place of articulation.

By working with environmental issues, our work aligns with humanistic geography by highlighting the experiential ties to a space and understanding the subjectivities that cross it. In this sense, the humanistic geographies define themselves against the objective, natural, and neutral pretentiousness of the scientific geographies of neopositivism (Ortega-Valcárcel, 2000). We explore human subjectivity and how it constructs the experience of space of each individual, and as Yi Fu Tuan says (2007, p 10):

> All in all, attitudes and beliefs cannot be excluded, not even from a practical approach, because it is practical to take into account human emotions in any environmental equation. Nor can the theoretic focus be excluded, considering that the human being is, in fact, the dominant ecology of excellence, and it is not enough to observe and document its conduct; it is imperative to understand it with much more clarity.

In order to approach environmental motifs, the workshops that we created articulate a standpoint that privileges a spectrum of diverse perspectives and ways to comprehend the world. We can affirm that we have placed ourselves to begin our dialogues through our lived realities; some of our experiences could be deemed problems or even socio-ecological conflicts.[5]

With this as our focus, the intention has been to take on environmental issues from a bodily dimension in a sensory, political, and actuating sense. We assume that environmental issues affect the possibilities of life itself, of health and the quality of life. Thus, they are intimately linked with the bodily experience and form part of our daily life: 'The experience is as much sensation as it is thought, and it refers to the distinct forms in which a person knows and constructs reality; sensation and thought are the constitutive parts of the human experiential continuum that involves all feelings and acts of symbolization' (Delgado, 2003, p 112).

In this 'human experience continuum', part of the creative process involves acts of symbolization, in which human practices are vinculated within the structure and the superstructure of production. Everyday life is the place through which social imaginaries and the construction of subjectivity are intertwined with contextual economic, political, and cultural practices and dynamics.

According to the feminist geographer Anna Ortiz (2012, p 117), 'the body is what we are, it is that in which we experience our emotions and where we connect with the world'. The trajectories of gender, class, origin, and ethnicities are embodied. They represent and are practiced constantly in our bodies; which at the same time, are continuously traversed by sensations that, afterwards, can be translated into emotions and feelings (Ysunza, 2021).

Before conceiving it in this manner, there has been a large epistemological and political journey, one of recognition; and so we must acknowledge that 'the body has been understood as a separate entity of space, while territory has been considered a spatial configuration of political administration, statistics and delineations of well defined borders' (Ysunza, 2021, p 122); just as the earth, from a capitalist vantage point, is seen and used merely as a resource for extraction.

In response to this modern and hegemonic understanding of the body, territory and earth, we are currently trying to dissolve these ontological borders in order to form a complex comprehension of the relationship with their totality, facing the distinct, cross-scale connections that arise simultaneously and spring from the body itself that we are, in constant relation with territories and the earth (Ysunza, 2021):

> Considering other decolonial proposals in the analysis of spatial categories, the visions of feminist geographers take up and revindicate Indigenous and Latin American experiences (Lorena K'abnal and Aura Lolita Chávez in Mayan territory, and Adriana Guzmán from Aymara territory in Bolivia) of the social-environmental struggles and against the violence against women from more intimate scales, on horizontal and micro levels, in order to proclaim that the body is also territory, a space that is materially and symbolically outlined and appropriated, constructor of identities and loaded with significations of power. Thus, as we say in GeoBrujas, the body is not only conceived, but it is our own and most immediate territory, our first stopover, which makes contact and interacts with the other body-territories. The body, being a territory, is a space of power, of existence and 'r-existence', as expressed by Porto-Gonçalves (2016). (Ysunza, 2021, pp 124–5)

In regard to the earth, it is not a resource nor a source of materials, but rather a refuge zone, according to Milton Santos. It is the sustenance that gives sense to the existence of many communities where they revindicate their struggles and preserve their memory and heritage, a concept that is highly questioned this day in age. Finally, with this circuit, we weave into and connect with *territorio-cuerpo-tierra* (territory-body-earth).

So the body, daily life, and living spaces are dimensions from which we position ourselves to observe environmental issues. We situate our sensory/bodily selves in both an individual and collective manner in order to travel through different territorial dimensions that help us to understand our critical and reflective stance about the world in which we live.

In order to weave in this thread, we revisit five workshops that we organized between 2015 and 2020 with distinct groups of people, mostly from Mexico, but also from other Latin American countries, Switzerland and the United States.

1. *Nuestros dolores y esperanzas: cartografías del despojo* (Our Pains and Hopes: Cartographies of Displacement) created with 'artivists' and activists that live in Mexico City.
2. *Mapeo de problemas ambientales desde la percepción sensorial* (Mapping Environmental Issues from a Sensory Perception) shared with the students of the Universidad Autónoma Metropolitana – Iztapalapa, Ciudad de México.
3. *Territorios interconectados* (Interconnected Territories), facilitated virtually with the students from the Faculty of Arts of the University of Basilea, Switzerland.
4. *Tras la Huella del racismo – Justicia Territorial para evidenciar el Racismo Ambiental* (Beyond the Footprint of Racism – Territorial Justice to Prove Environmental Racism), offered virtually, designed for students and activists from California, United States.
5. *Altermapeo de conflictos socioambientales en el contexto de pandemia* (Alter-mapping of Socio-economic Conflicts within the Context of Pandemia), realized virtually with people from different Latin American countries as part of the 'Utopias Liquidas' Festival organized by CLEA[6] and CoLEA.[7]

In each of our workshops, we begin by waking up the senses with an exercise that is used as a way to inhabit our body, feel it, become aware and in control of it, and from that centring point we begin our encounter. During the Alter-mapping workshop specifically, which centred on socio-environmental conflicts, it was interesting to feel and be embodied by such senses, and transmit to another body, inhabiting it imaginatively to practice a cross-species and cross-temporal empathy.

Each participant imagined being the non-human element involved in an environmental conflict and, from that perspective, lived the effects of environmental actions and those imposed by the actors upon them. This allowed, for a moment, to see the human species not as the key player, but rather as just another piece of the puzzle that makes up a much larger and complex ecosystem. We were able to put into perspective that even though we are just one of the components, we play a terribly destructive role. The effects of our acts can destroy structures and elements whose formations have occurred over thousands and millions of years.

Without a doubt, this involved a sensitizing exercise that was incredibly hard and disturbing because these abuses of the non-human elements were felt in a human body for just a moment. In the following collective creation activity, we offered an artistic leeway after this experience, above all, in order to hold space for *la escucha* (the listening) to be able to return to a place of feeling accompanied, a collective hug, and not being left in desolation. 'To hug life' is a political posture, understood as an act to defend and conserve life in its total biodiversity, proposed by Vandana Shiva. In her book written in 1988, she proposes different critical standpoints of ecofeminism starting with the *Chipko* (hug in Hindi) movement. This ecological movement was begun by women when they hugged the trees in order to defend the forests and set an example of consciousness in the world and caring for life.

Environmental movements give us political references for generating awareness of the political and economic background that is behind environmental problems, which produce inequalities and environmental injustices that eventually detonate socio-environmental conflicts. To uncover territorial plots and visibilize the implied actors in the problems and conflicts has been part of the workshops that we have offered, with the intention of purposefully contributing to unravel the complexity of the situations through possible strategies and alternatives.

Such is the case of our first workshop, *Nuestros dolores y esperanzas: cartografías del despojo* (Our Pains and Hopes: Cartography of the Dispossession) in which we reflected upon the geopolitical position in which Mexico finds itself. Many distinct megaprojects that have expanded displacement during the neoliberal phase of capitalism were analysed. We discussed the systematic violence that patriarchal capitalism imposes upon our *territorio-cuerpos*. In this case, feminist activist *compañeras* (women comrades) and academics articulated the advance of the femicide violence in our country. This demonstrated that it is not only important to visualize this panorama, but also that it is necessary to share our collective feelings, express our indignation and to manifest, by means of collective mapping and body mapping, our distinct forms of resistance and in this way to feel *acuerpada* (embodied, supported).

Structural analysis, raising consciousness and *acuerpamiento afectivo* (affective organizing) are braided together in our methodological proposals. Each action has been to mobilize not only the intellect, but also to be more sensitive when facing what is happening in our world in an empathetic way with all communities: human, animal, vegetable, fungal, mineral, and so on.

These proposals imply moving between the levels, and this we have done in different ways according to the diverse groups and contexts of our workshop, and also thanks to our experiences and learnings throughout the years. In the workshop *Mapeo de problemas ambientales desde la percepción temporal* (Mapping Environmental Problems from a Time Perspective) the approach was almost schematic, a species of *matryoshka* (Russian nesting dolls) where each scale fits within a bigger one. We think that this method helps to locate the implications of each scale, but at the same time it is difficult to conduct a continuous analysis; in certain moments the reflections and the analysis begin to fragment.

Contrastingly, in the workshop *Altermapeo de conflictos socioambientales en el contexto de pandemia* (Alter-mapping Socio-environmental Conflicts in the Context of Pandemic), conducted from the virtual reality in which we found ourselves shaped by the fact that the people came from distinct places, there was already a trans-scale positioning that was even more multifaceted and interconnected. This was reinforced by the way in which each participant presented themselves and 'brought their space to the meeting', the environmental conflict of their own interest and how each person articulated their feeling, their personal experience and at the same time the territorial entities and elements implicated in the mentioned conflicts. Afterward, with the main exercise in which our body was 'lent' to the non-human element being affected by the environmental problem, the scales then fused, were inverted. Following the *matryoshka* analogy, it would have been like fitting the biggest element into the smallest of them all.

Finally, another perspective from which we have approached the environmental problems has been from our daily practices that are oftentimes unquestioned, like the things we consume. That is to say, that is to propose an analysis of our consumption patterns to realize and ask ourselves, What responsibilities do we have? By doing this, we also raise awareness of how each one of us contributes to said problems, and thus we have the possibility to participate in its transformation by means of reflections and empathetic relations. This echoes Soja (2014) and the socialized geographies of (in)justice that significantly affect our lives creating lasting structures of opportunities and disadvantages distributed in an unequal manner, 'these geographies and their effects can be modified through forms of social and political action' (Soja, 2014, p 52). And it is precisely towards this last mark that we aim.

We approached this target using a dynamic activity with the students of Basilea, in which they had to recognize the place of origin of distinct objects of personal consumption by looking at their labels; like the exercise *Tras las huellas del racismo* (Behind the Footprints of Racism), taken from a methodology of *Ecofeminismo para principiantes* (Ecofeminism for Beginners) designed by one of our *compañeras*.[8] This body mapping exercise begins with standing on the soles of our feet and tracing their outline to create consciousness about the place of origin and mobility of the 'migratory footprint' and to recognize the environmental implications in the inhabited territory of the 'ecological footprint'.

A key element in this map was to question ourselves from a specific point in which we are situated: Where do we come from? Where are we? Who and how do we inhabit the city? Placing emphasis on the fact that cities are the places with a greater concentration of consumption, extraction and energetic requirements (food, goods, and services). That set of a reflection about the production-consumption chain of the goods and services: Where are they produced? Who are we dispossessing? What is the environmental impact of the local industry and infrastructure? We were able to dig deeper in the discussion about inequalities, displacement, and extractivism both in and out of the cities because, by way of the migratory and ecological footprint cartography, we oriented ourselves in the present and recuperated the memory with the objective of recognizing the changes in the inhabited territory and the modifications to the day-to-day landscape.

This methodology permits us to stand upon our life stories in order to name, represent, and recognize the forms of the production of space. As expressed by E. Soja (2014), spatial (in)justice is situated and contextualized in three overlapping levels of geographic resolution: 1) external creation of unjust geographies, borders, and political organization of space; 2) local distribution of inequalities that create discriminatory geographies; 3) the globalization of injustice.

The recognition of the footprints left by racism situates us in the analysis of discriminatory processes in the spatial dimension. On one level, the worldwide panorama, the majority of the countries located in the global north demonstrate a greater concentration of riches and resources that allow for the sustainment of their high acquisitive power at the cost of the global south. On another level, the centre-periphery relationship is reflected in the infrastructure, security, quality, and access to goods and services which privilege certain zones within the same city.

Transnationalization and business corporatism, which respond to a model of consumption and factory production, are situated above the structural relations of the economic and cultural system of hierarchies established over the social classes (entrepreneurs and workers), and go beyond a lifestyle. They imply political and commercial actors which impoverish territories by means of extractivism and systematic displacement. Awareness of our ecological footprint is not a question of individual culpability or responsibility because these feelings do not change the political structure of displacement, on the contrary, they promote a green 'eco-friendly' market that reinforces grand injustices, as well as social and ecological inequalities.

To synthesize, the methodological reflection between environmental levels and the many-tiered body has brought us to the sensitizing and the self-discovery of the world in which we live, the recognition of our ecological footprint from a political and self-critical questioning, the cultivation and practice of empathy, and the consideration of our social relationships and the natural ways of life, not in an individual manner, but rather collectively. By doing so, we prove that from the corporal dimension we can visibilize socio-environmental injustices and be conscious of them without merely being spectators.

The second thread: mapping violence to make resistance visible

Based on our experience, the workshops that have the spatiality of violence as the central theme have two main objectives. The first refers to bringing light to the naturalized violences that we, as women, live in daily, and the second is to generate and accompany sensibilization processes in relation to the diverse embodiments that we live in order to tell the unique story or the universality of history and geography. Both objectives come together in assuming, as a starting point, that space is an active agent in the construction of relations and identities. This is why in these workshops we turn to the production of alter-mapping and collective counter-cartographies in a horizontal dialogue between those of us who facilitate the workshop and those who share their experience, perception, and *senti-pensar* (thinking-feeling).

The *sentipensamiento* (thinking-feeling), 'a concept born from fishers of the *momposina* depression in the north of Colombia and diffused by Orlando Fals Borda',[9] is presented as a path that makes possible the integral formation of the human being in which the importance of the interrelation between the emotional and rational processes, that are as connected in the mind as well as the body, are taken into account. This consideration implies that people vinculate more complex and critical points of view in order to generate collective consciousness and to propose reflections that include the recognition of the other as a fundamental actor in social transformations.

In addition to the workshops, we use photography as another tool to that reclaim the *sentipensares* that cross our body to confront the violences against women. Several of these views, which we have compiled together as an allegation, are part of the photographic exhibition that we put together at the beginning of 2017.

Altermiradas Viajeras came about halfway through 2016 by way of a reencounter in the lives of two of the GeoBrujas (Karla and Valeria), while chatting and having a coffee. During this conversation, they agreed that both were unsettled and angered by the violence against women. In fact, none of the GeoBrujas feel separated from the lamentable tales surrounding the cases of femicides while travelling. Be it because of empathy, the feeling of collective care or the search for justice, we are each touched by these happenings because they have to do with women like any one of us that simply wants to exercise her right to mobility, transit, liberty, and leisure.

Based on this exchange of *sentipensamientos*, we called for sorority and an homage to the *compañeras* that are no longer with us. We opened the space to women from different coordinates and found even more voices resonated with the denouncement who also needed to share their views and stories of journeys they took as women travellers, the majority being geographers, anthropologists, and photographers, and who had been invisibilized in the patriarchal world in which the paths and trips seem to be exclusively for men.

So it was that we were able to compile various photographs by 23 women in five countries – Mexico, Brazil, Chile, United States and Italy – that were shown in an exhibition in *La Gozadera*, an emblematic point of feminist encounters and sexual diversity that existed in the centre of Mexico City. It was later on display in *El Paliacate*, a cultural space in San Cristobal de Las Casas, Chiapas. With this showing of *Altermiradas Viajeras*, we wanted to express that travelling is not only for or done by men, that our bodies are not limited by nor prohibited from travelling, and that we also have legs and wings to follow the course of the world and the movement of life, both of which are necessary to be free and feel alive.

The exhibition left us with great lessons and lots of desire to meet more women with whom we could exchange stories and experiences with in order to strengthen our connections and find paths together. Because of this experience, we continue to organize and/or facilitate workshops with the objective of bringing to light the violences we suffer, as well as to create awareness of the details of historic and geographical corporalities.

To explain the theoretical-methodological approach of this type of workshop, we take into account four experiences:

1. The workshop *Análisis territorial de un espacio de violencia en la ciudad* (Territorial Analysis of a Violent Space in the City) that took place in Morelia, Michoacan during the *II Taller Internacional de Creación Cartográfica: acciones para la construcción de nuevas narrativas territoriales* (II International Workshop of Cartography Creation: Actions for the Construction of New Territorial Narratives).[10]
2. The field study *Análisis territorial de un espacio de violencia* (Territorial Analysis of a Violent Space) done with students from the *Universidad Nacional Autónoma de México* (UNAM).
3. The workshop *Análisis territorial de un espacio de violencia en la ciudad* (Territorial Analysis of a Violent Space in the City) done with students from the *Escuela Nacional de Estudios Superiores* (ENES).
4. The workshop *Mapeo Corporal Cuerpo-Danza-Geografía* (Body Mapping-Dance-Geography) offered during the *Primer Encuentro de Mujeres (First Encounter of Women)* in San Pedro Atlapulco, Ocoyoacac, State of Mexico.

Now, let's consider the common threads of these four contexts: what do the women of Atlapulco have in common with the students of the UNAM in Mexico City or with the people from diverse latitudes united in the international encounter in the city of Morelia? It would be relatively easy to redirect the answer towards the fact that the violence that we live with these days is structural, and that is true; however, it is important to understand that the same violence manifests at the same time both directly and culturally. What's more, it is exercised in different manners depending on the social condition, the racialization of bodies, classism and gender, or any process vinculated to the production of otherness.

The execution of the workshop *Análisis territorial de un espacio de violencia en la ciudad* took place at the end of November, 2018 and had two fundamental antecedents. First, a field practice was done in the *Ciudad Universitaria* of the UNAM in which maps were used for the identification and representation of the perception of violence, insecurity, and spaces of fear on the university campus. The second was a workshop done the same month in the ENES-UNAM and was offered to undergraduate students of Social Studies and Local Administration, primarily working with techniques from the *Teatro del Oprimido* (Theatre of the Oppressed),[11] especially with the Human Machine exercise in which violent actions were represented with different bodies. The result of this workshop was the creation of a space that highlighted the violence that we live with in the cities and in educational environments.

In both experiences, the students went through sensitizing processes having to do with the same theme, which led them to identify and name manifestations of distinct types of assaults on their daily lives that they hadn't before recognized, like State violence, for example.

Using the previous experiences as a foundation, the dynamic for *Análisis territorial de un espacio de violencia en la ciudad* where the sensorial perception in the body was part of the conscientization of the violence that is lived as part of the construction of urban territories. To do this, we used methods like biodance and dance therapy; we moved through body and space perception exercises within urban ambiance, as well as including the confrontation of different models of understanding and living in the city which contradict one another and can become tense or even violent. Finally, we proposed a reflection about these conflicts and violent expressions, and in this way ended with a collective recollection that generated changes in the tensions provoked in the bodies (GeoBrujas, 2019).

On the other hand, with respect to the field study done in the *Ciudad Universitaria*, a visit to the campus was made, stopping in places where there were recognized cases of gender violence. There was consideration of the architectural design, the distribution and fragmentation of the spaces, and reflection upon how the solitary and dark spaces promote student insecurity. The purpose was to visibilize femicide violence, like had occurred when the body of Lesvy Berlín Osorio was found, strangled by her boyfriend in a telephone booth on the university campus in 2017. The intention of highlighting this act was to question: 1) the spatial message of fear that is created by femicide violence and 2) the possibility of action, denouncement, being alert and establishing one's own connections and safety strategies.

Contrastingly, but with similar tones, we had the opportunity to facilitate the workshop *Mapeo Corporal: Cuerpo-Danza-Geografía* (Body Mapping: Body-Dance-Geography) in San Pedro Atlapulco with Indigenous women, *campesinas* (women who work with the land) and women defenders of their territory. In the opening activity, we did dance therapy exercises with the objective of creating dialogue from the body in movement and artistic expression. The methodology led to creative processes that expanded the sensitivity of the participants to paint two silhouettes that they intervened with texts and graphic representations in order to recognize practices and discourses of violence, fear, and insecurity concerning their bodies. Inside the drawings, they painted the elements, practices, strategies and words that strengthen them from the collective body against the *machista* (misogynist, macho) violences of the community.

One of the differences between this workshop and the others mentioned was that the political practice of these women was established between the sharing of community wisdom and the broad knowledge that they have gained through herbalism. This marks a specific relationship with the landscape and the ways of living among it, because the cosmovision and the cultural codes are distinct with respect to the urban context. There exists a collective sentiment of belonging with the place, where the representation of the violences isn't lived from an individual perspective, rather they resound in a collective-community sense.

Another contrasting element between the workshop in Atlapulco and the other two that were held in academic spaces was the perception of violence that provokes the racialization of bodies. To be an Indigenous woman, and the use of the word *india*, are markings that appeared in the cartographies created by the women from Atlapulco. Meanwhile, with the students in the field practice, this violence was reflected in words like: nation-state, discrimination, and stereotypes.

Diverse perspectives exist that cover the typology of violence and, in some workshops, we have recovered as a tool the wheel diagram of control and power which categorizes and explains the forms of violence: physical, psychological, emotional, sexual, economic, and patrimonial. However, we problematize these categories and consider the central axis to be the violence of the state:

> Any violence causes fear, which can be resolved in different ways, but does not necessarily terrorize. To provoke terror, a violence of extermination, constant, massive and indiscriminate is required, visible but negated, a violence that no one knows exactly from where it arises, that is to say, a violence that potentially threatens the entirety, and is

able to immobilize it; because of these characteristics, the possibility of generating terror primarily stems from the State or cases that are protected by it. (Calveiro, 2014, p 196)

In Mexico and Latin America, violence against women increases each day and is produced in a systematic and generalized way in contexts of impunity; by consequence, we observe that these manners fragment 'the social collective with a consistent message: this which is happening, is happening to us. And from there the phrase: If you touch one of us, you touch us all. As a response to the violence of the state, the women, in their majority youth and students, decide to make allegations' (Guzmán, 2014, p 80).

And so, the planning and models that sustain the current design of the cities have excluded, in many occasions, the specific needs of diverse social groups (women, minors and elders, many people with diverse functionalities, minorities) in their daily use of the city and the manner of relationships that are established within the city (Genera Barri, 2018). This then generates gender biases that end up being violent for these excluded social groups (GeoBrujas, 2019).

From our vantage point, we cannot overlook the fact that power relationships operate on all spatial scales. As such, when analysing the *cuerpo-territorio* (body-territory), primarily among women, we take into account the importance of the power that is impressed upon the body – *corpolitica* (body politics):[12]

> It is in the feminine body where the territorial conflict is most intertwined and, therefore, it is the field in which the battles for the same are played out (Segato, 2014). Assassination, rape or any other form of torture or explicit domination of the feminine and feminized body ... represent the isolation, punishment and total marginalization of a person, losing sovereignty over their own body. (Ysunza and Mondragón, 2019, p 179)

So, during these experiences in the workshops, we have reaffirmed that violence is not only practiced, exercised, or lived, but also it is conceived, perceived, and imagined. Thus, an element that has led us to the design and collective creation of these activities is the search for methodologies that allow us to develop in a creative manner, what David Harvey (1977, p 17) has called 'spatial consciousness' or 'geographical imagination', in urban spaces:

> This imagination allows the individual to understand the role that the space and the place have in their own biography, to relate with the spaces that they see around them and to realize that the manner in which the transactions between individuals and organizations

are affected by the space that separates them ... This allows them to understand the relationship that exists between them and their surroundings ... 'their territory' ... It allows them to create ideas and utilize the space creatively and appreciate the significance of the spatial forms created by others.

In this manner, mapping the violence in the spaces and bodies, by means of the individual and collective experience, allows us to understand the relationship that is established between the social processes in the city and the spatial forms taken on by cities.

These learning processes help us discover diverse graphic representations and narratives about individual and collective experiences of occupying territory; this allows us to analyse violences from a territorial and critical perspective, from a theoretical positioning of the spatial trialect or the production of space (Lefebvre, 1974) in which exist latent tensions between the conceived space, the perceived space and the lived space.[13]

To understand violence from this perspective implies intertwining its structural, multilevel, and, of course, spatial and territorial dimensions. The incarnation in its being of 'the process of production of speciality or of "the construction of cartographies" begins with the body, with the construction and *performance* of being, of the human subject as a particularly spatial entity, implicated in a complex relation with its surroundings' (Soja, 2008, pp 33–4).

We consider it important to position ourselves politically and to denounce that if the production of space begins with the body, then the domination and colonization of the body must be questioned not only as individual and collective subjects, but also through these relationships of this oppression in which space is produced. The construction of spaces is not only differentiated, but it is also unequal and unjust. Our methodologies are based on our own questioning of hegemonic, academic theory because, for us, it is insufficient in order to respond to the specificity of each context. We are learning from activists, territory defenders, *mujeres que luchan* (women who struggle), the political voice of Indigenous women who teach us other ways to create theory, and the practice of *feminismos comunitarios* (community feminisms).

We must recognize that in the Latin American context, political feminist wisdom is extracted. A self-critique is necessary for those of us who participate in activism and academic research. There is an urgent need to construct our own epistemologies and reflect upon body mapping not as a theoretical fad, but rather as a profound questioning of and in contestation to the current context, looking instead towards multiscalar analyses. It is a critical and radical process of reflection.

Body mapping offers us distinct, subversive possibilities of narrating for ourselves and creating other symbols and meanings of non-imposed representation which allow us to be in constant, internal exploration and to dive into our emotional depths; therefore, they are not static, they produce sensations and shift bodily memories that arise in the skin (Ysunza, 2021):

> The countercartagrophies which come about from the resistance and the *alteridad* (otherness) of the other voices previously invisibilized, but which now collectively participate in the dialogue of the construction process, extend the invitation to disorient the maps and call for them to be created from our own scales. The idea is to break with the lectures and hegemonic discourses of the territorial representations, including the corporeal ones. It has to do with shifting into acto in order to carry out many mappings between, amongst and for everyone starting from the micro, beginning with our own territory: the body. (p 126)

It bears mentioning the importance that working with emotions is for GeoBrujas from the geopolitics of the *cuerpos sensibles* (sensing bodies), a concept taken from Ivaldo Lima (2020), who speaks of the geopolitics of bodies that exist, work, age, attract, and care for one another. From this vantage point, the author proposes the reflection of affected bodies by geopolitics that act within multiple spatial scales. Lima (2020) mentions sensitively perceived geopolitics in daily life, altered by the social control of bodies. Therefore, power is expressed in those bodies, that is to say, the *corpolitica* (body politics). Not only is it a limitation that is imposed from outside, but also it is a personal and internal factor that is stimulated by exercises like body mapping, where power emanates a search for bodily, territorial, and social transformation.

In regards to the political project that is reflected in bodies, the continued positioning of *feminismos* and their social transformations has allowed us to redefine concepts and question the traditional division that has been elaborated around the spheres of public space and private space. The same has occurred with geography and its androcentric dichotomies: masculine/feminine, public/private, out/in, work/home, culture/nature, reason/emotion (Ortega-Valcárcel, 2000). García Ramón argues, 'Feminist Geography looks for sources of information and analysis methods that reveal experiences of women and their vision of the world' (1987, p 150). Therefore, the growth of one or various feminist discourses in geography has diverse manifestations (Ortega-Valcárcel, 2000) that we can appreciate throughout our workshops.

As Rogério Haesbaert (2006) mentions, it would be pertinent to overcome the material/ideal dichotomy, and better to make the shift towards the conceptual complexity of duality, which the territory envelops, at the same time, the concrete, spatial dimension of social relations and the conjunction of representations about space or the geographic imaginary that also moves these relationships. Ortega-Varcárcel (2000) proposes considering the processes, the agents (or better phrased the actors), alongside their practices, representations, and, we would add, spatial and territorial imaginaries, that belong to a renovated perspective and critique of geography. This is what we bring forth to reflect upon based on our geographic action-participation; even more so if we take into account that we are actually living a crisis of the already established systems of imposed representation, but that are in a process of deconstruction because each day they are being questioned more and more.

Weaving bridges, threading reflections

At this point we take up the two threads of ecology and of violence, to finally weave them into this tapestry of methodologies, pedagogies, epistemologies, and politics that we, as GeoBrujas, have created and that also sustains us, clothes us and allows us to become 'tangled up' with other people, collectives, and spaces. In our warp, we highlight the complexity of the body and its multiscaled range that is represented in the mappings, which include collective and critical construction. From this intersecting point, we have been able to weave discussions, experiences, feelings, different ways of resistance, and counter-hegemonic alternatives. It is essential that we emphasize some of the lessons and challenges that this weaving has offered us along the way, and how we have been transformed, as well.

Each workshop opens a space-time to allow for trust and empathy, of sharing and self-permission to incorporate new visions about daily phenomena and to dive deeper into some aspects of one's own biography in order to embrace and/or revindicate them. These workshops also allow for an opportunity to 'mirror' oneself and with others, weaving symbolically networks that inspire different paths.

For the participants, as well as for us, this space-time was cultivated due to the creative process and open dialogue during the planning of the workshops. The inclusion of debate about epistemologies, interpretations, and personal expectations allowed us to know each other on a different level.

The workshop in Atlapulco was challenging. Despite its proximity to Mexico City, Atlapulco has its own, distinct framework of communities, of which we are not a part. This caused an intergenerational, cultural clash. We had a greater empathy towards the youngest participants, primarily concerning our position against *machismos* (misogyny). We learned that, despite the rooted differences between each person's life story and context, each and every point of view and perspective are included in the mapping.

Contrastingly, we share a language and similar life contexts riddled with colonialism and structural violences with university students from Latin American countries. We also share certain sentiments about the political posturing against the contemporary world order. In this case, the challenge was, perhaps, focusing on the transition from the profound analysis of the oppressing structures and not remaining in a sentiment of impotence. In fact, we invite these reflections, experiences, and/or representations to act as a collective catharsis, as a call to action and organization.

On the other hand, the workshops that we facilitated for the students of the University of Vasilea presented some of the greatest challenges. Not only were they realized in a language that is not native to us, the workshop was held in a virtual setting, which was a context totally unfamiliar to the majority of the GeoBrujas. In addition, we felt that our difficulties in communicating with the group were not only due to the language, but also to the fact that it seemed that the group was not very used to participatory dynamics and expected us to give very precise instructions. We, as instructors using the principles of popular education, were only trying to be triggers or facilitators of processes that should start with them. By this we learned that participation is also something that must be learned and practiced, and that our ability to perceive how much can be asked of a group is fundamental.

However, we were able to overcome these instances because of three main elements. We felt supported by one another concerning the language. We also had previously experimented with the methodology; that is to say, there was a process of self-reflection, passing through the sensations that we hoped to carry through to the participants for them to experience. And finally, we just let the river take its course, without being focused on any one fixed result or destination.

Looking at the themes that we work with, it is evident that, in consonance with the *feminismos comunitarios* (community feminisms) and ecological feminist politics, environmental problems cannot be approached without delving into the connection between the dispossession of native lands and the injustice that is born from them, a product and foundation of the capitalist, neoliberal, and patriarchal economic system. The *compañeras* Zapatistas remind us[14] that the four wheels of capitalism are: dispossession, disdain, repression, and exploitation. They are the same that support the environmental injustices and the distinct forms of violence that we, as women, encounter daily.

We have learned to interweave diverse disciplines, enriching our geography, subverting it, conjuring it.[15] To do so, feminist geography has given us important elements thanks to the fractures that have occurred throughout the field. This questioning has not only arisen from these cracks, but from the very activists, from the women who take their bodies to the streets, to the *barrios*, to the mountains, and, in many moments throughout Latin American history, have stood up because we feel that we carry an inherited responsibility to continue along the beaten bath, naming those who came before us, citing them, and remarking their steps.

The last loose thread: in conclusion

During the development of our workshops, we have nurtured a dialogue with art, lacing together sensitivity and structure in order to create a wide fan of methodologies that, despite maintaining certain political principles, are always situated within a learning space. The reflections have reached levels so deep that they connect with *sentipensares* beyond the multi-levels that criss-cross our body. For this reason, we have chosen techniques, like biodance, dance therapy, aromatherapy, *el teatro del oprimido*, *la escucha*, and *el apapacho*, which have allowed us to contain emotional processes and offer us hope and an impulse towards action.

Before the COVID-19 pandemic, the workshops had been in-person, utilizing paper and pens, dance therapy techniques, and physical closeness. But now, we have adapted to the circumstances of the virtual, revamping our methodologies and finding digital platforms that allow for creative interaction. Even with the limitations of cyberspace, we have encountered ways to foster political closeness by creating spaces of reflection, hope, and collective *acuerpamiento* (embodiment).

The photographic exhibition served to show that every day there are more of us who travel and take the initiative to discover new landscapes despite the fact that, in many countries, aggression – be it abuse, rape and even murder – against us for being women has expanded considerably in recent years. Such circumstances have left us more vulnerable than men, for simply following our dreams.

We believe in a world that is more inclusive, just, and safe for all people, one in which each perspective and each path is respected. That is why we consider that it was of utmost importance to create this activity, sharing our experiences and *sentipensares* of our travels as an homage to our assassinated *compañeras,* and as an allegation against the violence that affects us day to day.

Finally, we would like to reiterate that this tapestry of theoretic reflections and methodologies is permanently being woven and un-woven, always braiding in what has been learned in the process. This is remembrance from the collective *sentipensar.* It affirms how important it is for us to make memory from a self-critical view, in order to walk towards new experiences, embrace our errors, our pleasures, our creativity, our silences, and our manner of changing and living the daily spaces in their many-scaled articulations.

There are still lots of roads ahead for us to wander, along different routes and towards various horizons, always concerned with creating collective, autonomous, and divergent geographies, always acting in alignment both in community and politically, without disorienting from the *autogestiva* (self-organizing) and feminist compass.

Notes

1. To find out more about this appalling case, visit: www.plataforma-ayotzinapa.org/
2. To speak of *geografías otra* and not *otras geografías* is suggested from a political positioning according to the Zapatista proposal in which the order is symbolically transformed, not only to create contrary meanings but ones that are also different, emergent, new, and transgressive.
3. This approach is a political principle proposed by *Feminismo Comunitario* of the Xinka women from Mayan territory, which integrates the historic and daily struggle of our *pueblos* for the recuperation and defense of the *territorio tierra* as a guarantee of concrete territorial space where the life of the bodies manifests (Cabnal, 2010, p 23).
4. It is necessary to understand the term 'coloniality' as a profound process, related to 'the means of knowing, the process of knowledge, of producing perspectives, images and imaging systems, symbols, signification methods, about resources, patterns, and formalized and objectivized instruments of expression, intellectual or visual' (Quijano, 2007, p 12); contrastingly to colonialism, as an explicit, political order in a determined time. According to the proposal of Anibal Quijano, 'the coloniality of power is one of the elemental components of the global pattern of capitalist power. It is founded in the imposition of racial/ethnic classification of the world population as an angular stone in the said pattern of power, and operates in each one of the material and subjective levels, planes and dimensions of daily life and the social sectors' (Quijano, 2007, p 93).

    As far as the coloniality of being goes, it is a term coined by Walter Mignolo (2007) that refers to the colonization of being and its impact on language. Nelson Maldonado-Torres comments 'it responds to the necessity of clarifying the question about the effects of coloniality in the lived experience, and not only in the mind of subalternate subjects' (2007, p 130).
5. An environmental problem arises from individual and collective perception and identification of the effects of an environmental phenomenon. It has to do with the recognition of our surroundings and our historically lived experience. Similarly, 'an environmental problem occurs because it has roots of social dimensions, there are those who conceptualize it in this way and a society that originates it' (Bautista et al, 2011, p 34). Confronting the environmental problems can cause distinct reactions, from disgust, disagreement, apathy, indignation, and/or political organization.

    However, a socio-environmental conflict refers to the opposition and confrontation of differing interests and power relationships. Paz and Risdell (2014) analyses that for an environmental problem to convert into a socio-environmental conflict, the variables of aggravation and the object in dispute must be present. The people must be conscious of an aggression in the form of some type of social injustice and must take action as a result of this organization.
6. Coordinadora Latinoamericana de Estudiantes de Arquitectura.
7. Coordinadora Latinoamericana de Estudiantes de Arquitectura del Cono Sur.
8. The ecofeminismo course was designed by Karla Helena Guzmán Velázquez in October 2019 as part of an alternative project of popular education about 'Ecology and Feminism'; the methodology was adapted for this workshop in collaboration with Frida Rivera and Karina Flores.
9. Manifesto *'Otras formas de existir'* Other Ways to Exist, 2021.
10. Organized by the investigation group ESTEPA (UNAL), CIGA-UNAM, ENES-UNAM, UCR, Universidad de Antioquia, GET-UNAL Amazonía, Altépetl and in collaboration with GeoBrujas. www.humanas.unal.edu.co/estepa/
11. This is a theatrical proposal developed by the Brazilian playwright Augusto Boal and born out of the context of repression in which she lived in Brazil in the dictatorship era (at the end of the 1960s); because of this, oppressive situations are represented but also

[12] mechanisms of liberation through body expression are experimented with by using the stage as a space of liberty and creativity.

[12] As a basis, Valeria Ysunza (2021), who revisits what was discussed in *Corpoliticas* (an organized event in Buenos Aires, 8–17 June 2007), the *corpolítica* refers to symbolic and physical power of society that is reflected both in the body and territory. This concept focuses on the body that is intervened by social forces, body politics, political bodies and the relation between them; as such, the body is considered as a place where negotiations take place and that is disciplined; that is to say, *corpolitica* is used as a 'medium of expression and significance' (Werth, 2007, p 1). Because of this, Valeria Ysunza (2021) clarifies that this power also can be transformative, resignified, and can even change direction through the manifestation of subversive bodily practices like dance, performance, activism, or artistic and social protests.

[13] In the spatially conceived plane, the structures of power are materialized and the hegemonic ideology is expressed in respect to the political and economic order; it is a space that is designed by the planification of urbanists, architects, technocrats, administrators, and so on. The perceived space is, therefore, that in which spatial practices are realized, it refers to the daily, social use of a space, always within a determinate historical timeframe; while the lived space is that of the representations, where symbolic systems, codes, and the social imaginary of diverse social groups that inhabit the territory are integrated and superimposed.

[14] Ejército Zapatista de Liberación Nacional, 2005. *Sexta Declaración de la Selva Lacandona*. Sixth Declaration of the Lacandon Jungle.

[15] GeoBrujas-Comunidad de Geógrafas, and Liz Mason-Deese (2021). 'Bodies, Borders, and Resistance: Women Conjuring Geography through Experiences from the Other Side of the Wall', *Journal of Latin American Geography* 20(2): 168–18. Project MUSE. doi:10.1353/lag.2021.0033.

References

Bautista, F., Balancán-Zapata, A., Navarro-Alberto, J., and Bocco, G. (2011). 'Percepción social de los problemas ambientales en Yucatán, México una visión desde la geografía'. *Teoría y Praxis* 9: 33–54.

Cabnal, L. (2010). *Feminismos diversos: el feminismo comunitario*. Madrid: ACSUR-Las Segovias, colección Feminista Siempre.

Calveiro, P. (2014). 'Repensar y ampliar la democracia. El caso del Municipio Autónomo de Cherán K'eri'. *Argumentos. Estudios críticos de la sociedad* 27 (75): 193–212. México: UAM-Xochimilco.

Delgado, O. (2003). *Debates sobre el espacio en la geografía contemporánea*. Bogotá: Red de Estudios de Espacio y Territorio. Universidad Nacional de Colombia.

García-Ramón, D. (1987). 'Geografía Feminista: una perspectiva internacional'. *Documents d'Análisi Geográfica* 10: 147–57.

Genera Barri. (15 November 2018). 'La ciudad con perspectiva de género: lo específico y lo diverso'. Available from: www.generabarri.com/genero-urbanismo-y-ciudad/ [Accessed 6 July 2021].

GeoBrujas (2019). 'Análisis territorial de un espacio de violencia en la ciudad', in Fenner-Sánchez, G., Monroy-Hernández, J., Aguilar-Galindo, J.E. y Barrera-Lobatón, S. (eds) *II Taller Internacional de Creación Cartográfica. Acciones para la construcción de nuevas narrativas territoriales. Memoria y guía metodológica*. Bogotá: Universidad Nacional de Colombia.

Guzmán, K. (2014). 'Género, espacio y participación en Atenco. Mujeres en defensa del territorio'. Tesis el grado de licenciatura en Geografía Humana, Universidad Autónoma Metropolitana, Iztapalapa. Available from: http://dcsh.izt.uam.mx/licenciaturas/geografia_humana/wp-content/uploads/2015/01/Tesina-Karla-Guzman-2014.pdf [Accessed 8 July 2021].

Haesbaert, R. (2006). 'Concepções de território para entender a desterritorializaçao', in M. Santos, B. Becker, C. Silva, C. Porto Gonçalves, E. Limonad, F. Almeida et al (eds) *Território, territórios: ensaios sobre o ordenamento territorial*, 2nd ed. Brasil: PPGEO/UFF, DP&A Editora, pp 43–70.

Harvey, D. (1977). *Urbanismo y desigualdad social*. Madrid: Siglo XXI de España Editores.

Lefebvre, H. (1974). 'La producción del espacio'. *Papers: revista sociológica* 3: 219–29. Universidad Autónoma de Barcelona.

Lima, I. (2020). 'A condição geopolítica dos corpos sensíveis', *Paisagens Híbridas*. Available from: https://paisagenshibridas.eba.ufrj.br/2020/04/01/a-condicao-geopolitica-dos-corpos-sensiveis/ [Accessed 22 July 2021].

Maldonado-Torres, N. (2007). 'Sobre la colonialidad del ser: contribuciones al desarrollo de un concepto', in Santiago Castro-Gómez and Ramón Grosfoguel (eds) *El giro decolonial. Reflexiones para una diversidad epistémica más allá del capitalismo global*. Bogotá: Iesco-Pensar-Siglo del Hombre Editores, pp 127–67.

Mignolo, W.D. (2007). 'Introduction: Coloniality of power and de-colonial thinking'. *Cultural Studies* 21(2–3): 155–67.

O´Connor, J. (2001). *Causas Naturales: ensayos de marxismo ecológico*. México: Siglo XXI.

Ortega-Valcárcel, J. (2000) 'Los horizontes de la Geografía. Teoría de la Geografía', *Ariel Geografía*. Available from: www.cervantesvirtual.com/descargaPdf/ortega-valcrcel-j-2000-resea--los-horizontes-de-la-geogr afa-teora-de-la-geografa-ariel-geografa-barcelona-604-pp-0/ [Accessed 23 July 2021].

Ortiz, A. (2012). 'Cuerpo, emociones y lugar: aproximaciones teóricas y metodológicas desde la Geografía'. *Geographicalia* 62: 115–131.

Paz, M.F. and Risdell, N. (eds) (2014). *Conflictos, conflictividades y movilizaciones socioambientales en México. Problemas comunes lecturas diversas*. Cuernavaca: UNAM.

Porto-Gonçalves, C.W. (2016). 'Lucha por la Tierra. Ruptura metabólica y reapropiación social de la naturaleza'. *Polis: Revista Latinoamericana, Santiago de Chile* 45(15): 291–316.

Quijano, A. (1992). 'Colonialidad y Modernidad/Racionalidad'. *Perú Indígena* 13(29): 11–20.

Quijano, A. (2007). 'Colonialidad del poder y clasificación social', in S. Castro-Gómez and R. Grosfoguel (eds) *El giro decolonial: reflexiones para una diversidad epistémica más allá del capitalismo global*. Bogotá: Iesco-Pensar-Siglo del Hombre Editores, pp 93–126.

Santos, M. (2000, 1996). *La naturaleza del espacio. Técnica y tiempo. Razón y Emoción*. Barcelona: Ariel.

Segato, R. (2007). *La Nación y sus Otros: raza, etnicidad y diversidad religiosa en tiempos de Políticas de la Identidad*. Buenos Aires: Prometeo.

Segato, R. (2014). *Las nuevas formas de guerra y el cuerpo de las mujeres*. Puebla: Pez en el árbol, Tinta Limón.

Smith, N. (2008, 1984). *Desarrollo Desigual. Naturaleza, Capital y la Producción del Espacio*. Madrid: Traficantes de sueños.

Soja, E. (2008). *Postmetrópolis. Estudios críticos sobre las ciudades y las regiones*. Madrid: Traficantes de sueños.

Soja, E. (2014). *En busca de la justicia espacial*. Valencia: Tirant Humanidades.

Tuan, Y. (2007, 1974). *Topofilia. Un estudio de las percepciones, actitudes y valores sobre el entorno*. España: Melusina.

Ulloa, A. (2020). 'Ecología política feminista latinoamericana', in De Luca A., Fosado E. and Velázquez M. (eds) *Feminismo socioambiental Revitalizando el debate desde América Latina*. Mexico, DF: CRIM-UNAM, pp 75–104.

Werth, B. (2007). 'Cuerpo, interdisciplinaridad y política. Acerca de Corpolíticas en las Américas: Formaciones de raza, clase y género'. *Telondefondo: Revista de teoría y crítica teatral* 6: 1–7.

Ysunza, V. and Mondragón, D. (2019). 'Germinando en el asfalto, del encierro a la libertad del cuerpo, una propuesta a través de la danza'. *Revista de Arte Contemporáneo* 8: 176–83.

Ysunza, V. (2021). 'Propuestas metodológicas a partir de las cartografías corporales y de la danza para reflexionar sobre los cuerpos-territorios en las Geografías Feministas', *Geografía Cultural do femenino: enfoques e perspectivas*. Santa María: Arco Editores.

3

Critical Geography Collective of Ecuador as Feminist Geography Collective Praxis

Sofia Zaragocín, Soledad Álvarez Velasco, Guglielmina Falanga, Amanda Yépez, and Gabriela Ruales

Introduction

The Critical Geography Collective of Ecuador (or *el Colectivo*) is exemplary of contemporary feminist collective geography praxis happening in Latin America. The geographical reach of our activism is mainly within Latin America, with a lot of our work focusing on the Amazon region. We accompany social movements and collectives in the defense of their territories against extractive industry, militarization, migrant criminalization, and patriarchal formations of space. Currently our work focuses on denouncing the negative consequences of extractive industry, gender-based violence and most recently the relationship between structural racism, the reinforcement of racist border regimes and COVID-19 from critical cartography and geography perspectives. We focus on implementing critical geography methods and developing geospatial analysis based on the needs of the communities with whom we work. Since 2012, the Critical Geography Collective of Ecuador has organized around geographical critiques of extractivist industry, patriarchy, and the connection between the two. As of 2020, we have also delved into the geographies of human mobility, which will also be addressed in this chapter.

Many of the collective's members are research activists, and are members of both academic institutions and activist groups. We are about 25 members in total. About half our members hold a PhD or are studying in a PhD program. Many have participated in social movements since youth, in particular feminist and ecology movements. And almost all belong to another activist collective aside from *el Colectivo*. Our members are also spread out across the world in Spain, Brazil, Germany, Norway, Colombia, Mexico, and the Netherlands and members residing in Ecuador are from the USA, Italy, and non-urban centres within Ecuador. At some point each member has lived in Ecuador but now find themselves in other parts of the globe. And while we are called the Critical Geography Collective of Ecuador, our reach is transnational given how our own bodies have moved through multiple scales and with that bring different geographical epistemologies, ontologies, methodologies, methods, and activist praxis into conversation. As will be further explored in this chapter, we understand the embodiment of human mobility by most of the collective's members to be part of the translocation of feminist geographical praxis and feminist geography activist practices (Zaragocin, 2021; Falanga, 2022).

Aside from developing and implementing critical cartography methods, we publish on multiple scales from academic articles in geography journals to methodological guides (Bayón and Zaragocin, 2019) as well as in various languages and engage with different actors ranging from academic to global activist counterparts. We have also spent a lot of time focused on how we work as a group and how we want to organize internally. We are deeply reflexive concerning issues of power, recognition, and distribution of work and care among all members. As a gender mixed group, we have reviewed how our gender make-up affects our internal dynamics. There is a subgroup within *el Colectivo* that focuses on masculinity issues and has carried out a study among the members of the collective analysing if the responsibilities are spread out equally between all members. Likewise, we are constantly in conceptual and methodological formation. Most recently we have included decolonial, anti-racist, and migrants' mobilities and spatial struggles into our collective formation processes.

This chapter will address the feminist geography activist work we carry out with regards to migrants' mobilities, extractivism, and aquatic space. It is structured as follows: first we situate our work within feminist geography praxis and activism more broadly; then we underscore two key examples that are demonstrative of our feminist geographical activist praxis; and, last, we reflect on the link between Latin American feminist geographical activist process and *cuerpo-territorio* (body-territories) on the move.

Feminist geography praxis and activism

As many feminist geographers have previously noted, the link between activism, research, and feminism has long been present in our discipline (Wright 2008). We wish to shed light on what the link between activism and feminist geography means for the Critical Geography Collective of Ecuador in the Latin American context and in conversation with Anglophone feminist geography. Feminist geography collectives mean different things to Anglophone feminist geography than to Latin American Critical Geographies. In a recent publication by different feminist collectives in the US context, it is apparent that collectives organize within and against the neoliberal university (The Feminist Coven et al, 2021). In Latin America, critical geography and feminist collectives are mainly organized outside the university to assure autonomy. Nevertheless, there are important parallels between Anglophone and Latin American feminist geographies from activist perspectives, mainly that of prioritizing the body, which will be drawn out in this text.

Most of the discussions on activism and academia written in English have been concerning Anglophone feminist geography (Wright, 2008, Burke et al, 2017). However Latin American feminist geography collectives have gained presence in all the Americas. The inclusion of both the Critical Geography Collective of Ecuador and GeoBrujas of Mexico in this edited collection is demonstrative of an incipient dialogue between Anglophone and Latin American feminist geographies from research-activist perspectives. Two of the five authors in this chapter are immersed in both Latin American and Anglophone critical geography debates. However, the immersion in US and Anglocentric feminist geographies is not a priority of the collective. Our conversations with Anglocentric feminist geography are not a collective process. Up till now, individuals in the collective have sustained dialogue with some feminist geographers in the global north but from an individual reflexive process. This text is our first collective action to situate ourselves with Anglocentric feminist geography.

Being part of a collective provides unquestionable legitimacy within certain pockets of progressive academic and social movements in Latin America. This is in line with how critical geographies understand themselves in the region. Being simultaneously in academia and social activist circles is in some ways expected in Latin American feminist geography circles. Another central feature of feminist geography praxis in Latin America is placing the body, and in particular *cuerpo-territorio* (body-territory), at the centre of our research-activist work.

Cuerpo-territorio is not only a theoretical concept, but at the same time represents a method that consists of collectively mapping a body and, within it, territory offering a methodological opportunity to further the study of embodiment in Anglophone feminist geography (Zaragocín and Caretta, 2020). As researcher activists in Latin American feminist geography, *cuerpo-territorio*[1] includes constant resignification of the issues that are worked on within the Collective, but also of self-reflection on how we are carrying out our work. As previously mentioned, many Collective members live distinct migration scenarios, which therefore supposes both a transnational and dislocating experience, involving a constant exercise of translation of languages, cultures, knowledge, values, emotions, and feelings across scales. Thus, each one of us politicizes continuous translation and constant resignifications of *cuerpo-territorio*.

The concept and practice of embodiment represents the politicization of experiential processes and provides us with a roadmap of identity as constantly changing in cultural and spatial terms. Through these processes, we not only discover a fluid identity, but we can also see how this fluidity takes on various shapes and colours at the same time, according to our sociospatial disposition (Álvarez, 2009; Falanga, 2022). For example, the figure of the *transloca* (Álvarez, 2009) is a metaphor that seeks to account for this fluidity, and that implies much of the nomadism already proposed by Rosi Braidotti (2000), but adding the continuous experience of translation and a hemispheric rather than transnational perspective (Zaragocín, 2020). The proposal by Sonia Álvarez (2009) and the collective project 'Translocalities/Translocalidades: Feminist Politics of Translation in the Latin/a Américas' (Feminist Translation Policies in Latin America), proposes an approach no longer based on the movement between nations, but between historically and culturally situated places.

The movement between places and borders directly impacts the construction of subjectivities. The borders that are crossed are also emotional, cultural, and symbolic. Translocal movements allow the dissemination of theories and emotions shared and translated based on place (Falanga, forthcoming). Movement, as already illustrated by Massey (2005), does not affect only the agents of mobility (for example, migrants), but also the shaping of place. Influence is not unidirectional, but rather reciprocal and porous: there are cultural, symbolic, and political influences between places and not from a pre-established place towards another passive receptor. Hence, Álvarez talks about translocalities.

The translocal perspective proposed by Álvarez (2009) allows us to read the crossings between various types of borders as translocal movements to encompass the relational, processual, and dynamic complexity of places and to be able to capture various dimensions that are not included in the analysis of transnational migrations. Furthermore, it offers a hemispheric perspective and allows us to overcome a conceptual geographic binary that locates all colonial knowledge production in the north and decolonial production in the south. As Zaragocín (2021) states, the process of translocal translation occurs through the figures of *translocas* and through the inclusion of new epistemologies in northern theorizations, demonstrating how 'the flow of knowledge is multidimensional and travels through transcultural subjects' (Zaragocín, 2021).

Translocal processes suppose a continuous transformation and repositioning of subjectivities according to movements and passages through space-time locations (Álvarez, 2014; Zaragocín, 2021). 'Our subjectivities are, at the same time, based on the place and misplaced or misplaced' (Álvarez, 2009, p 745). Translocal feminism can be defined as a 'multilocalized practice' (Álvarez, 2009; Millán, 2009), where the categories of race, gender, and class are always subject to the practices and porous contexts of places that intersect. In fact, the translocal perspective disturbs the conceptualizations of race, class, gender, sexualities, and other 'locational politics', since these conceptualizations are continually re-signified, changing 'when we move through these different locations' (Álvarez, 2009, p 749). Sonia Álvarez exemplifies from her own body as a Cuban-American from South Florida: considered an 'ethnic' Latina in the United States, she then becomes 'white' in Latin America.

Based on this theoretical premise, the Translocaties/Translocalidades collective proposes translocation as a process that cannot be locked into the old migratory or identity categories, nor in the oppositional relationship of 'us' versus 'them', continually challenged by the very existence of a transloca figure 'for we are, simultaneously and intermittently, ourselves and the other' (Grewal and Kaplan, 1994, p 7). The name plays with the double meaning of moving between towns and going through senses of madness due to the need for continuous translation and the impossibility of identifying with existing categories or feeling at home anywhere. Translocas are agents of political, theoretical, and practical translation, 'we are cultural mediators ... agents of transculturation', says Álvarez (2009, p 749). Translation is a strategic political act that entails the possibility of constructing 'connected epistemologies' (Laó-Montes, 2007, p 132) that strengthen a Latin American feminist alliance not on the basis of the existence of a single subject or on fixed categories.

For this chapter, our *compañera* Sofia Zaragocin has had to translate linguistically and culturally parts of this chapter so that it can be read in English and understood from an Anglocentric feminist geography perspective. She has written about being a transloca in Anglophone feminist geography from the perspectives of Latin American feminist debates on territory before (Zaragocin, 2021) and Guglielmina Falanga has proposed that as a collective we take on these reflections and further relate them to our feminist geography activist praxis. Guglielmina Falanga has used the transloca perspective in her doctoral dissertation to further understand *cuerpo-territorio* in healing processes by organized women's groups in Ecuador (forthcoming).

In what follows, we present two case studies that highlight collective reflections on translation, migration, identity, and *cuerpo-territorio*. The first case focuses on the politicization of the experience of human mobility in a context of the feminization of migration and a counter-hegemonic proposal for the co-production and dissemination of counternarratives in this context. The second example shows the collective defense of the *cuerpo-territorio* from water basins of the Anzu and Jatunyacu rivers of the Napo province, in Ecuador. As a Colectivo, we acknowledge that since both experiences are embedded in transnational dynamics with multi-scale consequences in the *cuerpo-territorios* that we work in, we should identify, conceptualize, and politicize the possible interconnections and articulations between them. This is an analytical task that is beyond the scope of this writing piece. Our future research agenda includes this conceptual challenge related to our praxis.

Feminist geography activist praxis: migrant women's transnational struggles

The feminization of migration speaks to the fact that since the end of the 20th century the presence of women has multiplied, equalling or even exceeding the number of migrant men: this is one of the defining features of contemporary migratory dynamics (De Haas et al, 2019). The deepening of systemic inequality together with changes in labour regimes in countries of origin and the high demand for women in the care economy of the 'global north' can explain this trend (Yates, 2009). Feminist geography (Hofmann and Buckley, 2013), has insisted, however, on the importance of refocusing our gaze on the scale of the body and emotions (Zaragocín, 2020) to make this analytical approach more complex.

From the scale of the body and in intimate relationship to emotions allows us to go beyond the argument that migrant women are just a demanded workforce. Rather, they reveal themselves as autonomous and politicized subjects who, on the move, unfold transnational spatial struggles to preserve their lives in countries of origin, transit and destination (Varela, 2015). Their migrant mobilities, embodied in diverse racialized bodies, differentiated by age, gender orientation, class origin and nationalities, respond not only to the violence of systemic inequality, but at the same time, to patriarchy, systemic racism, and the border control regime (Cordero et al, 2019; Gago, 2019).

At the turn of the 21st century, Ecuador's migratory pattern took a turn. From being predominantly a country of origin of migrants, it became a country of reception of regional and extra-continental migrants, of refuge, voluntary and forced return, and of transit to various destinations in the Americas (Velasco, 2020). The presence of migrant women has been decisive in explaining this turn, since not only Ecuadorean women, adults, and minors have emigrated notably to the United States in a sustained manner at least since the late 1980s and to European destinations since the 2000s (Herrera, 2012); but also South American, Caribbean, Asian, and African women have immigrated to or transit through the Andean country since the first decade of the 21st century (IOM, 2020). These embodied mobilities have spatially transformed Ecuador within the new geography of migration in the Americas.

At the beginning of 2020, we created the activist research line named *Migrant Justice*. Inspired in the continental slogan, *Nada de Migrantes, Sin Migrantes* (Nothing from Migrants, without Migrants), we proposed a *migrant pedagogy* as the foundation of our knowledge production regarding the role that the migrant struggle has had in changing the migratory pattern of Ecuador. From this analytical-political framework, the encounter with diverse migrant subjects has been the basis for a dialogue of *saberes* or a dialogue of knowledges which, based on their testimonies, lived experiences and embodied knowledge, allowed us to co-produce counternarratives around migratory dynamics. For us, these narratives have a clear objective: to dismantle the hegemonic understanding of migrants as only a demanded workforce, passive 'victims' of migrant smugglers, or even worse 'criminals' who irrationally cross borders clandestinely or live without documents.

Aligned with feminist geography and critical migration studies (Mezzadra and Neilson, 2013; De Genova et al, 2014), in particular with the theoretical perspective of the autonomy of migration (Papadopoulos and Tsianos, 2013; Tazzioli, 2014), we centred our analysis on the bodies and emotions of migrants. We understand migrants as subjects that are politically diverse, racialized, and differentiated by age, sexual and gender orientation, class, and nationality. We also understand migrants as having the capacity of decision, agency, and as interlocutors with a wealth of knowledge and resistance strategies that emerge from their own migrant experience and memory, and whose struggle has multi-scalar repercussions in individual, communal, local, regional, national, and global space.

Due to the context of the pandemic, our dialogue of *saberes* took place via digital space. Through long conversations on Zoom or WhatsApp we reconstructed the trajectories of 27 migrants, of which 15 were women between 20 and 50 years of age. A part of them were Ecuadoreans living in New York, Genova, and Barcelona who emigrated in the 2000s in the context of one of the biggest Ecuadorean economic and political crises that ended up dollarizing the national economy. The rest were immigrants and refugees from Colombia, Haiti, and Venezuela, countries marked by armed conflict, the violence of poverty exacerbated by the 2010 earthquake, and socioeconomic and political collapse. Our gatherings with them confirmed that their presence has been decisive indeed in the migratory turn of contemporary Ecuador and they had woven a transnational space of care and struggle to sustain their lives.

This research process was carried out in collaboration with the, *Migrante Universal*, a migrant organization based in Quito which provides legal and economic advice to migrants, and *Red Clamor*, a network of Catholic and civil society organizations working on migration issues. Through both instances, we met the migrant women who dwelt in Ecuador and took part in our research because they were either members of *Migrante Universal* or beneficiaries of the programs of *Red Clamor*. Likewise, we got to know all the participants through the snowball method or by reaching out to migrant women suggested by other migrant women already in dialogue with us. In the case of the migrant women residing outside of Ecuador, we made contact through fellow researchers who were also migrants in the US or Spain. The networks of trust between women researchers and migrants made it possible for our interlocutors to be part of this process.

Although emigrating from Ecuador or from their countries of origin to Ecuador was an autonomous response that our 15 interlocutors gave against collapsed national contexts, there were other underlying and compelling reasons. As one of the Ecuadorian migrants in New York remembered it:

'I come from an Indigenous and peasant community. When I went to school, my classmates used to tell me that I smelled like smoke, and to stay away. The girls were super racist and classist. [In Ecuador] if you don't have a certain surname and leverages, it is difficult to get a job. When I graduated I told myself: I will not have a future, I will be discriminated for being an Indigenous women ... Coming to that realization decided my departure.'

Like this participant, who clearly suggests that the violence of systemic racism triggered her departure, the rest of the migrant women pointed to patriarchal violence as another cause for their departures. In their voices: "In Colombia you live in war. They threatened to take my land away from me, to rape me, to attack me. There comes a time when threats are no longer tolerated and that's why I left," said one of the Colombian migrant woman; "The country was falling on us, we had to leave, but in our case we also went out because at home there was a lot of conflict, a lot of pain from my father's attacks, my mother came out first and then I arrived," insisted an Ecuadorean in Genova; while one of the Haitian migrants reiterated that "after the earthquake, Haiti was left in ruins and women there have few opportunities to survive, worse if we are single mothers. That is why I emigrated to Ecuador."

Out of their embodied mobility, a battle against the violent contemporary border control regime is revealed. In the case of the Ecuadorean women, they had been outside of Ecuador for two decades. Although all of them had regularized their immigration status and nationalized in Spain, Italy, and the United States, their testimonies told of difficult and costly legal battles against anti-migrant and racist systems. They insisted that the path to regularization is a fight that must be won to guarantee other living conditions, as reflected an Ecuadorean woman in Barcelona, in her own words: "without citizenship, we are second-class citizens and we cannot claim rights, that's why we have to fight until we have papers". For them having a regularized migratory status was also their major protection against possible deportation, as stated by another Ecuadorian in New York: "having documents is the only way to not live with the fear that at any moment you will be detained and deported".

In the case of immigrant women in Ecuador, becoming legal was a difficult road. In 2019 the Ecuadorian government imposed a visa on Venezuelan citizens and doubled control along the Ecuador-Colombia border. This propelled Venezuelan migrants to enter through illegalized points of entry, therefore entering as illegalized migrants (Herrera and Cabezas, 2019). Among our Colombian interlocutor women, some were refugees and others were still awaiting the resolution of their papers and documents; while Haitian women no longer had a residence permit, as it had expired, and they did not meet the requirements for renewal. They all agreed and stressed that legalization of immigration status in Ecuador was incredibly difficult because of the costs and that the requirements were unattainable.

The experience of immigrant women in Ecuador revealed a contradictory national context. Despite a progressive constitution on immigration matters, since 2010 the Ecuadorian state has reinforced its anti-immigrant turn by re-imposing selective visas, such as those imposed on the Venezuelan population, and making the migratory legal process more complex (see Herrera and Cabezas, 2019; Álvarez Velasco, 2020; Álvarez Velasco et al, 2022). Undaunted by the hostility of the state, these immigrant women insist on fighting for legalization. In the words of one of the Venezuelan migrants: "We have no other choice then to be patient, figure out how to legalize ourselves and demand our rights every time we go to the ministry. They don't want to help us because we are Venezuelan. Without papers, our are lives are more complicated, but together we hold one another."

As she mentions, "figuring out how to legalize ourselves" was part of a strategy that Colombian and Haitian migrants also deployed. In their stories they realized that via digital platforms, especially via Facebook pages, they exchanged a lot of strategic migration information that aids them in that battle and in the face of the Ecuadorian border control regime. Speaking out and denouncing the difficulties of that process was part of their struggle.

The case of one of the Venezuelan migrants is exemplary. As the leader of the Glovers-Ecuador delivery service,[2] she is highly political and aware of the hyper-precarious situation that migrants live in Ecuador as they are exposed to various forms of labour exploitation. In her words:

'Here they say that we come to take jobs from Ecuadorians, but it is not like that. Even if you are legal, here you work on the street, without access to social security. Bosses pay you what they want and always for a low salary. There have been cases of migrants who work and then get fired and are never paid. This is exploitation and abuse. Whenever we can within our organization, we tell them that they have to report and not stay quiet. This is the only way things will change.'

Her story was marked by the strength of her outrage at the injustice that she experienced in hearing the stories of permanent abuse that other migrants faced. She has not stayed quiet and has made her criticisms public from the streets, leading hundreds of undocumented migrants to publicly protest for their rights.

Like her, another of our interlocutors, an Ecuadorian woman in Barcelona, also mentioned how for a long time she was an activist fighting for the rights of Ecuadorians in Spain: "We have to help the community, we have to protect ourselves because here the Ecuadorian state is not present. So we have to demand that the Spanish state protects our rights, and that is what we do." From New York, another Ecuadorian woman mentioned: "here we have to fight against the system that wants us to be undocumented and against racism, which is not the same as Ecuador, but which is present. I fight and I teach my daughters to fight."

Those bodies in resistance that partake in activisms and publicly fight a continuous, simultaneous battle of surviving on a daily basis be it during transit to Ecuador, residing in that country or from another destination. Venezuelan migrants recounted how travel on foot from Venezuela to Ecuador was "a journey full of dangers where the only thing left is to take care of each other". Faced with the complete lack of state protection for migrant routes that connect the Americas (Velasco, 2021), these migrants formed spontaneous families, set up camps on the highways and developed protection strategies with other migrants. In their voice: "we eat together, set up places to sleep or we stay in shelters along the way".

Solidarity, care, and protection were also present when arriving at destinations. That was the common experience for both migrant Ecuadorian women and for Colombian, Haitian, and Venezuelan women in Ecuador. This is how one of the testimonies of a Venezuelan woman summarized it: "Here we share everything: Food, house, care. Just as we invented life." She realized that "this collective invention" for survival marked by solidarity among family members, friends, and acquaintances was what allowed them to gradually create a safe place to live: they shared a house, communal kitchens, spaces for the care of their children, temporary informal jobs, and migratory survival strategies. Generating a collective life of care was the basis of that struggle to confront the hostility of the Ecuadorian state.

In this 'collective invention' to take care of their lives there was also a double concern and a double care: not only for the migrant lives in the country of destination but also in the country of origin. In fact, something common among our 15 female interlocutors, be they Ecuadoreans dwelling abroad or immigrants in Ecuador, is that they all sent remittances to their countries and maintained constant communication via cell phone and digital platforms with their families. In their voices: "Since I set foot in the US I have been very concerned about my family in Ecuador and I have always sent them packages of clothes, toys and money," while a migrant woman in New York said: "Since I came to Spain, I never stopped worrying about my family, that's why I always send some money from my job"; and "I communicate with them all the time and send whatever dollars are left over to Venezuela, there people have no way of living," said a Venezuelan migrant. Their double concern and the construction of digital communities of affect is a nodal part of the existence of the transnational space resulting from the migrant struggle in Ecuador and other countries in the Americas and Europe.

Based on the testimonies and lived experience mentioned, it is evident that the autonomous cross-border movement of migrant women that are either leaving or entering Ecuador is not only a response to the violence of systemic inequality, but also, at the same time to patriarchy, systemic racism and the border control regime. In doing so they are moving beyond being part of international labour force, rather they are bodies in resistance and activism in spatial disputes.

Even though their trajectories are diverse, these bodies in resistance show latent or manifest actions, collective or individual, subjective or communitarian actions practiced in the public or private space, by the migrant women practice at specific moments to sustain their lives (Varela, 2015). Moreover, the movement of migrant women reconfigures spatial dynamics, producing transnational territories of protection and care, re-signifying the ways of belonging and membership that disrupt outdated forms of control and territorial nationalism (Wimmer and Schiller, 2002).

As the Critical Geography Collective of Ecuador, our strategy of collective activism with migrant women is reflected in two ways. The first is through the co-production of counternarratives on migratory dynamics that resulted in the migration guidebooks and infographics for popular education purposes.[3] The previous reflections are just a synthesis of the joint work developed based on a profound dialogue of *saberes*. Moreover, the fact that as feminist geographers we have put our body and voice further a process of awareness in which members of the Critical Geography Collective of Ecuador together with some of the migrants disseminate public counternarratives in independent media.[4] Our participation in public spaces is intended to reveal the anti-migrant sentiment present in contemporary Ecuador while at the same time acknowledging the diverse and strong migrant struggle. This is the path that together we have opened to draw attention to the urgency of migrant justice for women migrants across the Americas.

Feminist geography activist praxis: Naporuna river territories, women and the struggle for life

The people of the different Naporuna settlements and communities of the Napo and Pastaza provinces, as well as of Indigenous Kichwa peoples of the Ecuadorian Amazon, have historically inhabited the banks of rivers and streams of this region. Myths and symbols that originate from their communal life live in the different aquatic spaces present in their territory. Their diverse water sources provide enormous abundance to sustain life. The arrival and settlements of colonial domination for resource extraction and in particular gold via the use of intense mining caused massive devastation to local populations and nature. Local communities also partake in artisanal forms of mining as an economic alternative to the abandonment of the colonial state, particularly in the context of the COVID pandemic that left these communities in oblivion.

Artisanal forms of gold mining are of low intensity and have caused minimal contamination of nature and water systems of communal territories. Nevertheless, in the last 25 years, mining activity has diversified on multiple scales in the Napo province. The investment of capital by settlers that have made their life in the province, as well as by foreign capital and peoples, has propelled the entry of other aggressive technology such as: dredgers of various sizes and heavy excavation machinery. This type of machinery initiates new forms of mining extraction (mainly by men), and they are the cause of one of the most complex environmental and social conflicts on various river basins found in the Napo province.

Mining extractive activity has implied the advancement of the commercialization and destruction of the common goods of the Naporunas. The rivers have become a source of interest for miners, who use water for the sole purpose of gold extraction without any consideration of its impact on the health, food, symbolic values, and other life forms that inhabit these aquatic spaces. The increase in mining activities, both legal and illegal, has generated concern among women in the Naporuna communities that inhabit the riverbanks. In seeing that their everyday lives and bodies have been affected by contamination and internal displacements within their communal territories, women have organized as part of *guardia indígenas*, autonomous indigenous security forces. *Guardia indígenas* propose alternative productive activities, and are informed and socialized between women to stop the entry of mining activities in communities of Serena and Tzawata that inhabit the riverbanks of Jatanyacu and Anzu.

Concerning the dynamics mentioned, the *Colectivo* proposed a collective reflection with women affected by mining activity along the Jatunyacu and Anzu rivers that involved a reading and revision of maps to explain and identify water basins. Collective reflection with maps made visible water ways that, in turn, highlighted women's struggles for the defense of water.

The water basins are fluvial territories built on the history and symbols of the Naporuna communities. In the construction of participatory maps of the past, present, and future, we could construct the maps of fluvial territories of water basins. The maps of the past and present helped us compare the changes occurring on territories and rivers and the consequences for women's lives in order to identify the challenges they are facing. In constructing the maps of the future, the women shared their collective proposals to generate and deepen the defense of life through water. Their ecological concerns regarding the reproduction of life required the involvement of all the communal members to demand that the state carry out its role in controlling mining activities.

The *Colectivo* has systematized information on the layout of mining concessions along rivers in Ecuador as well as processed studies on the environmental impacts of mining companies to locate the sampling points of contamination on water, air, and land. Along with this, the *Colectivo* has generated information in the field to verify the contamination that mining extractive activities are generating in fluvial territories. All of this information has been shared with the women of the Anzu and Jatunyaco river communities. The prior collective reflection regarding what is a water basin, and the construction of their present, past, and future maps have allowed a simple assessment of the maps presented by the *Colectivo*. In these collective reflections the enormous amount of mining activity in the water basins and the multi-scalar forms of conflict on the everyday life of the community that it produces, is evident.

Collective reflection has been essential in order to assume a strong commitment that can articulate different water systems and communities that can generate a collective concern about the speed and contamination of mining activities. The possibility of reading impact maps and territorial diagnostics as well as being aware of official reports on mining activities, rarely occurs for indigenous women inhabiting these territories. For a long time, women have demanded this information from the leaders of their communities, since it is this information that allows for a more profound reflection concerning mining, waterways, and territory.

We have carried out this collective reflection with the *Guardia Indígena de Mujeres 'Yuturi Warmi'* of the Serena Community in the Jatunyacu River. Their contributions have been valuable in exposing their experience in defending river waters and demanding a good life regarding their fluvial territories as well as the right to decide over their territories and bodies, that we can ultimately define as ecofeminist. The Tzawata community along the Anzu river was rebuilt 11 years ago by recovering their ancestral lands from the Canadian mining company *Merendon of Ecuador*. Women have been key in creating organizations dedicated to ecotourism and the harvesting of land to sustain families. The community has undergone reforestation processes for over a decade giving results such as the recovery of once occupied land by mining activities. Today the threats from mining are still present. In August 2021, the company Terra Earth Resources illegally and violently entered their ancestral territory with the aim of evicting the Kichwa communes of

Tzawatalla Chukapi and San Clemente. Women in large numbers were at the forefront of resistance of further intervention of the mining company.

Collectively reflecting on these experiences with other women from different communities, who are also experiencing the intervention of mining activity in their territories, has made it possible to strengthen the politization of rivers as common goods. The rivers mentioned are generally administered by men, although it is the role of women to produce and reproduce life along fluvial territories. The methodologies of collective reflections on official mining maps as well as the social cartography maps we developed with the women provoked a multi-scalar reflection on women in extractive spaces. The importance of daily and intimate spaces has been evidenced in relation to the individual and collective use of rivers, as well as a larger scale when reflecting on how rivers can also articulate struggles beyond the colonial gaze of the nation-state.

The water basins were treated as a natural geographical unit that does not pretend to hierarchize human and non-human forms of life from the perspective of all the ecosystems that inhabit fluvial territories. This means that the care for water systems is a co-responsibility that eliminates borders and for which the reproduction of life is central.

Discussion and conclusions

The two examples previously mentioned are just a glimpse of the feminist geographical activist praxis we have undergone since 2014, when feminist geography became a pillar of the work carried out by the Critical Geography Collective of Ecuador. There are three underlying characteristics of our work, the first being that the body (and understandings of cuerpo-territorio) is at the centre of our research–activism, the second is that this work is always done from a collective perspective and, third, that we are acutely aware of the translocation (cultural and linguistic translation) of feminist geography activist praxis from a multi-scalar perspective. As feminist geographers, we set our bodies in motion, to accompany the struggles and plights of women in other challenging scenarios that are deeply determined by territorial struggles. Moreover, developing feminist geography methodologies from the understanding that body, territory, and mobilities are intimately interlocked influences how we relate bodies and territories in the different contexts where we carry out our work. As is evident from the examples presented in this text, whether we are dealing with critical migration studies or the gendered effects of extractive industries the emphasis on the experience of the body is drawn out and reflected on from a collective scale. Our bodies as feminist geographers doing feminist geography praxis activism are directly related to the research that takes place in every context where we are needed. This furthers feminist geography research-activist praxis that has long depended on feminist methodological principles such as strong reflexivity and horizontal research relationships. When we apply moving cuerpo-territorio understandings that not only our bodies are placed at the centre of the research but more importantly the intrinsic relationship between bodies and territories, then our methodologies are possible on a collective scale. Collective scale here means the understanding that our body-territories as feminist geographers are connected to the women struggling against extractive industry or from human rights abuses because of their legal status. Notwithstanding, we acknowledge important differences between ourselves and the women we accompany. Still our hope is to create a collective scale where we can focus on connecting our body-territories.

In the first example, our *compañera* Soledad Álvarez Velasco stresses that doing critical migration geography praxis from feminist geography research-activist perspectives requires an emphasis on the relationship between bodies, emotion, and mobilities. Explorations into the role of emotions in how women's bodies travel across borders unsettle outmoded nation-state fundamentalisms and challenge uneven planes of human mobility. Moreover, Soledad underscores the relationship between our cuerpo-territorios as research activists and the transnational women migrants that co-produce knowledge resulting in conceptual and methodological guides that were developed together in 2020. She emphasizes that activist researchers in this scenario can use their bodies to publicly denounce human rights abuses on news media outlets and other public platforms, to enact feminist solidarity praxis.

In our second example, Amanda Yépez and Gabriela Ruales reflect on the importance of collective methodological frameworks in drawing out the fluvial territories of indigenous women in the Ecuadorian Amazon that are organized around the defense of river territories. Different social cartography methods were used to discern where mining has affected different water systems from the embodiment of water by indigenous women that are organized through *guardias indígenas*, which are autonomous security forces. Collective reflections among both researcher activists and indigenous women on where mining contamination is located and how it affects water systems provokes deeper understandings of the connections between life, the non-human, and fluvial territories.

Finally, Guglielmina Falanga and Sofia Zaragocin as feminist geographers who embody migratory experiences look to translation processes across the Americas, from the translocation of feminist geographical praxis. As is evident, there are many cuerpo-territorios involved in doing feminist geographical activist praxis and therefore a constant need for cultural and linguistic translation within the collective and with the populations we work with. Our effort in bringing these experiences and reflections to an edited collection in English and with mainly Anglocentric feminist geography praxis, is an effort to bring our collective knowledge in new directions.

Notes

[1] Cuerpo-territorio has been developed in collective spaces that have fostered reflections and debates from political and methodological perspectives. This has occurred within communitarian feminisms in Guatemala and from the Collective Miradas Criticas del territorio desde el feminismo. Latin American feminist geography has drawn from these reflections and others.

[2] Glovo is a Spanish quick-commerce start-up founded in Barcelona in 2015. It is an on-demand mobile application that offers the service of purchase and delivery of products and food ordered through its mobile app. It operates on a global scale and in Ecuador the delivery drivers are known as *glovers*, most of whom are migrants, usually undocumented migrants, working by motorcycle, bicycle and even car.

[3] During 2020, we produced five thematic monographs or *Cartillas Migratorias* and more than a dozen infographics, including maps of migrant mobility in Ecuador. See the *Migrant Justice Microsite*, from the Critical Geography Collective of Ecuador. https://geografiacriticaecuador.org/justiciamigrante/.

[4] Our interviews can be reviewed at the *Migrant Justice Microsite*, from the Critical Geography Collective of Ecuador. https://geografiacriticaecuador.org/justiciamigrante/.

References

Álvarez, S. (2009). 'Construindo uma política feminista translocal da tradução'. *Revista Estudos Feministas* 17(3): 743–53.

Álvarez, S. (2014). 'Introduction to the Project and the Volume/Enacting a Translocal Feminist Politics of Translation', in S. Álvarez, C. De Lima Costa, V. Feliu, R.J. Hester, N. Klahn and M. Thayer (eds) *Translocalities/Translocalidades: Feminist Politics of Translation in the Latin/a Américas*. London: Duke University Press, pp 1–18.

Álvarez, S. (2020). 'From Ecuador to Elsewhere: The (Re)Configuration of a Transit Country'. *Migration and Society* 3(1): 34–50.

Álvarez, S. (forthcoming). 'En búsqueda de un lugar: tránsitos irregularizados por las Américas', in M.G. Rivera, G. Herrera and E.E. Domenech (eds) *Movilidades, derecho a migrar y control fronterizo en América Latina y el Caribe*. Mexico, DF: CLACSO-Siglo XXI.

Bayón, M. and Zaragocin, S. (2019). 'Activisimo geográfico crítico y feminista, contra la explotación del Yasuni y la escala del cuerpo frente a la criminalización del aborto'. *Journal of Latin American Geography* 18(3): 210–14.

Braidotti, R. (2000). *Sujetos nómades: Corporización y diferencia sexual en la teoría feminista contemporánea*. Buenos Aires: Paidós.

Burke, S., Alexandra, C., Casson, H., Coddington, K., Colls, R., Jollans, A., Jordan, S., Smith, K., Taylor, N., and Urquhart, H. (2017). 'Generative Spaces: Intimacy, Activism and Teaching Feminist Geographies'. *Gender, Place & Culture* 24(5): 661–73.

Cordero, B., Mezzadra, S., and Varela, A. (2019). *América Latina en movimiento. Migraciones, límites a la movilidad y sus desbordamientos*. Mexico, DF: Traficantes de Sueños.

De Genova, N., Mezzadra, S. and Pickles, J. (2014). 'New Keywords: Migration and Borders'. *Cultural Studies* 29(1): 55–87.

De Haas, H., Miller, M.J. and Castles, S. (2019). *The Age of Migration: International Population Movements in the Modern World*. London: Red Globe Press.

Falanga G. (2022). *El cuerpo en disputa: procesos de politización y despolitización en entornos feministas y New Age en la ciudad de Quito*. Tesis para obtener el título de Doctorado en Ciencias Sociales con especialización en Estudios Andinos. Quito: Flacso Ecuador.

Gago, M.V. (2019). *La potencia feminista: o el deseo de cambiarlo todo*. Madrid: Traficantes de Sueños.

Grewal, I. and Kaplan, C. (eds) (1994). *Scattered Hegemonies: Postmodernity and Transnational Feminist Practices*. Minneapolis: University of Minnesota.

Herrera, G. (2012). 'Repensar el cuidado a través de la migración internacional: mercado laboral, Estado y familias transnacionales en Ecuador'. *Cuadernos de Relaciones Laborales* 30(1): 139–59.

Herrera, G. and Cabezas, G. (2019). 'Ecuador: de la recepción a la disuasión. Políticas frente a la población venezolana y experiencia migratoria 2015–2018', in L. Gandini, A. Lozano and V. Prieto (eds) *Crisis y migración de la población venezolana. Entre la desprotección y la seguridad jurídica en Latinoamérica*. Mexico, DF: UNAM, pp 125–55.

Hofmann, E.T. and Buckley, C.J. (2013). 'Global Changes and Gendered Responses: The Feminization of Migration From Georgia'. *International Migration Review* 47(3): 508–38.

International Organization of Migration (2020). *World Migration Report*. Available at: https://publications.iom.int/books/world-migration-report-2020 [Accessed 5 July 2021].

Lao-Montes, A. (2007). 'Decolonial Moves: Trans-locating African Diaspora Spaces'. *Cultural Studies* (7): 309–38.

Massey, D. (2005). *For Space*. London: Sage.

Mezzadra, S. and Neilson, B. (2013). *Border as Method, or, the Multiplication of Labor*. Durham: Duke University Press.

Millán, M. (2009). 'Revistas y políticas de traducción del feminismo mexicano contemporáneo'. *Revista Estudos Feministas* 17: 819–46.

Papadopoulos, D. and Tsianos, V.S. (2013). 'After Citizenship: Autonomy of Migration, Organisational Ontology and Mobile Commons'. *Citizenship Studies* 17(2): 178–196.

Sabido Ramos, O. (2016). 'Cuerpo y Sentidos: el análisis sociológico de la percepción'. *Debates Feminista* 51: 63–80.

Tazzioli, M. (2014). *Spaces of Governmentality: Autonomous Migration and the Arab Uprisings*. London: Rowman & Littlefield.

Varela Huerta, A. (2015). 'Luchas migrantes: un nuevo campo de estudio para la sociología de los disensos'. *Andamios* 12(28): 145–70.

Velasco, S.Á. (2020). 'From Ecuador to Elsewhere: The (Re)configuration of a Transit Country'. *Migration and Society* 3(1): 34–49.

Velasco, S.Á. (2021). 'Mobility, Control, and the Pandemic across the Americas: First Findings of a Transnational Collective Project'. *Journal of Latin American Geography* 20(1): 11–48.

Velasco, S., Bayón Jiménez, M., Hurtado Caicedo, F., Pérez Martínez, L., Baroja, C., Tapia, J. and Yumbla, M.R. (2021). *Viviendo al Límite: Migrantes Irregularizados en Ecuador. Quito: Colectivo de Geografía Crítica de Ecuador.* Quito: Red Clamor y GIZ. https://geografiacriticaecuador.org/justiciam igrante/cartillas/cartilla-2-migrantes-irregularizados-en-ecuador/

Wimmer, A. and Schiller, N.G. (2002). 'Methodological Nationalism and the Study of Migration'. *European Journal of Sociology/Archives Européennes de Sociologie* 43(2): 217–40.

Wright, M.W. (2008). 'Gender and Geography: Knowledge and Activism across the Intimately Global'. *Progress in Human Geography* 33(3): 379–86.

Yeates, N. (2009). *Globalizing Care Economies and Migrant Workers: Explorations in Global Care Chains.* London: Palgrave Macmillan.

Zaragocin, S. (2020). 'Geografía feminista descolonial'. *GEOPAUTA* 4(4): 18–30. Available at https://doi.org/10.22481/rg.v4i4.7590 [Accessed 24 July 2021].

Zaragocin, S. (2021). 'Challenging Anglocentric Feminist Geography from Latin American Feminist Debates on Territoriality', in C. Gokariksel, M. Hawkins, C. Neubert and S. Smith (eds) *Feminist Geography Unbound: Discomfort, Bodies and Prefigured Futures.* Morgantown: West Virginia University Press, 235–52.

Zaragocín, S. and Caretta, M. (2020). 'Cuerpo-Territorio: A Decolonial Feminist Geographical Method for the Study of Embodiment'. *Annals of the American Association of Geographers* 111(5): 1503–18.

4

Legacies of Black Feminist Activism in the US South

LaToya E. Eaves

> Our perception of the black freedom struggle changes when we place the worldview and deeds of black women activist educators such as Septima Clark at the center.
>
> Charron (2009, p 3)

Septima Earthaline Poinsette Clark was born in 1898 in Charleston, South Carolina. Her life and work can be characterized as being 'for the people'. Her long career as an educator, which began with her accepting her first teaching position in 1916, was activist in its orientation, advocating for better conditions for African American schools and increased pay for African American teachers along with promoting education for the masses. After being fired from her teaching position due to her involvement with the National Association for the Advancement of Colored People (NAACP), she began working for the Highlander Folk School, a multi-racial social justice training centre then located in Monteagle, Tennessee. Among numerous interventions in reshaping the United States Southeast, Clark is the orchestrator of 'literacy-based citizenship pedagogy' (Hall et al, 2010) which is revealed through examining the structure of the Citizenship Schools Program. Through the Highlander, and later through the Southern Christian Leadership Conference, Clark launched the Citizenship Schools Program with Esau Jenkins, opening the first in Johns Island, South Carolina, in 1957 then expanding throughout the southeast. The Citizenship Schools were characterized as focusing on eliminating illiteracy, as voter literacy tests became common throughout the southeastern US to keep African Americans from voting, though the work of the schools extended to economic literacy, civil rights, and democracy education. By 1970, over

28,000 African Americans had gone through the Citizenship Schools, a powerful accomplishment highlighting 'the nature of Clark's work in the movement: using education to empower grassroots people, particularly African American women, so they might become leading citizens in their communities' (Hall et al, 2010, p 32). Re-orientating commonly held understandings of histories of inequality, oppression, exploitation, and white supremacy in the US Southeast reveals deep and long legacies of Black feminist activism and praxis.

Feminist geographers have prioritized inquiries and analyses that trouble normative notions of women's lives, politics, and location in the production of space, Feminist geographers have introduced the gender question in order to challenge hegemonic understandings of socio-spatial interactions, disrupting the dominance of patriarchal, masculinist methods and analyses in the discipline (Domosh, 1999; McDowell, 1999; Massey, 1994; Moss and Al Hindi, 2008; Johnston et al, 2020). As epistemological scaffolding, the field of feminist geographies has interrogated the politics of domination and positioning of space, place, and landscape. Feminist geographers have challenged cisheteropatriarchal politics in relations of power, notions of freedom, and hierarchical challenges to geographic imagination (Moss and Falconer Al-Hindi, 2008). Within feminist geographies, Black human geographies become contingent upon – and therefore respatialized – through real-imagined white spatialities. In alignment with the call to dismantle systems that have rendered transnational Black feminist contributions invisible, this chapter recognizes Black women as underacknowledged producers of feminist geographies and centralizes the 'unknowable figures' (McKittrick and Woods, 2007) that name place, and therefore the self, and asks: 1) What role does the unknowable geographies of Black subjects have in/on renovating dominant spatial processes? 2) Can/should Black feminist theoretical and spatial intimacies – focusing on resistance, histories, and the everyday across space and time – augment geographic thought? I use Evans-Winter's (2019) description of Black feminism, in that it is used 'to describe a long tradition of Black women's intellectual labour and community endeavours in the US and across the African Diaspora' (p 12).

This chapter is centred on the legacies of Black feminist activism in the United States Southeast (after here, referred to as the South), elucidating Black women's liberation work revolving around racial, economic, gender, and sexual justice. Because disciplinary practices have concealed and erased Black women's histories, scholars interested in Black feminist spatialities must turn to multidisciplinary sources to understand their activist legacies and orientations. Some sources are more accessible to geographers, such as examining the lives of widely known Black women. Indeed, several prominent activist figures in the United States and globally are Southern-born Black women, including Angela Y. Davis, Zora Neale Hurston,

Septima Clark, Alice Walker, Ella Baker, Dorothy Height, Fannie Lou Hamer, Ruby Bridges, Anna Julia Cooper, Ida B. Wells-Barnett, and Rosa Parks, among others. And still, sites of knowledge production occur in the quotidian experiences of Black women's living. Collectively, Black Southern women's spatialities unveil an organizing framework built on intellectual and grassroots organizing that has created a counternarrative to the idea that the US South and its people are stagnant, backwards, and lack bodily and spatial agency, which is included in accounts of people including Septima Clark (see Charron, 2009) and Ella Baker (see Ransby, 2003).

At the same time, scholars of racialization have increased attentiveness to the imagination of racial disparateness and its material consequences along social, political, and economic lines (Wilson 2000a, 2000b; Bressey and Dwyer, 2009; Price, 2010; Inwood, 2011; Lipsitz, 2011; Pulido, 2017; Alderman, 2018). Geographers studying race have delved into research that exposes the oppression of racialized peoples by highlighting connections to histories of colonization (Bond and Inwood, 2016; Pulido, 2018). As such, race has served as a social construction through which imperial movements can be achieved through the annihilation, enslavement, and hierarchical arrangement of peoples across the globe, which has continuing effects in modern operations and viewpoints (Stannard, 1992). In the past two decades, geographers have turned to Black geographies, a burgeoning (but not new) subfield of the discipline (Bledsoe et al, 2017; Bledsoe and Wright, 2019; Hawthorne, 2019; McCutcheon, 2019; Allen, 2020). In their groundbreaking work *Black Geographies and the Politics of Place*, McKittrick and Woods' (2007) discussion on Black geographies is articulated through what they call 'the unknowable figures' (that is, the Black Atlantic) that shifts dominant narratives of spatial production. Black geographies recognizes the undergirding of race and racism in socio-spatial formations, but also works to decentre pathologizing narratives as the limit of Black space. Black geographies moves beyond difference and (mere/lack of) representation towards taking Black ways of knowing as the intellectual and methodological agents, which parallels the ontological and epistemological groundings of Black feminist theory (Collins, 2000). Black geographies augments what we consider to be archives (which not only includes qualitative work but also natural archives, the humanities and the arts) and where we think Black people/communities belong or do not belong and where their knowledges are legible and valid in geography. A central characteristic of Black geographies scholarship is that it foregrounds Black knowledges in the production of space and place is the attention to the body and geographical embodiment, which aligns with Black feminist practice in centring Black women's embodied knowledges.

The geographies of the South are complex and their discursive configurations of the South are powerful. As such, the chapter highlights the history and challenges of organizing in/along/for US Southern spaces alongside the opportunities presented for new forms of socio-spatial knowledges through Black feminist spatial practices. The climate of the South lends itself to clear multi-issue activism that incorporates racial, gender, environmental, and sexual justice alongside spatial and class liberation struggle. Bobby Wilson (2002) writes that race-connected patterns and structures are deeply engrained and not easily discernible without an understanding of the larger structural and institutional forces that shaped and moulded them (p 1). To further Dr Wilson, both Black women's embodiments and lived experiences and the South as a subject of analyses provides us a conceptual framework through which complex and cumulative relations of power are analysed to reveal and redress structures of oppression embedded in/across place and scale. In this chapter, I amplify the right to theorize through Black feminists by drawing on several texts elucidating the quotidian experiences of Black women since the 1800s. Then, the chapter briefly engages contemporary activist work being undertaken by organizations led by and/or including a strong contingency of Black feminist, queer, and trans organizers in the South.

Black feminist geographies

> There is also undeniably a personal genesis for Black Feminism, that is, the political realization that comes from the seemingly personal experiences of individual Black women's lives. Black feminists and many more Black women who do not define themselves as feminists have all experienced sexual oppression as a constant factor in our day-to-day existence ... The fact that racial politics and indeed racism are pervasive factors in our lives did not allow us, and still does not allow most Black women, to look more deeply into our own experiences and, from that sharing and growing consciousness, to build a politics that will change our lives and inevitably end our oppression. Our development must also be tied to the contemporary economic and political position of Black people.
>
> The Combahee River Collective (1977)

The Combahee River Collective (CRC) was formed by a group of Black lesbian socialist feminists in Boston at the height of the women's movement, the gay and lesbian movement, and the African American civil rights movement in the 20th century. They took their name from the Combahee River Raid, a military expedition at the Combahee River in South Carolina during the US Civil War led by Harriet Tubman, the abolitionist who escaped slavery herself and led over a dozen missions to free other enslaved people through the Underground Railroad (Taylor, 2017). The CRC developed The Combahee River Collective Statement, an organizing document which anchors contemporary Black feminism, highlighting its radical intervention into understanding interlocking systems of oppression, which they call identity politics. Their standpoint and activist orientations are elucidated in the guiding quote excerpted earlier. In it, the CRC develops a focus on the role of embodied knowledges in pursuing liberation for Black women and Black feminists. Black women's spatialities and knowledges are essential for engaging activist feminist geographies because the legacies of Black women's erasure have curbed geographic understandings of place. As Katherine McKittrick writes, 'Concealment, marginalization, boundaries are important social processes. We make concealment happen; it is not natural but rather names and organizes where racial-sexual differentiation occurs' (McKittrick, 2006, pp xi–xii). Patricia Hill Collins describes, 'The humanist vision in Black feminist thought has deep historical roots in the political activism of African-American women' (2000, p 224). Here, I turn to recent examples of how Black feminist praxis in geography has demonstrated McKittrick's and Collins' insistence of Black women working to actualize a 'humanist vision' of space and place.

Priscilla McCutcheon's examination of Black woman activist Fannie Lou Hamer demonstrates how Hamer's embodiment and positionality grounded her politics and acts of resistance. She writes, 'In speeches, Hamer constantly weaved together her experiences of oppression in the rural Mississippi Delta to her activism. Simply, Hamer was engaged in a lifelong, fierce battle to nurture and protect her body and believed this story to be an important part of her mission' (2019, p 209). In McCutcheon's analyses, she echoes McKittrick's work in understanding how the body is a geographic location of struggle. Similarly, Brittany Meché's (2020) discussion of Black feminist legacies in the Birmingham-based upbringings of Angela Davis and Condoleezza Rice, based on analysing autobiographical material from each woman. Davis' and Rice's material overlaps, though conceptualized differently based on their vision of society, draw us to understand the subjectivities of Black girlhood and the negotiations of Black citizenship. Meché's analysis draws on Black feminist geographies to consider power, positionality, and 'overlapping historical specificities related to race, gender, and class' (p 477). McTighe and Haywood's (2018) analysis of Black feminist activism in New Orleans does just that. They examine the nonprofit Women With A Vision (WWAV) and elucidate how WWAV's epistemological approach centres Black women's knowledge by giving them authority over the post-Hurricane Katrina story of displacement and violence. It centres how individual experiences are transformed into collective consciousness through connective processes, and emphasizes the importance of space.

Black women's knowledge production and Black feminist placemaking practices are inclusive of those who have not risen to large-scale recognition and/or are public intellectuals (Collins, 2000). What follows in the next section contains some of both, recognizing the contributions of Black women associated with the legacies of Black feminism in the South as well as accounts of Black women whose words and actions over the last two centuries demonstrate the quotidian possibilities of Black feminist praxis.

Black feminism in the South from slavery to civil rights

> To be recognized as human, levelly human, is enough.
> The Combahee River Collective (1977, np)

Understanding the legacies of Black feminist activism, the struggle for being 'recognized as human' in the South, means recognizing Black women's relationship to Southern and United States histories and institutions, reinforcing the assertion that 'geography and black women have *always* functioned together and that this interrelated process is a new way to "enter" into space (conceptually and materially), one that uncovers a geographic story predicated on an ongoing struggle (to assert humanness and more humanly workable geographies)' (McKittrick, 2006, p xxiv). Here, I turn to an example from *Born in Slavery: Slave Narratives from the Federal Writers' Project, 1936–1938*, more commonly referred to as the WPA Slave Narratives. The narratives were collected as the United States was grappling with the Great Depression as part of the New Deal, a set of programs launched by President Franklin D. Roosevelt intended to stabilize the economy and provide jobs. Out of work writers were commissioned to gather stories of everyday life, and some were specifically sent to gather stories from formerly enslaved African Americans in the South. Included in the narratives are stories of everyday expressions of power and resistance, even under the conditions of enslavement. Mrs Fannie Berry, at the time a resident of Petersburg, Virginia, was interviewed on 26 February 1937, by Susie Byrd, a member of the Virginia Writers' Project, a division of the Federal Writers' Project. Mrs Berry had been enslaved in Virginia and described her experiences hearing about resistance and rebellion, including the anxieties it caused white slaveowners and other white people who supported the 'peculiar institution'. Early in her interview, Mrs Berry describes an encounter with a white man:

> I wuz one slave dat de poor white man had his match. See Miss Sue? Dese here ol' white men said, 'what I can't do by fair means I'll do by foul.' One tried to throw me, but he couldn't. We tusseled an' knocked over chairs an' when I got a grip I scratched his face all to pieces; an dar wuz no more bothering Fannie from him; but oh, honey, some slaves would be beat up so, when dey resisted, an' sometimes if you'll

'belled [rebelled] de overseer would kill yo'. Us Colored women had to go through a plenty, I tell you. (Federal Writers Project, 1936, p 2)

Black women who endured slavery were frequently subject to multiple scales of bodily violence, exploitation, and coercion. Their rights and capacities as childbearing people were stolen for the cause of reproducing empire, providing more labour for American industries. A tactic of preserving the hierarchies of slavery was to separate Black women from their children through the practice of selling enslaved people. And Black women were subject to rape by white men, slaveholders, overseers, and otherwise (Davis, 1983). Mrs Berry's account of fighting back against potential sexual violence unveils the exercise of agency and power she commanded, even in the face of potential future danger, including her own death.

Born into slavery in North Carolina, Anna Julia Cooper was 'an internationally renowned African American feminist educator, activist, orator, and scholar' (May, 2007, p 1). Of many remarkable aspects of her life, the publication of Cooper's *A Voice from the South* ([1892] 1998) is an important one, as it provides a crucial archive of Black feminist praxis in her own words and reflected through her socio-political advocacy at the intersection of racism-sexism:

> The colored woman of today occupies, one may say, a unique position in this country. In a period of itself transitional and unsettled, her status seems one of the least ascertainable and definitive of all the forces which make for our civilization. She is confronted by both a woman question and a race problem, and is yet an unknown or unacknowledged factor in both. (p 134)

Cooper's argument is the foundation of the Combahee River Collective's identity politics (1977), France Beal's double jeopardy (1970/2008) and Kimberlé Crenshaw's intersectionality (1991). Importantly, Cooper dedicated her life to the cause of recognizing that uplifting Black women's positions in society would improve the conditions of Black communities, seeing Black women as essential to pursuing a more just society. Her activism, pedagogy, and public engagement clearly linked 'dissident thought with transformative practice' (May 2007, p 45) solidifying her position as the 'Mother of Black feminism'.

Cooper and Septima Clark, who was discussed in the opening of this chapter, had a commonality in that they were activist educators. After slavery was abolished in the United States through President Abraham Lincoln's 1863 presidential proclamation and executive order, the Emancipation Proclamation, the creation of primary and secondary schools as well as colleges for Black students was one of the areas at the forefront of civil rights work for newly freed people. Many of the new so-called freedmen's schools were developed collectively with and funded by African Americans, both in and outside of the South, federal government agents in the Bureau of Refugees, Freedmen, and Abandoned Lands (mostly referred to as the Freedmen's Bureau), abolitionists, and missionary associations. Initially, mostly white teachers, typically women, from outside of the South were placed in these new Black schools. However, as new Black teachers were trained through Black colleges in the South, they took over the responsibilities of educating Black youth in the South. Learning to read and write was forbidden for enslaved people in the South. After emancipation, Black schools faced a number of additional challenges, such as funding, teacher pay, lack of adequate textbooks and other pedagogical materials, classroom space, and overpopulation. Yet, Black teachers (who were overwhelmingly women) served as sources of hope and empowerment for Black communities.

Anna Bernice Dewees Kelly was born in Charleston, South Carolina, in 1913. She was first educated in a private school, then at Immaculate Conception, a Catholic school, graduating in 1928. She then matriculated to the Avery Normal Institute, the first secondary school for Black youth in Charleston. There, she completed a teacher training program. After she graduated from Avery in 1932, she taught Black youth in Colleton, Dorchester, and Horry Counties in South Carolina, enrolling at Fisk University, an historically Black college in Nashville, Tennessee, to pursue an undergraduate degree. In an oral history interview recorded in 1984, she described her experiences teaching in rural South Carolina. She spoke of living with Black families in the communities where she taught, mostly sharecropping families, and learned how to farm and about other aspects of rural life. When the interviewer asked Kelly about the literacy rates in the community, she replied:

> I would imagine that most of the people were rural and if they went to school it was just for four or five months during the year. But I would say the intellectual rate was high in that many of them seemed to be able to use what they had and they seemed to be doing pretty well. (Kelly, 1984)

Here, Kelly demonstrates a Black feminist praxis of acting in solidarity with Black communities. Her relationships with communities involved the sharing of knowledge, through her role as a teacher in the schools and through her role as a learner from community members. She recognized and elevated indigenous knowledge production, valuing Black peoples 'intellectual rate', akin to what Clyde Woods terms blues epistemology (1998).

Examining the first-hand accounts of Black women spanning nearly two centuries reveals three clear themes to consider in Black feminist activist theorizations. The first is a foundational understanding that Black women activists in the South were acting in defense of their lives. Black women all advocated for dismantling the interlocking structures of racism-sexism through wide-ranging campaigns including the abolition of slavery, anti-lynching activism, women's suffrage, access to education, and labour rights. Black women's participation exposed the overlapping structures of racial-sexual domination within each area of human and civil rights and revealed the details of disenfranchisement. Second, Black women activists developed methods of forging communal visions that birth new practices of placemaking. Ida B. Wells-Barnett was an educator, activist, and investigative journalist, most widely known for her anti-lynching campaign. Her career legacy includes numerous publications that provided trenchant analyses of anti-Black violence in the South, such as *The Red Record* (1895) and *The Arkansas Race Riot* (1920). Wells-Barnett's early journalism was written in a way that was accessible to the Black people of Memphis during that time. In *Crusade for Justice: The Autobiography of Ida B. Wells*, she recalls the invitation to write in *the Living Way*, a weekly religious periodical published by a local Baptist pastor, Rev. R.N. Countee:

> All of this, although gratifying, surprised me very much, for I had had no training except what the work on the *Evening Star* had given me, and no literary gifts and graces. But I had observed and thought much about conditions as I had seen them in the country schools and churches. I had an instinctive feeling that the people who had little or no school training should have something coming into their homes weekly which dealt with their problems in a simple, helpful way. So in weekly letters to the *Living Way*, I wrote in a plain, common-sense way on the things which concerned our people. Knowing that their education was limited, I never used a word of two syllables where one would serve the purpose. (2020, p 22)

Finally, Black women's activisms in the US South worked for socio-spatial liberation in ways that prioritized solidarity in the work of tracing power structures and dismantling oppression. Mississippian Fannie Lou Hamer was said to be a strong mediator, working along trans-racial lines to transform place, such as the fundraising campaign for the Freedom Farms Cooperative – a project 'envisioned ... as a secure food source for Black people' in the late 1960s (McCutcheon, 2019, p 209). For South Carolinian Septima Clark, the vision was education in the most grassroots sense: 'This is what I feel as I work in a community. I don't think that in a community I need to go down to the city hall and talk; I think I train the people in that community to do their own talking' (Hall et al, 2010, p 48).

The work of Black women, engaged in Black feminist praxis, left a blueprint for the contemporary freedom struggles in the South today. To elucidate, I highlight three Southern feminist organizations pursuing liberatory placemaking practices through Black feminist epistemologies and ontologies.

Contemporary engagements with Black Feminist activist legacies in the South

> Redemption: because we believe that while the South is a physical geography of white supremacy and poverty and how they form plantations, mountaintop removal, and slave labor, it is also more than that. It is a place of redemption and hope for many: a place where folk reconcile with the past in an honest and painful way; a place where people can stay in lands riddled with pain and remember old traditions; and birth new ways.
>
> Southerners on New Ground (2013, np)

Approaching its thirtieth anniversary, Southerners on New Ground (SONG) is a queer liberation organization founded by three Black lesbians and three white lesbians. Since its founding in 1993, its organizing framework has engaged with and built on Southern Black feminist and womanist legacies in that they connect the material survival of LGBTQ+ Southerners, as guided by developing a justice infrastructure required for the liberation for all people through unravelling interlocking systems of oppression and linking axes of race, gender, ethnicity, class, and culture into their multi-racial, multi-issue actions, as shared in the quote excerpted above. Further, their history summarizes the nature of their activism:

> Some of SONG's major accomplishments include: crafting the first-ever Southern, LGBTQ-led, traveling Organizing School for small towns and rural places all over the South; training over 100 Southern and national racial and economic justice organizations to integrate work around homophobia and transphobia into their work; holding over 50 Southern sub-regional retreats for Southern Queer People of Color; continuing to be one of the only LGBTQ organizations in the US that truly listens, responds, and represents LGBTQ folk in small towns and rural places; and in 2008 holding the largest gathering specifically for Southern LGBTQ organizers in the last 10 years. (Southerners on New Ground 2022, np)

SONG focuses on the shared needs of LGBTQ+ people and their allies, engaging in 'Southern intersectional movement work'. For them, the actualization of liberation includes coalitional, solidarity work, which Cathy Cohen makes the case for in her well-known essay 'Punks, Bulldaggers, and Welfare Queens: The Radical Potential of Queer Politics?' (1997). Black women's intellectual traditions have impacted the ways in which life- and placemaking can happen across the South. SONG is not the only organization engaged in this movement work. As demonstrated in the previous section, the role of Black feminist activism in the South cannot be understated. From abolition movements and freedom colonies to desegregation, labour rights and land rights, and to reproductive justice and environmental justice, the South is a site of struggle in the United States. The depth of Southern Black feminist activist legacies is often rendered into monolithic terms, particularly in terms of civil rights, but the contemporary moment asks for a deeper examination. Perhaps one of the lesser engaged modes for Southern activism takes place on billboards.

The aesthetic of presumed regional cultural mores that pervades the South can be unquestionably revealed through billboards dispersed throughout the region. Billboards are purchased or rented by entities and used to disseminate a wide array of information, from goods and services to social issues to commuters. One of the most common issues disseminated by private groups is related to abortion. Anti-abortion billboards deploy a range of discursive strategies and images, including descriptions of the foetal heartbeat timeline, Bible verses related to the Christian God and conception, and the construction of future regret for the woman.

Gender and reproductive justice issues have long been subjects of regional activist efforts, with a range of Black feminist organizations, such as SisterSong, Sister Reach, and Access Reproductive Care – Southeast, taking up reproductive justice activism to employ sustained acts of resistance to oppressive political systems that have sought to limit sexual and reproductive health and bodily autonomy along pronounced gendered lines. In recent years, community and faith organizations have sought to change the public messaging, or to create counternarratives, to local policies and religious rhetoric. In Tennessee, the organization Healthy and Free Tennessee has built a coalition of individual members, agencies, and community groups to do just that. The organization's mission is 'to promote sexual and reproductive health and freedom in Tennessee by advancing policies and practices which recognize these elements as essential to the overall well-being of all individuals and communities' (Healthy and Free Tennessee, 2020). Healthy and Free Tennessee operates under an organizing model that collocates reproductive justice as having varying impacts based on race and ethnicity, gender identification, sexualities, age, education level, and socioeconomic status. Healthy and Free Tennessee centres a reproductive justice approach to their work. Reproductive justice is a term long utilized by women of colour organizations in defense of themselves 'to recognize that the control, regulation, and stigmatization of female fertility, bodies, and sexuality are connected to the regulation of communities that are themselves based on race, class, gender, sexuality, and nationality' (Silliman et al, 2016, p 10).

In 2019, Healthy and Free Tennessee erected billboards across the state. Many of them were along interstates but some, like the case of Murfreesboro, were erected along busy streets within city limits. Murfreesboro is one of the fastest growing cities in the nation and among the list of largest cities (by population) in Tennessee. Home to employees of a local university and to an increasing number of new commuters displaced by the increased cost of living in Nashville, the development of the city of Murfreesboro has rapidly shifted in response to population growth. Certainly, Healthy and Free Tennessee recognized the need to publicly engage reproductive justice in a city that has long maintained through white, conservative political strongholds sustained through political Southern power strongholds, including its churches (Murfreesboro is home to multiple megachurches with wide influence in the city) and the sustaining of the city's racial, ethnic, and economic divisions. In late 2019, a Healthy and Free Tennessee billboard appeared on Church Street (Figure 4.1), one of Murfreesboro's main thoroughfares. Among Church Street's institutions are the city's United States Postal Service location and a prominent local mortuary. The billboard faced downtown and the Murfreesboro Square and was impossible to overlook as commuters travelled from downtown to Interstate 24. The intersection of Church Street and Interstate 24 opens Murfreesboro to Nashville metro to the northwest, the town of Shelbyville to the southwest, and other small towns including Manchester and Monteagle to the southeast, all common destinations for commuters.

The spatial strategy of placing their billboards within city limits, like that of Church Street in Murfreesboro, is a direct disruption of the power structures

Figure 4.1: Billboard facing Church Street, Murfreesboro, Tennessee

Source: Reproduced with permission of Healthy and Free Tennessee

that have imposed homogenous, racialized [hetero]sexual and gender norms within Murfreesboro, the state, and the South.

Such a strategy was immediately relevant. During the early months of the COVID-19 pandemic, Tennessee Governor Bill Lee attempted to block abortion care, signing a heavily restrictive abortion law impacting decisions made at every stage of pregnancy in July 2020. A lawsuit filed by a group of organizations, including the American Civil Liberties Union, had (at least temporarily) blocked the law from taking place. However, before the pandemic, in 2019, Lee signed a so-called trigger law, one in which abortion would immediately become illegal should the Supreme Court of the United States (SCOTUS) reverse *Roe v. Wade*, the 1973 landmark decision that provided constitutional protection for abortion. The Tennessee law is significant, given that a draft of case pending SCOTUS decision was leaked to the press in early May 2022, indicating the constitutional right to an abortion might soon be overturned. A few days later, the governor signed another law, this time regulating abortion pill distribution by criminalizing access through telehealth and mail order. In June 2022, the SCOTUS ruled on abortion, repealing 50 years of national protection on the bodily right to choose, leaving the decision to allow abortion care to individual states. Consequently, the Tennessee laws have since been solidified.

Prior to the pandemic, Healthy and Free Tennessee had offered training for conducting self-managed abortion by pill. Just before the SCOTUS ruling, they launched a social media campaign, #SMAy, providing education around as 'an exercise of bodily autonomy' (Figure 4.2).

Healthy and Free Tennessee's work, grounded in Southern Black feminist orientations and emphasizing economic, racial, gender, and sexual justice, became more pronounced and urgent in the wake of the COVID-19 pandemic and, separately but related, in the fight against Tennessee lawmakers, for the cause of reproductive justice.

Finally, I want to briefly mention another organization whose work I have been following, Southern Movement Assembly (SMA). I argue that their work takes up Ruth Wilson Gilmore's (2017) notion of placemaking and its relationship to abolition:

> freedom is a place. Place-making is normal human activity: we figure out how to combine people, and land, and other resources with our social capacity to organize ourselves in a variety of ways, whether to stay put or to go wandering. Each of these factors – people, land, other resources, social capacity – comes in a number of types, all of which determine but do not define what can or should be done. Working outward and downward from this basic premise, abolitionist critique concerns itself with the greatest and least detail of these arrangements of people and resources and land over time. (p 227)

Figure 4.2: Screenshot from Healthy and Free Tennessee's #SMAy campaign (2022)

Source: Reproduced with permission of Healthy and Free Tennessee

Launched in 2012, SMA is a collective of organizations and individuals committed to shaping a multi-racial, multi-issue alliance to uplift frontline communities. The collective has been in community with more than 100 organizations from across the region, including the global south. Anchor organizations, those which have undertaken long-term commitment to SMA, represent all southern states, such as the Southern Rural Black Women's Initiative, SpiritHouse, Stay Together Appalachian Youth Project (S.T.A.Y.), and the Highlander Research and Education Center, formerly known as the Highlander Folk School and the same Highlander where Septima Clark launched the Citizenship Schools Program. SMA works as a collective and, like Healthy and Free Tennessee and SONG, and is informed by the legacies of Black women's organizing efforts in the South over the past several centuries. Their organizing framework specifically names the importance of history, stating, "We believe remembering, learning, and growing from our movement history is critical. We commit to recognize our long-term legacies and the most recent work that led to this moment' ('Principles of Unity', 2022, np). In one of SMA's recent campaigns, they set out to support Southern communities in the wake of the COVID-19 pandemic, the racial uprisings of 2020, the 2020 US election, and continued crises impacting Southern people's lives. They called the campaign the People's First 100 Days to set the into motion shared visions for 2021 – to practice a People's Democracy, build a New Social Economy, and Protect & Defend our communities. The launch of the campaign was timed with US President Joe Biden's inauguration and first 100 days in office, a time during which the performance of a newly installed president is unofficially but publicly evaluated. SMA's tactic included monthly strategy sessions during general assembly calls, held via Zoom in English with Spanish and American Sign Language interpreters included to increase accessibility to interested members. The strategy sessions included presentations from organizers recapping People's First 100 Days success so far, introducing various parts of the campaign – such as the April 2021 discussion of the SMA Toolkit for The People's First 100 Days (Figure 4.3) – breakout rooms for small group discussions, and opportunities for new people to get connected and engaged with the work.

The SMA's monthly assembly calls during 2021, beyond the People's First 100 Days, continued to provide support and training for southern organizers. In one additional example, the October 2021 assembly discussed the American Rescue Plan Act of 2021, a federal government program to provide public monies to communities across the United States in the wake of the COVID-19 pandemic. The conversation was facilitated by organizers from Spirit House and the Back in the Black Coalition in North Carolina who shared their organizing plan to secure community control of American Rescue Plan Act funds locally in the South through direct training attendees how to develop a plan for their towns and cities, to alleviate the oversights of state and local governments.

Conclusion

> '[W]e who believe in freedom cannot rest.'
>
> Ella Baker

It has been well documented in the story of this nation that Black womanhood has been devalued for centuries, even within slavery abolition, women's suffrage, and the African American civil rights movements (hooks, 1982; Davis, 1983; Collins, 2000). Yet, as Katherine McKittrick argues, 'black women have an investment in space, and spatial politics, precisely because they have been relegated to the margins of knowledge and have

Figure 4.3: Excerpt from the SMA Toolkit for The People's First 100 Days (2021)

#P100 #HearThePeople

ACTION DATE: APRIL 9-11TH, 2021

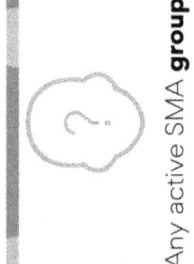

SOUTHERN MOVEMENT ASSEMBLY

Any active SMA **groups** plus other groups recruited to work with us. **Goal: Expand our base and our power.***

HOW?

Use arts + culture to **send a strong message** about one or more of those areas with a group of folks who are committed to working together – **Goal: Show our energy and our visions for change by sharing these events through a coordinated communication strategy.**

WHAT?!

public actions that lift our Southern voices to name **what we want to build in** our communities for our health, safety, work and land. **Goal: show our vision for the world we want to be**

Source: Reproduced with permission of Southern Movement Assembly

therefore been *imagined* as outside of the production of space' (2006, p 54). Examining the long legacy of Black women in the South, beginning with chattel slavery, makes this 'investment in space' more apparent. Black women, historically (and, in ways, contemporarily) denied the right to healthcare, education, employment opportunities, housing, voting, and more, developed their own systems for connectivity, community, care, and dignity (McCutcheon, 2022).

Visionary Ella Jo Baker was born in 1903 in Norfolk, Virginia, and raised in Littleton, North Carolina, a rural farming community near the North Carolina/Virginia border. Baker 'was nurtured, educated, and challenged by a community of strong, hard-working, deeply religious black people – most of them women' (Ransby, 2003, p 28). Her upbringing contributed to her life's work in grassroots organizing and radical change, which as historian and Black feminist organizer Barbara Ransby describes, 'was about a persistent and protracted process of discourse, debate, consensus, reflection, and struggle' (2003, p 18). Referred to as one of the most important, and most underrecognized, Americans of the 20th century, Baker's organizing legacies and impact as a civil rights leader cover the entire South, from her home in North Carolina to the Gulf Coast towns of Alabama. She held leadership roles in NAACP during the 1940s and 1950s and the Southern Christian Leadership Conference (SCLC) in the 1950s. She gathered and mentored a new generation of activists in the Black freedom struggle by organizing a meeting of students for what became the Student Nonviolent Coordinating Committee (SNCC) in 1960. Ransby's biography of Baker includes a partial list of her organizational affiliations between 1927 and her death in 1986, numbering more than 40. One of the most commonly cited lines from Baker's massive legacy of movement work opens this section. The quote is excerpted from a 1964 keynote speech given at the Mississippi Freedom Democratic Party. There, she eulogized the lives of three murdered civil rights workers, whose bodies had been found days before the gathering. She urged the crowd to continue the work of radical social change, saying, 'Until the killing of black mothers' sons is as important as the killing of white mothers' sons, we who believe in freedom cannot rest' (Ransby, 2003, p 266). 'We who believe in freedom cannot rest' endures as generations of movement activists have found strength and vision in Baker's life and work.

The legacies of Black feminist luminaries in the South are expansive. Black feminist activist geographies have reshaped the landscape of human rights, through Black women, like Ella Baker, engaging in collective organizing, community action, and building kinship networks, all establishing the groundwork for movement work for abolition, reproductive justice, voting rights, education, healthcare (including HIV), disability justice, environmental justice, LGBTQ+ rights, housing justice, and beyond. Through the examples included in this paper from SONG, Healthy and Free

Tennessee, and Southern Movement Assembly, we can draw connections to the work of Black feminist fore-mothers, doing as Chicago-based Black feminist activist Charlene Carruthers suggests in *Unapologetic: A Black, Queer, and Feminist Mandate for Radical Movements*: 'Our luminaries deserve more than to be distilled into pithy quotes. Their intellectual labour should be used to guide our strategies to build movements' (2018, p 6).

So, it is past time for feminist scholars and feminist geographers to take Black women's lives and work more seriously, not just use their theoretical frameworks (that is, intersectionality). Further, it is critical to understand the Black feminist roots that undergird much of feminist activism, both in the United States and globally. And finally, feminist geographers must not engage the American South monolithically, but as an active site of Black feminist placemaking, resistance, and movement. Building on the legacies of Black women's lives and work and in elucidating contemporary Black feminist organizing in the South, this chapter points towards the geographical insights of Black feminist activists, engaging their practices of resistance and change and denaturalizing the geographic imagination about Black women in the South.

References

Alderman, D. (2018). 'The Racialized and Violent Biopolitics of Mobility in the USA: An Agenda for Tourism Geographies'. *Tourism Geographies* 20(4): 717–20.

Allen, D.L. (2020) 'Black Geographies of Respite: Relief, Recuperation, and Resonance at Florida A&M University'. *Antipode* 52(6): 1563–82.

Beal, F.M. (1970/2008). 'Double Jeopardy: To Be Black and Female'. *Meridians* 8(8): 166–76.

Bledsoe, A. and Wright, W.J. (2019). 'The Pluralities of Black Geographies'. *Antipode* 51(2): 419–37.

Bledsoe, A., Eaves, L.E. and Williams, B. (2017). 'Introduction: Black Geographies in and of the United States South'. *Southeastern Geographer* 57(1): 6–11.

Bonds, A. and Inwood, J. (2016). 'Beyond White Privilege: Geographies of White Supremacy and Settler Colonialism'. *Progress in Human Geography* 40(6): 715–33.

Bressey, C. and Dwyer, C. (2009). *New Geographies of Race and Racism*. Abingdon: Taylor & Francis.

Carruthers, C.A. (2018). *Unapologetic: A Black, Queer, and Feminist Mandate for Radical Movements*. Boston: Beacon Press.

Charron, K.M. (2009). *Freedom's Teacher: The Life of Septima Clark*. Chapel Hill: University of North Carolina Press.

Cohen, C.J. (1997). 'Punks, Bulldaggers, and Welfare Queens: The Radical Potential of Queer Politics?'. *Gay and Lesbian Quarterly* 3: 437–65.

Collins, P. (2000). *Black Feminist Thought: Knowledge, Consciousness, and the Politics of Empowerment*. New York: Routledge.

Combahee River Collective. (1977). 'The Combahee River Collective Statement'. Available from: www.blackpast.org/african-american-history/combahee-river-collective-statement-1977/ [Accessed 10 March 2022].

Cooper, A.J. (1892/1988.) *A Voice from the South*. New York: Oxford.

Crenshaw, K. (1991). 'Mapping the Margins: Intersectionality, Identity Politics, and Violence against Women of Color'. *Stanford Law Review* 43(6): 1241–99.

Davis, A.Y. (1983). *Women, Race, & Class*. New York: Random House.

Domosh, M. (1999). 'Sexing Feminist Geography'. *Progress in Human Geography* 23(3): 429–36.

Evans-Winters, V.E. (2019). *Black Feminism in Qualitative Inquiry: A Mosaic for Writing Our Daughter's Body*. London: Routledge.

Federal Writers' Project: Slave Narrative Project, Vol. 17, Virginia, Berry-Wilson. (1936). Manuscript/Mixed Material. Available from: www.loc.gov/item/mesn170/ [Accessed 1 September 2021].

Gilmore, R.W. (2017). 'Abolition Geography and the Problem of Innocence', in G.T. Johnson and A. Lubin (eds) *Futures of Black Radicalism*. Brooklyn: Verson, 225–40.

Hall, J.D., Walker, E.P, Charron, K.M., and Cline, D.P. (2010). '"I train the people to do their own talking": Septima Clark and Women in the Civil Rights Movement'. *Southern Cultures* 16(2): 31–117.

Hawthorne, C. (2019). 'Black Matters Are Spatial Matters: Black Geographies for the Twenty-first Century'. *Geography Compass* 13: e12468.

Healthy and Free Tennessee (2020). 'Mission, Vision and Values'. Available from: www.healthyandfreetn.org/mission_vision_values [Accessed 10 March 2022].

Healthy and Free Tennessee (2022). 'Healthy and Free Tennessee presents … #SMAy'. Instagram, 1 May. Available from: www.instagram.com/p/CdCOY5xNuNR/?igshid=MWI4MTIyMDE= [Accessed 11 April 2023].

hooks, bell (1982). *Ain't I a Woman: Black Women and Feminism*. Boston: South End Press.

Inwood, J. (2011). 'Geographies of Race in the American South: The Continuing Legacies of Jim Crow Segregation'. *Southeastern Geographer* 51(4): 564–77.

Johnston, L, Datta, A., Hopkins, P., Silva, J.S., and Olson, E. (2020). 'Introduction: Establishing, Placing, Engaging and Doing Feminist Geographies', in A. Datta, P. Hopkins, L. Johnston, E. Olson and J.M. Silva (eds) *Routledge Handbook of Gender and Feminist Geographies*. London: Routledge, 1–14.

Kelly, Anna (20 August 1984). Interview by Edmund L. Drago. AMN 500.001.014, Avery Research Center Oral Histories, Avery Research Center at the College of Charleston. Available from: https://lcdl.library.cofc.edu/lcdl/catalog/lcdl:23394 [Accessed 1 September 2021].

Lipsitz, G. (2011). *How Racism Takes Place*. Philadelphia: Temple University Press.

Massey, D. (1994). *Space, Place and Gender*. Minneapolis: University of Minnesota Press.

May, V. (2007). *Anna Julia Cooper, Visionary Black Feminist: A Critical Introduction*. New York: Routledge.

McCutcheon, P. (2019). 'Fannie Lou Hamer's Freedom Farms and Black Agrarian Geographies'. *Antipode* 51(1): 207–24.

McCutcheon, P. (2022). '"When and Where I Enter": The National Council of Negro Women, Black Women's Organizing Power, and the Fight to End Hunger'. *Annals of the American Association of Geographers* 112(8): 2486–500.

McDowell, L. (1999). *Gender, Identity and Place: Understanding Feminist Geographies*. Minneapolis: University of Minnesota Press.

McKittrick, K. (2006). *Demonic Grounds: Black Women and the Cartographies of Struggle*. Minneapolis: University of Minnesota Press.

McKittrick, K. and Woods, C. (eds) (2007). *Black Geographies and the Politics of Place*. Cambridge, MA: South End Press.

McTighe and Haywood, D. (2018). 'Front Porch Revolution: Resilience Space, Demonic Grounds, and the Horizons of a Black Feminist Otherwise'. *Signs: Journal of Women in Culture and Society* 44(1): 25–52.

Meché, B. (2020). 'Memories of an Imperial City: Race, Gender, and Birmingham, Alabama'. *Antipode* 52(2): 475–95.

Moss, P. and Falconer Al-Hindi, K. (eds) (2008) Feminisms in Geography: Rethinking Space, Place, and Knowledges. Lanham: Rowman & Littlefield, pp 155–70.

Price, P. (2010). 'At the Crossroads: Critical Race Theory and Critical Geographies of Race'. *Progress in Human Geography* 34(2): 147–74.

'Principles of Unity' – Southern Movement Assembly. (2022). Available from: www.southtosouth.org/about [Accessed 30 March 2022].

Pulido, L. (2017). 'Geographies of Race and Ethnicity II: Environmental Racism, Racial Capitalism and State-sanctioned Violence'. *Progress in Human Geography* 41(4): 524–33.

Pulido, L. (2018). 'Geographies of Race and Ethnicity III: Settler Colonialism and Nonnative People of Color'. *Progress in Human Geography* 42(2): 309–18.

Ransby, B. (2003). *Ella Baker and the Black Freedom Movement: A Radical Democratic Vision*. Chapel Hill: University of North Carolina Press.

Silliman, J., Gerber Fried, M. Ross, L. and Gutiérrez, E.R. (2016). *Undivided Rights: Women of Color Organize for Reproductive Justice*. Chicago: Haymarket Books.

Southern Movement Assembly (2021). SMA P100 Toolkit. Available from: www.southtosouth.org/resources/sma-p100-toolkit [Accessed 5 May 2022].

Southerners on New Ground (2013). 'Why the South?'. Available from: https://southernersonnewground.org/who-we-are/why-the-south/ [Accessed 30 March 2022].

Southerners on New Ground (2022). 'Our Mission, Vision, and History'. Available from: https://southernersonnewground.org/who-we-are/vision-mission-history/ [Accessed 20 April 2022].

Stannard, D.E. (1992). *America Holocaust: The Conquest of the New World*. Oxford: Oxford University Press.

Taylor, K.Y. (2017). *How We Get Free: Black feminism and the Combahee River Collective*. Chicago: Haymarket Books.

Wells, I.B. and Duster, A. (2020). *Crusade for Justice: The Autobiography of Ida B. Wells*, 2nd ed. Chicago: University of Chicago Press.

Wells-Barnett, I.B. (1895). *A red Record: Tabulated Statistics and Alleged Causes of Lynchings in the United States, 1892–1893–1894*. Chicago: Donohue & Henneberry.

Wells-Barnett, I.B. (1920). *The Arkansas Race Riot*. Chicago: Hume Job Print.

Wilson, B.M. (2000a). *America's Johannesburg: Industrialization and Racial Transformation in Birmingham*. Lanham: Rowman & Littlefield Publishers.

Wilson, B.M. (2000b). *Race and Place in Birmingham: The Civil Rights and Neighborhood Movements*. Lanham: Rowman & Littlefield Publishers.

Wilson, B.M. (2002). 'Critically Understanding Race-Connected Practices: A Reading of W.E.B. Du Bois and Richard Wright'. *The Professional Geographer* 54(1): 31–41.

Woods, C. (1998). *Development Arrested: The Blues and Plantation Power in the Mississippi Delta*. New York: Verso.

5

LGBT+ Activism and Morality Politics in Central and Eastern Europe: Understanding the Dynamic Equilibrium in Czechia from a Broader Transnational Perspective

Michal Pitoňák

It was during the time of first writing of this chapter when I lost my father. I stay forever grateful for his support and unconditional love.

A note on my positionality

This research is part of my independent work. In 2015 I defended my PhD thesis in the field of human geography and became the first human geographer to focus on the field of geographies of sexualities in Czechia. Although I have not been the first to attempt to introduce feminist thought into Czech(oslovak) geographical thinking (Blažek and Rochovská, 2006; Matejsková, 2007) these approaches have, so far, remained far from accepted by the 'mainstream' geographers and have a long way to go before they become established within local geographical academia. Issues related to sexual and gender minorities are, so far, mostly regarded as peripheral within Czech (Osman and Pospíšilová, 2019) as well as other Central and Eastern European geographical academia which resists feminist and queer scholarly approaches (Timár and Fekete, 2010). I have discussed this lasting disciplinary resistance toward feminist and queer thought in detail elsewhere (Pitoňák, 2019; Pitoňák and Klingorová, 2019).

Many researchers who focus on this field in the region of Central and Eastern Europe often lack institutional support and continue with their work as independent researchers or seek scholarly opportunities abroad. Some of us work in other disciplines or earn their living by working in different jobs. For me, this chapter is a result of my independent and lasting interest in contributing to the field of geographies of sexualities, informed by queer and feminist perspectives. To be able to focus on this task, I have worked in my free time, sacrificed time that I could otherwise spend with my life-partner, my family, or friends. Sometimes I had to take a vacation to be able to write or reschedule my paid-work activities and other research project duties. Oftentimes I had pondered introspectively about my lasting motivations and questioned my involvement. Yet, I remain hopeful that this work will contribute to the large field of sexuality and gender studies in geography. In a way I feel that scholarly work in this area relates to some sort of responsibility and fits into a web of both formal and informal scholarly interactions that simultaneously receive support and give it to others.

Brief history of Czech(oslovak) LGBT+ activism

When considering the history of Czech(oslovak) LGBT+ activism, I should start with frequently overlooked development in 1930s Czechoslovakia. Even though at this time 'homosexuality' or more precisely 'homosexual conduct' was illegal, there were already social developments and a proto-LGBT+ movement with a clear goal that aimed to decriminalize 'homosexual conduct' (Himl et al, 2013). The fact that the Czechoslovak movement was relatively vibrant at this time has so far remained disregarded and 'beyond translation'. Remarkably, between 1931–1932, advocates managed to publish a several unique sexual-minority-oriented semimonthly magazines, including *Hlas sexuální menšiny* (Voice of the Sexual Minority) and *Nový hlas: List pro sexuální reformu* (New Voice: paper for sexual reform). This proves that the sexual minority, both as a concept and basis for the societal movement existed at this time, predating the post-Stonewall gay and lesbian movement by decades (cf Jagose, 1996). Indeed, this pre-WWII Czechoslovak 'homosexual movement' was closely connected to neighbouring German-speaking circles, which are widely recognized as a cradle of 'homosexual' activism with lasting legacies of Magnus Hirschfeld (Seidl et al, 2012). This connection is perhaps best demonstrated by the *International conference of World League for Sexual Reform* (Weltliga für Sexualreform) that took place in 1932 Brno, the second-largest city in Czechia.

However, these promising tendencies were thwarted in the 1940s by the intervention of Nazism in Germany and after the onset of WWII through the whole region. Post-war Europe left little space for continuation, and the emerging communist regimes in Central and Eastern Europe (CEE) almost completely interrupted the earlier liberalizing tendencies at both the cultural and civil-societal levels.

During this period, Czechoslovakia, as well as other countries under the influence of Soviet communism, became reshaped economically, socially, and culturally. The totalitarian regimes firmly censored discourses that questioned the societal homogeneousness and subsequently entrenched heterosexuality as an unquestioned norm of citizenship. Despite this censorship and normative social taboo, the medical fields of psychiatry and sexology, scientific disciplines interested in studying sexuality from an essentialist perspective, continued to develop progressively in Czechoslovakia (Sokolová, 2012; Lišková, 2018). Although many scholars at the time adhered to methods that would today be considered unethical, the early interest of researchers such as Kurt Freund and his research in the field of 'sexual orientation change efforts' (for example, aversion therapy), paradoxically contributed to the development of a robust medical consensus on incurability/immutability of sexual orientation (Freund, 1962). These early experiments had an undeniable impact on decriminalizing 'homosexual conduct' in Czechoslovakia and potentially elsewhere in the region, such in Hungary (Takács and Tóth, 2021). 'Consensual homosexual intercourse' was legally decriminalized in Czechoslovakia in 1962. The importance of the Czechoslovak school of sexology and the Cold War developments beyond the Iron Curtain has only recently been noticed by scholars who argue that the Iron Curtain was, in fact, relatively permeable for some (Szulc, 2018; Davison, 2021).

However, the 1962 decriminalization of homosexuality should not be read as an end of censorship or stigmatization of sexual minorities within the communist state. Strict censorship remained, whereas 'homosexuals' were still discriminated against and persecuted. For example, the homosexual age of sexual consent remained set at 18 years of age (compared to 15 years for heterosexual intercourse), and 'homosexuals' were expected not to 'cause a public nuisance'. According to recent investigations utilizing archival work and oral histories, the communist state police (*Státní bezpečnost – StB*) kept so-called 'pink lists' to keep files about 'homosexuals' to serve potential purposes of politically-motivated blackmail (Himl et al, 2013).

Cold War politics and sexuality

Until the 1970s, 'homosexuality' was regarded as pathology, a mental health diagnosis, globally. It was removed as a diagnosis for the first time from the *Diagnostic and Statistical Manual of Mental Disorders* (DSM III) in the US. In Europe, pathologizing of 'homosexuality' lasted until the early 1990s, when the new *International Classification of Diseases* (ICD) took effect. For this reason, even during the 1980s, some sexologists and psychiatrists continued to provide so-called 'heterosexual adaptation therapies' to patients who sought 'help' with their efforts to conform to the heteronormative pressure promoted by dominant heteronormative culture (Brzek and Hubalek, 1988). These 'therapies' typically resulted in coupling people of different sex typically those who agreed to some form of asexual relationships or an idea of successfully conceiving a child with their 'mate' under the supervision of the therapist to fulfill their 'duty to the society' as part of the pro-natalist policies (for example, related to access to housing) during the communist period (Sokolová, 2012).

The normative influence of state-socialist and the communist regime should not be underestimated. For example, Czechoslovakia was affected by the aftermath of the Prague Spring in 1968, which was a failed attempt to overthrow the communist government and challenge Soviet hegemony. In response, Soviet military interventions resulted in a period of so-called 'normalization' that strengthened communist rule and its norms. According to scholars, this period substantially impacted societal morale and had a lasting effect that lowered people's willingness to participate in public life (Holý, 2001). Under their respected medical authority, selected sexologists like Dagmar Bártová founded so-called 'socio-therapeutic groups' that allowed for early socializing among mostly gay community members (Sokolová, 2012). Some sexual minority men may have also been motivated to join these groups because it was one of the few officially sanctioned ways to avoid the mandatory two-year military service (Nedbálková, 2016).

The firm censorship regarding LGBT+ people thawed for the first time during the late 1980s due to the global HIV/AIDS pandemic. During this time, the first public articles covered 'homosexuals' and 'homosexuality' and represented them as 'nonconforming' and 'anti-social' citizens prone to spreading the emergent disease (Kolářová, 2013). Following the political events in November 1989, known as the *Velvet Revolution*, and subsequent dismantling of the socialist regime in Czechoslovakia (as well as in neighbouring countries through similar processes), a long post-socialist period of uneasy transition toward a deregulated and neoliberal democratic future began. In the area of LGBT+ activism, it is undeniable that sexologists played a sustained and affirmative role in facilitating the organization of an LGBT+ subculture from a basis of the 'socio-therapeutic groups'.

These opportunities then gave rise to first communities and initiatives that quickly mobilized into post-revolutionary activism through a newly formed Association of Homosexual Citizens' Organisations in the Czech Republic (SOHO, *Sdružení organizací homosexuálních občanů v České republice – SOHO v ČR*) by 1990.

The first significant step of SOHO was equalizing the legal age of same-sex and different-sex intercourse to 15 years (achieved in 1990). In 1993 Czechoslovakia broke up into Czechia and Slovakia. This is known as the

Velvet divorce. During the 1990s, a vivid activist scene emerged and focused primarily on several then pressing issues such as the growth of sex work at the former Iron Curtain border and the HIV/AIDS pandemic prevention. Activists were also intimately aware of the pressing need to improve public opinion regarding sexual minorities and promoted the introduction of anti-discriminatory protections. In order to build up the local LGBT+ community, SOHO organized several private, semi-public, and public events. These events included: annual community event *Gay man*, a beauty contest exclusively for men, and *Apríles* festival of lesbian culture organized mainly as semi-private events that did not aim for broader public participation or visibility (Procházka et al, 2003). In 1998, SOHO organized the first Czech public pride parade named the *Rainbow festival* (*Duhový festival*) in Karlovy Vary. The primary reason for this parade was to show support to the first proposal of the same-sex partnership bill, which became the most important goal for activists during the following two decades due to the uneasiness of passing this legislation.

According to my interview with the former activist leader Jiří Hromada, the activists knew that public support was essential. Thus, the activist focused on advocacy work and support of anti-discrimination legislation which was also facilitated by the necessity to meet the European Union accession criteria, which Czechia joined in 2004. Meanwhile, the advocacy of the same-sex partnership bill (later known as the Registered Partnership Act) became a more lengthy and tiring process. After almost two decades of repeated negotiations, the Registered Partnership Act was adopted in its minimal version in 2006. However, scholars concur that this 'achievement' eventually ended the first chapter of the modern Czech 'LG+' activism era because it effectively led to the dissolution of the formerly active and relatively well-organized (although mostly gay male) activist networks (Nedbálková, 2016).

The 2006 registered partnership law became immediately criticized for its weak legal and symbolic status. The law did not create grounds for joint property or joint rent, it did not entail any tax advantages nor granted widow/widower pension, and even in cases of inheritance and gift taxes, the partners were not treated the same way as wife or husband would have been. Most importantly, the law completely omitted same-sex families' recognition and directly prohibited registered partners from accessing individual adoptions that were otherwise accessible to all eligible individuals regardless of their sexual orientation. The Czech law thus enabled a paradoxical situation in which any eligible person could apply for individual adoption, except for individuals who entered into a same-sex legal partnership. In March 2009, a gender studies NGO published a legal analysis by constitutional lawyer Jan Wintr which substantiated that the Registered Partnership Act contradicts the constitutional order (Wintr, 2009). Eventually, based on a separate lawsuit with the Czech constitutional court, this contested legal provision was repealed in 2016 based on a decision recognizing it to have been an infringement of human dignity and violation of the right to protection of private life.

Aside from this development, however, the first decade of the 21st century remained relatively inactive of LGBT+ activism. The organization of the first significant pride parades in the public space was among few notable exceptions. In 2008, two years after the registered partnership legislation was passed, several formerly underrepresented groups organized an event called *Queer Parade* in Brno, the second-largest city in Czechia. This event was the first major LGBT+ event attracting hundreds of non-heterosexuals, their family members, and allies. This event was the first to gain high visibility and substantial media coverage. However, the higher visibility of the event was met with first major mobilizing effort by the opposition, which resulted in far-right extremist groups disrupting this event. In 2009 a similar event called *Queer Pride* took place in Tábor second-largest city in Southern Bohemia. Again far-right radicals and adherents of the radical Workers' Party (Dělnická strana) also tried to interrupt the parade, this time unsuccessfully because the organizers learned from the last years' experience in Brno successfully cooperated with police.

In the following year (2010), another parade retook place in Brno, which over the first decade of the new millennium became home to the first queer cultural and social events of its kind in Czechia, namely the *Mezipatra queer film festival* (since 2000) and the *Queer Ball* (since 2013).

Remarkably, the first major public pride parade organized in the capital took place only in 2011. As I analyse it in more depth elsewhere (Pitoňák, 2022), this 'delayed organization' was partly a result of a deliberate strategy in which activists' organizing in public space were carefully weighted by public support that steadily grew over the years. Several years ago, I attended a public discussion with Jiří Hromada, the former activist leader of the SOHO, during which he explained: "In Prague, SOHO resisted doing something like this [organizing of pride parade] at the time because [our strategy/goal] was about promoting the registered partnership and we didn't want to irritate politicians and the public with such exhibitions" (Jiří Hromada, public discussion).

It is evident that organizing first major pride parades in Brno and Tábor thus only took place when the activist networks decided that it was the right time to increase the LGBT+ people's presence in the public space. The organizers of these events typically did not follow any concrete political goal and, in line with this argumentation, primarily meant to increase the societal visibility of LGBT+ people, mobilize the 'LGBT+ community', and enhance its solidarity networks (Pitoňák, 2022). The 'societal acceptance of *homosexuals*' grew steadily from 28 per cent in 1995 to 56 per cent in

2010. Interestingly, this figure has remained relatively stable since then (57 per cent in 2020) (Public Opinion Research Centre, 2020).

With exception of largely apolitical annual organizing of Prague Pride, the Czech LGBT+ activists mobilized once more in 2014 when a novel organization, *Platforma pro rovnoprávnost, uznání a diverzitu* (Platform for Equality, Recognition and Diversity) which uses an acronym PROUD came to the fore and started advocating for LGBT+ rights, most notably attempted to advocate for introduction of stepparent adoptions. Despite painstaking efforts, this goal was unsuccessful as it was met with substantial opposition and lack of interest on the part of the wider society as well as with low support on the side of politicians. Following the four-year cycle of parliamentary elections in Czechia, the proposed laws repeatedly remained undeliberated nor were taken up by the newly elected parliament in 2017. It became evident that in a climate where, on the one hand, the public lacks awareness and sensitivity to LGBT+ people's situations and, on the other hand, politicians are resisting attempts to spark discussion and block any legislation that could improve the recognition of LGBT+ people's families and parental rights, any change would require tremendous effort. Despite the failure of PROUD's four-year work, their activities focused on public-oriented advocacy and media representation became mirrored in the increases in support of same-sex family rights in public opinion polls.

In 2017 activists decided to build wider coalition which they named *Jsme Fér* (*We are fair*). This new initiative, in which Prague Pride and PROUD played the most audible roles, revised the existing advocacy strategy and, instead of aiming at singular adoption-related legislation goals, defined a broader goal of achieving marriage equality in Czechia. This new goal received substantial support from several organizations and became understood as the primary community goal one which may simultaneously lead to recognition of same-sex families' existence and their legitimacy. Indeed, I must note that marriage equality did not become any singular LGBT+ movement goal and other organizations and initiatives focused on other goals, most notably on trans people's rights or concerns of elderly LGBT+ people. Especially, trans and gender diverse people's activism was also developing vividly at this time, and it particularly focused on resisting pathologizing and oppressive practices from the site of health professionals. In addition, trans activism has a long-term goal of removing legal requirement of sterilization as part of legal transition process.

Regardless of their goal, most activists have however recognized the importance of public support and societal mindset. Since its beginning in 2017, the *Jsme Fér* coalition focused on the public and started a petition for marriage for gay and lesbian couples. This helped create a momentum which climaxed on 13 June 2018 when first proposal to amend the Civil Code to allow same-sex marriage was submitted by 46 MPs led by Radka

Maxová (ANO party). Like all other proposals, this one was discussed by the Government of the Czech Republic. On Friday, 22 June, the Czech Government adopted a favourable opinion on it. In parallel to this hopeful development, on 27 June 2018, the Jsme Fér representatives handed over a successful public petition to the Chair of the House Petitions Committee, and on 23 October 2018, a public hearing was held in its regard in the Chamber of Deputies of the Czech Republic.

However, just a couple of days after the proposal to amend the Civil Code and other laws to allow marriage for same-sex couples was submitted, another group of 37 MPs led by Marek Výborný from Christian Democratic party submitted a counter-proposal to amend the Czech constitutional order to include 'protection of marriage clause' and define it only as a 'union between a man and a woman'. This development resulted from rapidly mobilized advocacy of a moral-entrepreneurial-type organization *Aliance pro Rodinu* (Alliance for family), founded in 2017. Although the counter-proposal did not receive equal support from within the Czech Government, a decision was passed that both submitted proposals are to be discussed by the MPs in the Chamber of Deputies jointly.

Since its submission in June 2018, the 'marriage-equality proposal' was debated in the Czech Chamber of Deputies only three times – its first hearing began in November 2018, as it was facing obstructions from the opposition the debate was continued in March 2019 and it was only after 1,052 days, on 29 April 2021, when the Chamber of Deputies finally committed to completing the first reading and sent the two competing proposals to the second reading. However, given the end of the parliamentary term and the long subsequent legislative process, it was clear that efforts to legalize marriage for same-sex couples, at least in the current parliamentary term, were thwarted. As a result of the fact that the new October 2021 election has significantly strengthened the conservative-minded and right-wing groups and, on the contrary, significantly weakened the Pirate Party which unanimously promoted marriage equality, further development became uncertain, to say the least.

Before I proceed to the next section, I find it apt to quote several statements presented by MPs in the Czech Chamber of Deputies during the 29 April 2021 debate. All following translations are my own: 'Marriage is dad, mom, and kids. Marriage should not be diluted, and the concept should not be relativized' (Marek Výborný, a member of the Christian-democratic party – KDU-ČSL). 'We consider it normal that there are two sexes. A family consists of a mom, a dad, and children. It is normal that marriage is a union of one man and one woman' (Zuzana Majerová Zahradníková, the chair of the Trikolóra party). 'I grew up in an orphanage for part of my childhood. If a same-sex couple adopted me as a little boy who cannot defend himself, I would rather jump out of the window' (Tomio Okamura, the chair of

Freedom and Direct Democracy party). 'This is not a gay and lesbian story. This is a culture war story. We don't have to try every stupid thing the West does' (Marek Benda, a member of Civic Democratic Party).

If there is a word that we can use to depict the current development of the LGBT+ movement in Czechia, it would be stalemate. As I will attempt to demonstrate in the following parts, this situation may not be viewed as a 'lack of progress' because other processes that activists and advocates had encountered were already underway, and these new challenges required adaptations and novel strategies.

From invisible and disunited advocacy toward united transnational opposition

Following the transformation of economies and political systems, most countries in CEE witnessed a period of vivid change. This is also related to relatively quick LGBT+ activist mobilizing and progress in terms of new legislative changes as well as new opportunities for civil society building. Perhaps one of the reasons why this process was initially relatively undisturbed, yet relatively small, was that most countries in the region focused on their accession to the EU (and partly to NATO), and thus this type of activism was partly shielded from reaching wider societal visibility and evaded potential disapproval at times when societal acceptance of 'homosexuality' was relatively low. Nevertheless, achieving a greater degree of visibility, acceptance, and integration was among the clear goals of all activists. In this respect, LGBT+ communities challenged societal exclusion, erasure from public discourses, and everyday stigmatization by organizing events such as pride parades in public space (Johnston, 2007; Bilić, 2016). These public gatherings are connected with building up LGBT+ communities and strengthening their solidarity networks via their transformative power that literally may substitute individual shame with collective pride (Britt and Heise, 2000).

As I mentioned, the first minor event in Czechia was organized in Karlovy Vary in 1998. As such pride parade organizing was intentionally avoided by Czech activists in the early 2000s as they decided to avoid 'arousing' public disapproval at times when they catered their advocacy of same-sex partnership legislation to politicians. However, it can be said that the first pride parades organized in the region of CEE were relatively small in scope and, hence, low profile. For example, the first pride parade in the Hungarian capital, Budapest, was organized in 1997. Similarly, the first Equality Pride in the Polish capital, Warsaw, was organized in 2001. None of these events gained significant media attention, and if they encountered some opposition, it only took the form of a minor incident (Rédai, 2012). One of the first examples of violent anti-LGBT+ mobilizations occurred in Serbia during the first

Belgrade pride in 2001. This event resulted in 40 injured and was infamously nicknamed 'massacre pride'. In his analysis of Belgrade Prides, Bojan Bilić explained that the violence might have been a consequence of unfavourable and underestimated spatial and social circumstances that occurred in hardly recovered post-Yugoslav war Serbia (Bilić, 2016). However, even in a societal climate undisturbed by war, the situation in Hungary and Poland also became more complicated as the visibility of LGBT+ activism increased while the public opinion remained relatively low. In Budapest, it was until 2007 that when first substantial protests disturbed pride organizing (Rédai, 2012). Similarly, the opposition in Poland started in the years 2004 and 2005 when local politicians for the first time openly opposed the *Warsaw Equality March*.

Naturally, activists employed various strategies by which they attempted to moderate the public response and mitigate the opposition. For example, in Poland, the very choice of the event name played a significant role. Rather than calling the event 'love parade' or 'gay pride', organizers appealed to 'equality', which, according to Graff, was a conscious turn to the discourse of human rights and civil liberties. Moreover, the term 'parade' was later substituted by 'march' to avoid associations with Berlin 'love parades' that may be regarded as sexually 'loose' (Graff, 2006, p 438). According to Graff (2006) it was only after the spring of 2003 when a campaign called 'Let Them See Us' organized by *Campaign against Homophobia* (*Kampania Przeciw Homofobii*) NGO triggered violence. An exhibit of 30 photographs featuring 15 lesbian and 15 gay male couples, each stamped with the words 'Let them see us', initially opened in five galleries around the country and was followed by a nationwide billboard campaign. As Graff (2006) explained: 'Within a few days most of the billboards were destroyed, torn or painted over. Yet, the media kept showing them, if only to express outrage at the "ostentatious" nature of the material' (Graff, 2006, p 438).

The full height of the newly emergent violent opposition appeared during the first *Cracow Equality March* in 2004. The most vocal opposition group, an ultra-nationalist organization *All-Polish Youth* (*Młodzież Wszechpolska*), which is a branch of the *League of Polish Families* (*Liga Polskich Rodzin*), confronted the Cracow March and chanted things like, 'pedophiles and pederasts-these are Euro-enthusiasts', 'labor camps for lesbians', or 'faggots to the gas' (Graff, 2006, p 439).

Graff focused on this substantial shift in public discourse and related it to a broader process of politicization of LGBT+ issues in Poland. According to her analysis, the critical topic in this shift was a question of 'Equality Parade' legality that became one of the key themes of the fall 2005 presidential elections in Poland. Poland's newly elected president Lech Kaczynski was a former mayor of Warsaw and a vocal opponent of gay parades. His opposition toward gay parades resulted in bans of Warsaw Equality Marches in 2004 and 2005. However, both marches took place despite these bans.

The controversy that was built around it ignited broader societal divisions, which demonstrated themselves during the November 2005 *Poznan Equality March* where even the police did not protect the Equality March participants from the violence of the All-Polish Youth and turned against the participants of the Equality March (Graff, 2006, p 441).

According to Graff, these events and politicization of LGBT+ issues were all part of well-planned moves in Lech Kaczynski's political career, whereas 'a candidate's attitude toward sexual minorities served as a litmus test for her or his views on modern democracy, Poland's Westernization, freedom of speech, and traditional Catholicism' (Graff, 2006, p 436). Hence, this politicization process aimed to reinforce what the government saw as 'traditional family values', 'patriotic sentiments', and 'prevention against the aggressive promotion of homosexuality' (Graff, 2006, p 436). As part of this politicization process, attitudes of Polish politicians have constructed an image of Polish moral superiority over the 'loose' attitudes toward sex and sexual minorities in the (western) EU (Graff, 2006). These events indeed stirred action at the level of EU institutions, and it became evident that Poland as a member of the EU (since 2004) became positioning itself differently than most of the EU. In January and June 2006, the EU Parliament passed resolutions against homophobia in Europe. Although the January resolution did not explicitly mention Poland, it 'was received as an attack against Polish moral standards' (Graff, 2006, p 441). Consequently, this resolution served as a blunt instrument and serviced further exacerbation of politicization of LGBT+ activism in Poland.

By the mid-2000s, it was evident that the situation in Poland does not represent a unique case but may be part of a larger process taking place at an international scale. In their diligent analysis of various illiberal/conservative mobilizations in Europe, Paternotte and Kuhar identified that although these mobilizations have only become visible in various countries in the past years, they can be traced to the mid-2000s (Paternotte and Kuhar, 2018). Specifically, they identified actions of various conservative groups, including the Catholic Church and political parties, against the same-sex marriage bill proposed by Spain's government in 2004. In addition, they also identified similar mobilizations against sex education in 2006 Croatia, mobilizations against the same-sex civil partnership in 2007 Italy, and mobilization against marriage equality in 2009 Slovenia (Paternotte and Kuhar, 2018).

Particularly vocal opposition mobilized in 2012 during the climax of French '*Manif pour Tous*' (*Demonstration for All*) protests against same-sex marriage and various liberal policy making related to gender and sexuality (Paternotte and Kuhar, 2018). Although the same-sex marriage legislation in France was successfully legalized in 2013, the scope and efficiency of the protesters mobilizing inspired similar opposition actions in other countries, including Czechia, Germany, Poland, Russia, Slovakia, Romania, and others. While specific debates varied according to different national contexts, they followed a similar pattern and were typically a reaction to a concrete policy proposal and attempted to cement the current status quo by introducing legislative changes such as constitutional amendments against same-sex marriage or opposition toward progressive sex education (Paternotte and Kuhar, 2018; Hesová, 2021). Indeed, this backlash has already been recognized by scholars in the field of geographies of sexualities who proposed to address it with a broader term *heteroactivism* (Nash and Browne, 2020).

Despite growing understanding that this opposition is increasingly transnational, authors caution from regarding this as a 'global right-wing' or employing a universalizing framework. Instead, it is essential to disentangle these processes to diverse phenomena in ways that remain sensitive to different national contexts together with different structure of involved actors as well as their dominant agendas (Paternotte and Kuhar, 2018). However, at the same time, it is undeniable that opposition that claims to mobilize against what it names 'LGBT propaganda' or 'gender ideology' may be connected by some more complex common ground.

Gender as a symbolic glue of novel morality politics

Phrases such as 'gender ideology' or 'gender theory' are not to be confused with the academic scholarship developed within the transdisciplinary fields of gender and sexuality studies. Instead, they need to be seen as terms created to oppose this scholarship and to a resistance of progressive support of women's and LGBT+ people's rights. Kováts (2017) traced the origins of 'gender ideology' as an anti-gender ideology to the Vatican and the impacts of the UN Conference in Cairo (1994) and the UN Fourth Conference of Women in Beijing in 1995. Also, other authors agree that these campaigns started as a conservative Catholic reaction to these conferences, which eventually expanded beyond (Paternotte and Kuhar, 2018). Interestingly, most if not all contemporary opponents of LGBT+ rights identify 'gender' as 'the root of their worries and the matrix of the reforms they want to oppose' (Paternotte and Kuhar, 2018, p 8). The idea of opposing 'gender(ism)' can thus be seen as a unifying topic within the increasingly polarized sociopolitical environment in which gender acts as a 'symbolic glue' or common denominator (Pető, 2015; Grzebalska et al, 2017). Having been symbolically turned into a 'glue' anti-genderism represents an *opportunistic synergy* (Graff and Korolczuk, 2021) of various opponents and heterogeneous groups such as Catholic (or other) traditionalists and/or fundamentalists, far-right or chauvinistic/nationalistic politicians or their entire parties, radical extremists, misogynists, and others.

In her analysis of recent populist conservative mobilizations in Central and Eastern Europe, Hesová (2021) argues that important aspect of this recent anti-gender mobilization is a wider process in which issues that have long been considered resolved or too moralizing such as access to abortion or contraception, sexual education, definition of marriage and so on have become subjects of renewed political conflict. One of the most visible conflicts in the EU emerged against so-called gender mainstreaming, an officially endorsed policy principle. As explained by Paternotte and Kuhar (2018), the gender mainstreaming principle incorporates gender equality in all policies at all levels by policy makers and became one of the core points of dispute in Germany and Austria, where it is opposed by activists such as Gabrielle Kuby. Kuby represented gender mainstreaming as 'totalitarian ideology and a non-democratic practice, imposed on European countries by the feminist lobbies and elites from Brussels' (Paternotte and Kuhar, 2018, p 10). A specific case of opposition toward gender mobilized around the ratification of *The Council of Europe Convention on preventing and combating violence against women and domestic violence* (that is, Istanbul Convention). This document became at the heart of heated mobilization in various countries, including Poland (Graff, 2014), Slovakia (Maďarová and Valkovičová, 2020), and Czechia (Hesová, 2021; Svatoňová, 2021), along with Turkey, which withdrew from the Convention by the presidential decree of Tayyip Erdogan in March 2021.

In Slovakia, Maďarová and Valkovičová (2020) described that this conservative turn relates not only to unfulfilled ratification of the Istanbul Convention but was also fuelled by populist political leadership representing it in terms of 'evil attack' on the 'traditional Slovak nation'. In their analysis, these events are part of a successful opposition toward 'gender ideology' taking form as a more systemic political backsliding from the formerly achieved gender equality policies:

> Over the last several years, we witnessed the adoption of 'family mainstreaming' or building of the state-wide infrastructure for 'family counseling' by the EU-funded conservative and church-based organizations. After the national election in 2020, the new Minister of Labor, Social Affairs, and Family restructured the gender equality department, which is now called the Department of Equality between Men and Women and Equal Opportunities and is led by a former employee of the Slovak Bishops' Conference (TASR, 2020b). The term gender has been gradually erased from the public administration and policies; the financial support for gender equality has in fact stopped. (Maďarová and Valkovičová, 2020, p 276)

Importantly, authors underscored the importance of understanding that the 'anti-gender mobilization' or 'conservative turn' may be fuelled by the former connection between the gender mainstreaming and various neoliberal policies, which may have, so far, together with shortcomings in narrow frameworks of human rights discourses failed to take broader societal processes into consideration. Consequently, the newly growing political opposition towards 'gender' has also targeted academic institutions in which gender studies became established as vibrant fields of academic inquiry. However, in some countries, 'anti-gender(ists)' succeeded in attacking these institutions using, either or both, direct and indirect strategies by which they interfered with freedoms of scientific inquiry and exploration. Examples include cuts in funding for gender studies programs in the French region of Ile-de-France (Paternotte and Kuhar, 2018), and more recent expulsion of Central European University by the Hungarian government. In this respect, 'gender studies' or 'gender(ism)' have become represented not only as spreading elitist discourses but also targeted as 'foreign' and 'incompatible' institutions which promote 'imported culture' and 'decadent values' (Grzebalska et al, 2017).

Today it is evident that various political anti-LGBT+ or anti-gender campaigns in Poland, Hungary, Slovakia, Czechia, or elsewhere are increasingly imbued by nascent 'morality politics'. As such, morality politics are rooted in late 1990s US political science discourse and refer to issues such as death penalty, abortion, same-sex marriage, gambling and drug policies, sex work, euthanasia and so on (Haider-Markel and Meier, 1996; Mooney and Lee, 1999). A critical factor in distinguishing conventional politics from morality politics is the intrinsic focus on ideological divisions between people for whom it may become the dominant topic of political conflict. Previous conflicts at the level of social or economic issues about 'who gets what', thus became replaced by topics about 'who believes that' (Doan, 2014). Hence, morality politics over time replaced more conventional topics such as economic or social issues with those related to values, mores, and norms (Hesová, 2021).

A precise definition of morality politics is elusive. Nevertheless, scholars agree that the term may be applied to situations and political disputes where at least one of the active advocacy groups portrays the issue as morality or sin and uses moral arguments in its policy advocacy. Haider-Markel and Meier, in their investigation of gay and lesbian rights in the context of US morality politics, explained, that: '[M]orality politics issues are highly salient with little need to acquire any information (technical or otherwise) to participate in the debate. Everyone is an expert on morality' (Haider-Markel and Meier, 1996, p 333).

Morality politics is then closely tied to populism, which is generally defined as an ideology in which the populists separate the society into two homogeneous and antagonistic groups – 'the pure people' and 'the corrupt elite', in addition populists argue that politics should be based on the *volonté générale* (general will) of the people (Mudde, 2014, p 543). However, despite populists' claim to represent 'the people', they simultaneously reject their diversity of opinions and deny protections of minority groups, a tactic visible in countries led by populist governments (for example, Poland, Hungary). In this way, populism is very close to morality politics because, according to Mudde (2014), populism is moralistic rather than programmatic. It not only normatively distinguishes between 'the people' and 'the elites' but divides all into irreconcilable camps: 'friends' and 'foes', 'good' and 'evil', 'liberals' and 'traditionalists', fundamentally limiting (or eliminating) the potential for achieving a compromise.

The populists' focus on the homogeneously imagined 'people' is closely tied with other ideologies, especially with nationalism and its specific subtype nativism. Mudde defines nativism as 'an ideology that holds that states should be inhabited exclusively by members of the native group ("the nation"), and that nonnative people and ideas are fundamentally threatening to the homogenous nation-state' (Mudde, 2017). Hence, the described situation in Poland (as well as other countries) and their dispute with the EU may be seen via a nativist lens and morality politics. Polish populist representatives construct the Polish mores as superior or different from those of the 'decadent West', which according to them became too 'loose' towards sex and too favourable to sexual minorities who have become symbolically represented in Poland as a symbol of this 'looseness' (Graff, 2006, p 436).

In the same breath, the progressive values represented by 'elites' (that is, queer, or feminist scholars or activists) have become represented by morality entrepreneurs as some novel modern version of (Western) colonialism – a threat 'people' deserve protection from (Graff and Korolczuk, 2021).

Ontological (in)security as an overlooked explanation framework

In a way, 'gender' has been discursively depicted by its opponents as a threatening concept that serves as an umbrella term for a whole set of issues that opponents want to resist. Phrases like 'gender/LGBT-ideology', 'genderism', 'political correctness', 'homosexual propaganda/lobby', 'traditional family', 'pro-life', and others have all become symptomatic of a broader resistance, of a particular conservative turn, a backlash or fundamentalist societal movement (Kováts, 2018; Paternotte and Kuhar, 2018; Maďarová and Valkovičová, 2020; Graff and Korolczuk, 2021; Hesová, 2021). This backlash often manifests itself as a violent reaction or resistance to change of the 'status quo', 'power geometries', or 'distribution of privilege' within the given society (Kováts, 2017, p 182). In this way, we may understand this process in terms of reaction towards change – one which is represented to be caused by feminist or queer/LGBT+ movements. These progressive movements often identify norms such as heteronormativity, male or white privilege, and criticize them as harmful. In turn, various actors and groups supported by populism and morality politics mobilize against these sociocultural changes and challenge them by representing them as *threatening*. In this context Graff and Korolczuk write: 'We argue that the anti-gender mobilization has played an important role in the consolidation of the populist right as a transnational movement, one that successfully harnesses the anxiety, shame and anger caused by neoliberalism' (Graff and Korolczuk, 2021, p 165).

The nascent anti-genderist mobilization thus allegedly offers *protection* and, based on the 'common sense', attempt to provide hope for the *preservation* of the 'status quo'. By connecting themes of security, threat, protection, and preservation, I believe the anti-gender discourses also tap into a wider process of people's desire to maintain their *ontological security* – a concept introduced by Giddens to explain the importance of people's reliance on language social conventions that underpin the predictability and stability of people's everyday interactions (Giddens, 1991, p 37). In other words, people's need to live in an understandable, predictable, and stable world. Giddens borrowed from Kierkegaard's understanding of *dread* to explain that ontological security is a way through which we may cope with anxieties that emanate from potential cognitive or emotional disorientation related to potentially lacking a coherent sense of 'being in the world' (Giddens, 1991, p 38 emphasis original).

In this way, it may be perhaps productive to contextualize the discourses related to sexual and gender diversity as potentially 'disorienting' and 'complicating' people's stable, understandable, and predictable lives – whereas their fear of losing this stability or 'comfort of not having to care' – may be understood as threatening the ontological security of some. Modernist and liberal discourses, together with civil rights, feminist, LGBT+ and climate change movements, all represent some vehicles of change – one which moral entrepreneurs readily represented as destabilizing and threatening force destructive of securities and rules of conduct to which people were used to. Indeed, complex discussions related to 'political correctness' or more recently to 'woke culture' need to be contextualized within these processes. In turn, a potential deficit of ontological security may explain the resurgence of religious convictions (post-secularism) as well as drive a return to traditionalism or nationalism. In this light, nationalist and religious authorities promise precisely that type of a sense of 'security and stability' as well as simple answers that emanate from moralistic and populistic discourses which allegedly protect 'them' (the people) against 'corrupt elites' and their 'decadent' or 'foreign discourses'.

Scholarly responses, challenges, and opportunities

Based on my own experience in Czechia – 'gender' and most of the 'LGBT+ issues' – still represent particularly opaque and ambiguous topics for many people. As scholars working in the field, we sometimes forget about the distance we may end up in after working in the academic 'ivory tower'. Yet, even as scholars who focus on these issues within our institutional environments in CEE, we are typically not shielded from the dominant societal temper, and we also face marginalization, resistance, or opposition not so different from one that permeated the wider societal situations even at their workplaces and departments. As I discussed in previous sections, in some cases, a whole university may become targeted by anti-gender and anti-LGBT opposition, and scholars interested in feminist and queer approaches in these national contexts need to carefully navigate their respective environments to minimize risks of being dismissed or replaced by someone who focuses on more 'mainstream' topics. What may some perceive as an 'ivory tower' may therefore represent a way of protection or a strategy of self-preservation. There is no doubt that much of the research on gender and sexualities in CEE is conducted by scholars who *decided* to work abroad where more resources and support may be available. Yet, many of us stayed for various reasons and continue with their work despite the environment and resultant lack of resources or support. Although we may recognize that the issues related to gender and sexual diversity are highly topical and there is strong societal demand for gaining understanding in these fields, our home environments may become increasingly politicized and hostile toward this scholarly work to effectively communicate its knowledge (Timár, 2019). Scholars who work in these conditions thus need to develop strategies by which they can maintain their jobs and stay accepted by their fellow colleagues and institutions. It may become challenging to pursue their goals and maintain comprehensibility from the public.

Nevertheless, academia is a specific environment, and there are various conditions that both restrict and enable scholarly work that may overcome some of these challenges. For example, as is well known, the academic culture is heavily Western-centric (Navickaitė, 2014; Pitoňák, 2019). Most journals are published in English, and there is no doubt that English has become academic lingua franca despite being resisted by various scholarly traditions. The very fact that academic performance is increasingly evaluated based on scientometric evaluation of scholarly productivity, in other words, on scholars' capacity for becoming published in high-ranking journals (primarily Western and English) makes it less motivating to publish in local and less prestigious journals. This situation is undoubtedly not favourable for the production of locally specific knowledge that may be important for actors who may only speak local languages such as local activists, and policy makers. Many of these stakeholders are thus unable to benefit from this knowledge in their decision-making roles. Here a paradoxical situation emerges – on the one hand the researcher may recognize the importance of informing the local activists, policy makers, and other relevant actors via channels and language that is accessible to them. On the other hand, the evaluation of the academic performance motivates the researcher to publish in foreign journals that are often out of reach and access to those who might otherwise benefit from it. Even though values and discourses that are common in the West may facilitate and increase the chance of publishing content that may be regarded as political/activist or otherwise biased by local actors influenced by morality politics, the very fact that the content is published 'abroad' and in 'foreign language' contributes to an unfavourable disjunction between the scholar's work and their local society. In other words, it may contribute to the isolation of the scholar within their academic bubbles and facilitate a perspective in which they are deemed elitist. It is therefore vital to recognize this power dynamic that not only involves questions related to immediate scholar's performance and success, but also addresses wider concerns and questions, such as in what ways can scholarly work contribute to the well-being of the local community? After all, research is often publicly funded, and these questions relate to broader problems surpassing questions related to gender and sexuality. Here another set of questions emerges – what constitutes a successful scholar? Is it one who reaches excellence by becoming published in top-ranking (foreign) journals? Does this success translate into influence on policy making and recognition by policy makers who may resist this knowledge based on morality politics? Should scholars seek to make a positive change in their local communities? If so, should they do it directly (for example, by becoming involved in the process of policy making) or become involved indirectly (for example, by empowering other actors)? Even though these choices are not mutually exclusive, they may all entail negotiating different scholarly work ethics and require different skills (for example, language proficiency, presentational, popularizing, diplomatic), whereas some of this work may not be recognized as part of scholarly work. Inevitably, a scholar who is influenced by feminist and queer thought may become conflicted by the plethora of dilemmas and negotiate their sense of *care/responsibility* as well as their job obligations and personal limits.

In the final part I will shortly describe my struggle in which I attempted to balance some of these complex conditions and sought ways in which scholarly work may reach its target audiences.

Introducing queer geography in Czechia

In concord with feminist and queer scholarly traditions, I accept that even as a researcher, I cannot detach myself from the subject matter I study. No one is a mere (or careless) observer, and it is crucial to openly admit being situated in a particular context in which we may produce knowledge (Haraway, 1988). Back in 2011, when I started my PhD research, I became a pioneer of the subject of geographies of sexualities in Czech human geography. At this time it was typical to focus on political geography, poverty, urbanization, and issues such as migration and tourism, but feminist topics were largely marginalized, whereas sexuality perspectives were completely invisible (Blažek and Rochovská, 2006). Thus, my initial positionality reflected a state of insecurity both caused by being a student who is evaluated by the departmental committee consisting of members with particular scholarly interests as well as someone who is introducing marginalized and potentially stigmatizing topics related to feminist thought, let alone queer topics (Pitoňák and Klingorová, 2019).

For this reason, I spent my first years of PhD studentship meeting the criteria set by the department (that is, in terms of methodology or publication performance) as well as carefully introducing the subject matter of geographies of sexualities and its relevance to the Czech geographical thought. I organized several conference sessions, workshops, and seminars and presented at many conferences both at the national and international levels. In addition, I wrote publications in Czech in which I focused on introducing the basic theories and goals of this field (Pitoňák, 2013a, 2013b, 2014a, 2014b). However, after some disillusions during which I realized that Czech scholarly space is relatively limited, I soon came to an understanding that there was not enough traction inside geography nor there were enough opportunities in other neighbouring disciplines for establishing a more significant presence of geographies of sexualities (for example, to apply for a project with some interested colleague). Thus, after completing my PhD in 2015, I followed an opportunity and moved to another field (public health and psychology) where I had a prospect of developing my previous research on socio-spatial heteronormativity and spatial negotiation of LGBT+ identities further. As seeking opportunities abroad was not an option for me, I became employed at National Institute of Mental Health. However, my new institutional setting did not prevent me from continuing with extra-work activities, including participating (mostly self-funded) at various geographical conferences such as European Geographies of Sexualities Conference (EGSC) or Czech sociological conferences and organizing several events for the public as part of Prague Pride festival or other events. It was during this time when I became convinced that public debates related to sexual citizenship (Richardson, 2000), such as same-sex parenthood and marriage equality, are highly topical and may benefit from the insight and geographical thinking intrinsic to human geographical perspectives. In part due to lacking resources and support in the local academia, I decided to establish a small NGO called Queer Geography (QG; starting words of my dissertation) in 2017 two years after completion of my doctoral study. All of this would hardly be possible without support of my partner Lukáš and our friend Jana. Working only in our free time, we dedicated our work in QG to the promotion of geographies of sexualities as a scholarly field as well as filling the gap between activist organizations and somehow distanced academia. At this time, we felt there was a deafening silence from the part of academia regarding topics such as marriage equality, same-sex parenting, LGBT+ psychology or stigma in people living with HIV. Having recognized this, I became convinced it might be fitting to establish an organization which could create more symbolic space for a field that is currently underrated (geographies of sexualities) and utilize its comprehension of humanities to connect the dots between various related subjects and by doing so support both – local activists as well as the wider interested public – by popularizing knowledge and making hard-to-reach data and content openly available online in the Czech language. One of my personal motivations for founding QG was a nomination to organize the V. EGSC in Prague (2019) that I received from members of the scientific committee of the IV. EGCS (2017) conference in Barcelona. Today I can write with a bit of relief that we managed to bring this international event to Prague and, at least within the context of Czechia, we created previously unprecedented space for a diverse set of topics, all united under an umbrella of geographies of sexualities. The conference included 158 participants from 38 countries around the globe.

The first five years of our work in QG consisted mostly of volunteering our free time to be able to organize various public events and popularize knowledge by publishing it in accessible ways. One of our main products became online, downloadable, cellphone friendly, and interactive maps. I believe that maps may mediate the often difficult to grasp and heated topics in approachable ways. This way we created maps about marriage-equality public opinion support in Europe; about same-sex parenting rights in Europe, or global world comparison of LGBT+ rights. We believe that these maps, as well as charts and articles written about them in Czech language, facilitated many discussions about these heated topics and potentially sparked critical thinking. For example, our map that synthesizes data from five international surveys on public opinion of marriage equality allowed viewers to find out about the level of public support by themselves, without us making any explicit or comparative arguments that may have been viewed as instructive or counterproductive by some. This strategy not only allowed us to avoid reproducing discourses of backwardness (for example, East vs. West narratives) that became criticized over the past years (Kulpa, 2014; Navickaitė, 2014; Pitoňák, 2019), but also enabled people – the viewers – to make their own associations of the meanings contained in the maps.

Despite not being engaged in any direct advocacy, our work had soon reached even to local politicians – it was a very nice symbolic moment for us when we saw an MP from a Pirate party present a printed version of our map in the Czech parliament during a parliamentary debate about same-sex marriages. Over the years, we published numerous other maps and articles, in which we always include references and use language that we deem accessible both for public as well as fellow scholars. Since the beginning, we were aware of the threat of misinformation and disinformation influences spread by conservatives over the internet and social media, in fact, the foundation of QG was a response to this growing threat. Perhaps our work represents a potential approach that may increase societal resilience towards these negative influences.

I will end this short introduction of our work by demonstrating one of our last materials. Figure 5.1 shows our visualization of data from Special Eurobarometer through which we wanted to communicate the often-underestimated relationship between the given society's contact with gay, lesbian, bisexual, trans, and gender diverse people and the actual legal recognition codified for example by the presence of partnership legislation. This chart demonstrates seemingly simple information – what is the proportion of any given society having friends among LGBTQ+ people – however, when we order all countries based on this proportion an interesting 'secondary story' becomes available to all viewers – that is a clear relationship between societal contact with LGBTQ+ people and the legal recognition in any given society. It may then come as no surprise that societies with the least contact with LGBTQ+ people are exactly those where LGBTQ+ people face the least support and most obstacles (for example, in form of 'marriage-equality bans').

Figure 5.1 may enable various conversations where people may re-think their assumptions regarding LGBTQ+ people. On the one hand, morality entrepreneurs may try to convince their audiences that the increasing *presence* of LGBTQ+ people and their *lifestyles* is indicative of some moral decline or modern decadence of Western societies. Yet, on the other hand, our chart may enable critical thinking and spark conversations regarding whether prejudices and stereotypes about LGBTIQ+ *people* in fact play a central role in the opposition against the authentic *presence* and *visibility* of LGBTQ+ people in *public* spheres – an opposition which is much more easily built against someone people don't *know* and don't *care* about.

Conclusion

In this chapter, I aimed to provide an in-depth but relatively restricted insight into Czech LGBT+ activism. I sought to overcome the discourses of progress narrative that permeate much of the literature and instead focused on developing a more sensitive story. Although, I must have omitted many of the achievements and nuances of local activism as well as discussion of topics that relate to specific conditions of Central and Eastern European civil society functioning. I believe I outlined a situation in which a seeming lack of progress represents a state of dynamic equilibrium between the

Figure 5.1: Share of population that reported knowing someone who is LGBTQ+

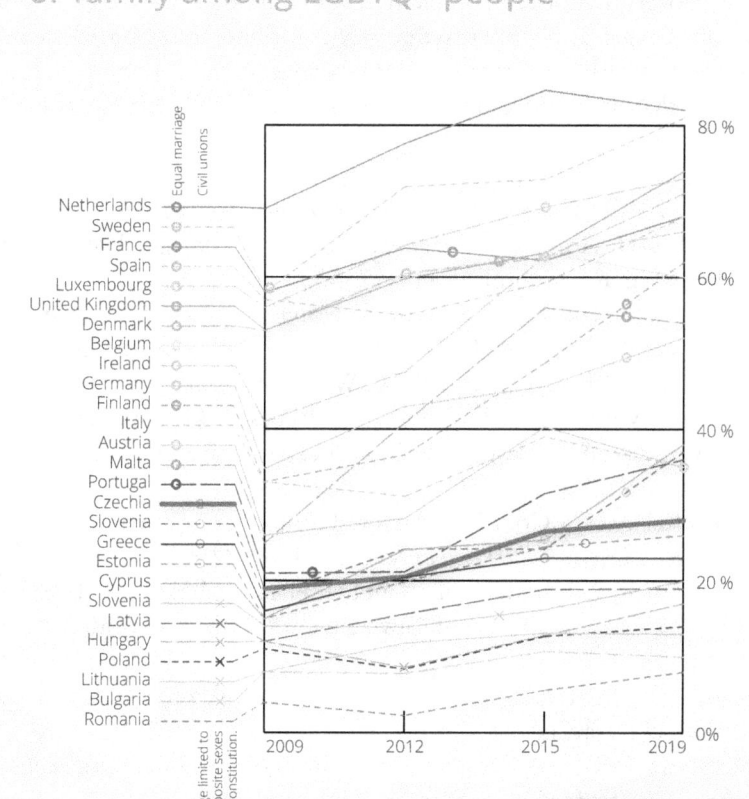

Source: Author's own work for Queer Geography

activists and LGBTQ+ people's needs, on the one hand, and the novel anti-LGBT and anti-gender mobilizations that have spread across the region over the past two decades, on the other.

Before I delved into aspects of opposition and tracking its nature and roots, I pointed out the delicate and fragile balance between the visibility of LGBT+ activism and public opinion and related opposition that activists in various contexts must negotiate. Yet, without attempting to provide an all-encompassing narrative, I offered a more in-depth theoretical dissection of the problem connecting the rise of populism and novel morality politics or morality entrepreneurship with the resurgence of nationalist discourses and various illiberal formations.

By employing Gidden's concept of ontological security, I did not intend to justify motivations for people's support of these oppositional groups, rather, I sought novel questions and problems that may have so far stayed overlooked. The shared experiences and practice may contribute to the broader feminist and queer scholarly conversations and related activism through which we all recognize that there is no such thing as impartial or powerless knowledge.

References

Bilić, B. (2016). *Europe ♥ Gays? Europeanisation and Pride Parades in Serbia, LGBT Activism and Europeanisation in the Post-Yugoslav Space*. London: Palgrave Macmillan, pp 117–53.

Blažek, M. and Rochovská, A. (2006). *Feministické geografie*. Geografika.

Britt, L. and Heise, D. (2000). 'From Shame to Pride in Identity Politics', in S. Srtyker, T.J. Owens and R.W. White (eds), *Self, Identity, and Social Movements*. Minneapolis: University of Minnesota Press, pp 252–68.

Brzek, A. and Hubalek, S. (1988). 'Homosexuals in Eastern Europe'. *Journal of Homosexuality* 15: 153–62.

Davison, K. (2021). 'Cold War Pavlov: Homosexual Aversion Therapy in the 1960s'. *History of the Human Sciences* 34: 89–119.

Doan, A. (2014). 'Morality Politics', in D.P. Haider-Markel (ed) The Oxford Handbook of State and Local Government. Oxford: Oxford University Press, pp 757–77.

Freund, K. (1962). 'Homosexualita u muže'. Praha: Státní Zdravotnické Nakladatelství.

Giddens, A. (1991). *Modernity and Self-Identity: Self and Society in the Late Modern Age*. Stanford, CA: Stanford University Press.

Graff, A. (2006). 'We Are (Not All) Homophobes: A Report from Poland'. *Feminist Studies* 32(2): 434–49.

Graff, A. (2014). 'Report from the Gender Trenches: War against "Genderism" in Poland'. *European Journal of Women's Studies* 21(4): 431–5.

Graff, A. and Korolczuk, E. (2021). Anti-Gender Politics in the Populist Moment. London: Taylor & Francis.

Grzebalska, W., Kováts, E., and Pető, A. (2017). 'Gender as Symbolic Glue: How 'Gender' became an Umbrella Term for the Rejection of the (Neo) Liberal Order'. *Krytyka Polityczna & European Alternatives*. Available from: http://politicalcritique.org/long-read/2017/gender-as-symbolic-glue-how-gender-became-an-umbrella-term-for-the-rejection-of-the-neo liberal-order/ [Accessed 11 April 2023].

Haider-Markel, D.P. and Meier, K.J. (1996). 'The Politics of Gay and Lesbian Rights: Expanding the Scope of the Conflict'. *The Journal of Politics* 58(2): 332–49.

Haraway, D. (1988). 'Situated Knowledges: The Science Question in Feminism and the Privilege of Partial Perspective'. *Feminist Studies* 14(3).

Hesová, Z. (2021). 'New Politics of Morality in Central and Eastern Europe: Actors, Discourse, and Context'. *Intersections* 7(1): 59–77.

Himl, P., Seidl, J., and Schindler, F. (2013). *Miluji tvory svého pohlaví*. Praha: Argo.

Holý, L. (2001). *Malý český člověk a velký český národ: národní identita a postkomunistická transformace společnosti*. Praha: Sociologické nakladatelstvá.

Jagose, A. (1996). *Queer Theory: An Introduction*. New York: New York University Press.

Johnston, L. (2007). 'Mobilizing Pride/Shame: Lesbians, Tourism and Parades'. *Social & Cultural Geography* 8: 29–45.

Kolářová, K. (2013). 'Homosexuální asociál a jeho zavirované tělo', in P. Himl, J. Seidl and F. Schindler (eds) *'Miluji tvory svého pohlaví': homosexualita v dějinách a společnosti českých zemí*. Praha: Argo, pp 411–52.

Kováts, E. (2017). 'The Emergence of Powerful Anti-gender Movements in Europe and the Crisis of Liberal Democracy,' in E. Kováts (ed) *Gender and Far Right Politics* in Europe. New York: Springer, pp 175–89.

Kováts, E. (2018). 'Conservative Counter-Movements? Overcoming Culturalising Interpretations of Right-wing Mobilizations against "Gender Ideology"'. *Femina Politica–Zeitschrift für feministische Politikwissenschaft* 27(1): 15–16.

Kulpa, R. (2014). 'Western Leveraged Pedagogy of Central and Eastern Europe: Discourses of Homophobia, Tolerance, and Nationhood'. *Gender, Place & Culture* 21: 431–48.

Lišková, K. (2018). *Sexual Liberation, Socialist Style: Communist Czechoslovakia and the Science of Desire, 1945–1989*. Cambridge: Cambridge University Press.

Maďarová, Z. and Valkovičová, V. (2020). 'Is Feminism Doomed? Feminist Praxis in the Times of 'Gender Ideology' in Slovakia'. *European Journal of Women's Studies* 28(2): 274–81.

Matejsková, T. (2007) 'Straights in a Gay Bar: Negotiating Boundaries through Time-Spaces', in K. Browne, L. Jason and G. Brown (eds) *Geographies of Sexualities*. Burlington: Ashgate, pp 137–50.

Mooney, C.Z. and Lee, M.-H. (1999). 'The Temporal Diffusion of Morality Policy: The Case of Death Penalty Legislation in the American States'. *Policy Studies Journal* 27(4): 766–80.

Mudde, C. (2014). 'The Populist Zeitgeist'. *Government and Opposition* 39(4): 541–63.

Mudde, C. (2017). 'Why Nativism, Not Populism, Should Be Declared Word of the Year'. *The Guardian*, 7.

Nash, C.J. and Browne, K. (2020). *Heteroactivism: Resisting Lesbian, Gay, Bisexual and Trans Rights and Equalities*. London: Zed Books.

Navickaitė, R. (2014). 'Postcolonial Queer Critique in Post-communist Europe: Stuck in the Western Progress Narrative?' *Tijdschrift voor Genderstudies* 17: 165–85.

Nedbálková, K. (2016). 'Idle Ally: The LGBT Community in the Czech Republic', in I. Jusová and J. Šiklová (eds) *Czech Feminisms: Perspectives on Gender in East Central Europe*. Bloomington, IN: Indiana University Press, pp 205–21.

Osman, R. and Pospíšilová, L. (2019). *Geografie 'okrajem': Každodenní časoprostorové zkušenosti*. Praha: Karolinum Press.

Paternotte, D. and Kuhar, R. (2018). 'Disentangling and Locating the "Global Right": Anti-Gender Campaigns in Europe'. *Politics and Governance* 6(3): 6–19.

Pető, A. (2015). '"Anti-gender" Mobilisational Discourse of Conservative and Far Right Parties as a Challenge to Progressive Politics', in E. Kováts and M. Põim (eds) *Gender as Symbolic Glue: The Position and Role of Conservative and Far Right Parties in the Anti-Gender Mobilizations in Europe*. Budapest: Friedrick-Ebert-Stiftung, pp 126–32.

Pitoňák, M. (2013a). 'Geografie sexualit, bílé místo v prostoru české geografie?' in R. Osman (ed.) *Geografický výzkum: participace a angažovanost*. Brno: Masarykova univerzita, pp 153–68.

Pitoňák, M. (2013b). 'Spatiality, Institutionalization and Contextuality of Heteronormativity: Study of Non-heterosexual Identity Negotiation in Czechia'. *Gender, rovné příležitosti, výzkum* 14: 27–40.

Pitoňák, M. (2014a). 'Queer prostor(y)', in R. Matoušek and R. Osman (eds) *Prostor(y) Geografie*. Praha: Karolinum Press, pp 123–46.

Pitoňák, M. (2014b). 'Urban Spatiality in the Context of (Homo/Hetero) Sexuality: Introduction to a Theoretical Debate in Geographies of Sexualities'. *Geografie* 119(2): 179–98.

Pitoňák, M. (2019). 'Lessons from the "Periphery": Countering Anglo-Geographic Hegemony Over Geographies of Sexuality and Gender'. *Documents d'Anàlisi Geogràfica* 65: 563–85.

Pitoňák, M. (2022). 'A Decade of Prague Pride: Mapping Origins, Seeking Meanings, Understanding Effects,' in M. Blidon and S. Brunn (eds) *Mapping LGBTQ Spaces and Places: A Changing World*. New York: Springer.

Pitoňák, M. and Klingorová, K. (2019). 'Development of Czech Feminist and Queer Geographies: Identifying Barriers, Seeking Progress'. *Gender, Place & Culture* 26: 1001–12.

Procházka, I., Janík, D. and Hromada, J. (2003). 'Social Discrimination of Lesbians, Gay Men and Bisexuals in the CR', *Gay Initiative in the CR*.

Public Opinion Research Centre. (2020). *Naše společnost 2020 – březen*. Available from: https://doi.org/10.14473/V2003 [Accessed 11 April 2023].

Rédai, D. (2012). Un/Queering the Nation? Gender, Sexuality, Nationality and Homophobia in the Media Discourse on the Violence against the 2008 Gay Pride in Budapest. *Sextures* 2(2): 2071–6834.

Richardson, D. (2000). 'Constructing Sexual Citizenship: Theorizing Sexual Rights'. *Critical Social Policy* 20: 105–35.

Seidl, J., Wintr, J. and Nozar, L. (2012). *Od Žaláře k Oltáři*. Brno: Host.

Sokolová, V. (2012). 'Skládání duhové mozaiky: Česká sexuologie a "gay" a "lesbická" orální historie v komunistickém Československu'. *Gender, rovné příležitosti, výzkum* 13: 28–40.

Svatoňová, E. (2021). '"Gender Activists Will Kidnap Your Kids": The Construction of Feminist and LGBT+ Rights Activists as Modern Folk Devils in Czech Anti-Gender Campaigns,' in M.D. Frederiksen and I.H. Knudsen (eds) *Modern Folk Devils*. Helsinki: Helsinki University Press, pp 135–56.

Szulc, L. (2018). *Transnational Homosexuals in Communist Poland*. London: Palgrave Macmillan.

Takács, J. and P. Tóth, T. (2021). 'Liberating Pathologization?: The Historical Background of the 1961 Decriminalization of Homosexuality in Hungary'. *Hungarian Historical Review* 10(2): 267–300.

TASR (2020b). 'Šéfkou odboru rovnosti žien a mužov v rezorte práce bude Z. Brixová'. *Teraz*, 27 July. Available from: www.teraz.sk/ekonomika/sefkou-odboru-rovnosti-zien-amuzov/483128-clanok.html [Accessed 28 July 2020].

Timár, J. (2019). 'Hungarian Feminist Geography in a Curved Space?' *Gender, Place & Culture* 26(7–9): 1094–102.

Timár, J. and Fekete, É. (2010). 'Fighting for Recognition: Feminist Geography in East-Central Europe'. *Gender, Place & Culture* 17: 775–90.

Wintr, J. (2009). Analýza české právní úpravy osvojení dítěte gayi, lesbami a bisexuálními lidmi ve světle práva Evropské unie a Evropské úmluvy o lidských právech a základních svobodách.

6

Sexual Harassment and Claiming the Right to Everyday Life

Kate Boyer

Introduction

Sexual harassment has become a high-profile issue in recent years across a range of cultural contexts, including through the global rise of the *#MeToo* movement and the *Everyday Sexism* project. The UK (and elsewhere) has seen regular media coverage of high-profile cases of sexual harassment and other forms of gender violence across many different sectors (organized sport; organized religion; social and child welfare services and the entertainment industry, to name just a few) (Anitha and Lewis, 2018, p 5), as well as the shocking rape and murder of Sarah Everard by an acting British Police Officer and murder of London schoolteacher Sabina Nessa in 2021. Meanwhile awareness about the prevalence of sexual harassment within spaces of higher education (including within geography programs specifically)[1] has also risen (Batty et al, 2017; Mansfield et al, 2019), with research suggesting that up to three out of every five university students in the UK have been sexually harassed or assaulted at some point (Busby, 2018).

From the perspective of the 'right to everyday life' (Beebeejaun, 2017) and right to the city (Fenster, 2005), this state of affairs can only be viewed as an abject failure. Fear of sexual harassment can limit movement for women and other feminized and gender diverse subjects, and freedom from harassment is a basic human right and precondition to mental and physical health and well-being. In the UK, concern about this issue has now attracted the attention of policy makers at the highest levels, leading to a Parliamentary Inquiry in 2018 on sexual harassment in public places,[2] and a briefing paper on sexual harassment in higher education from the House of Commons in

2018. All of this highlights the urgent need for both deeper understanding – and cultural change – on this issue.

This chapter provides a critical reading of contemporary scholarship on sexual harassment within and beyond geography in order to contextualize activisms combatting sexual harassment across different settings and spaces in the UK and beyond. With our expertise in understanding issues to do with gender, power, and space, I argue that feminist geographers have a potential role to play in this work. Sexual harassment connects to a number of key conceptual frames in contemporary human geography. In addition to being a question of rights to space and the right to everyday life, this issue relates to calls for greater attunement to the sexual politics of citizenship and belonging (Johnston, 2017); as well as calls to attend to the body as a locus through which power operates (Mountz, 2018; Hopkins, 2019). Harassment relates to embodied day-to-day spatial practice (Simonsen, 2010; Brickell and Maddrell, 2016), and reflects relational approaches to embodiment.[3] While harassment can occur through threatening or demeaning words or actions, it can also occur through non-verbal signs that pass between people, the theorization of which has been deepened by work within and beyond geography on affect (Anderson, 2009; Duff, 2010; Stewart, 2011). Each of these conceptual frames can help deepen our understanding of sexual harassment. Building on these approaches, I suggest that sexual harassment can be conceptualized (after Deleuze) as an apparatus of capture through which certain bodies are fixed affectively, materially, and discursively within cultural logics of gender power, limiting what they can do and where and how they can move. This chapter takes knowledge forward by providing a critical review of scholarship within and beyond geography on sexual harassment and concludes by briefly outlining an agenda for future research in this field, including a consideration of efforts to fight back against sexual harassment. While this field constitutes a rich corpus of scholarship its findings have not been drawn together to allow a consideration of key findings in the round: now is the time for such a review.

Sexual harassment operates as a mechanism for maintaining heteropatriarchy through the sexual objectification of women and other feminized subjects. It can be understood as forming a kind of cultural 'wallpaper' to patriarchy, serving as part of a 'continuum of violence' that normalizes both male power generally and more serious forms of sexual violence (Kelly, 1988 in Anitha and Lewis, 2018, p 1). Put another way, harassment stands in a reciprocal relationship to patriarchy in that it is both caused by and helps maintain this system of gender power, and it is in this capacity that it persists.

Starting with Pain and Valentine's foundational work on the geography of women's fear (Valentine, 1992; Pain, 2014), geographers have made important contributions to understanding sexual harassment and other forms of gender violence (Brickell and Maddrell, 2016; Brickell and Cuomo, 2020).

This work has advanced scholarship by arguing that women's fear of rape and subsequent avoidance of certain kinds of public spaces constitutes, at its root, a 'spatial expression of patriarchy' (Valentine, 1992, p 315). Despite the greater statistical likelihood of rape occurring in private space by a known attacker (Valentine, 1989; Pain, 2014) this scholarship powerfully illustrates the role that fear of stranger rape plays in limiting women's spatial freedom (Valentine, 1992; Pain, 2014). Conceptually this work casts harassment as a symbolic threat of sexual violence, and the failure of the state to intervene as an illustration of its complicity in the maintenance of patriarchy as a gender order (Valentine, 1992; Pain, 2014).

Scholarship on sexual harassment within and beyond geography has expanded over the last 30 years to highlight how harassment functions across myriad cultural contexts, creating environments in which more serious forms of gender violence[4] are more likely to occur (Logan, 2015; Park et al, 2013; Bhattacharyya, 2015; Duckel Graglia, 2016; Anitha and Lewis, 2018). This work has highlighted how intersectional difference shapes experiences of harassment (Browne, 2004; Doan, 2010; Lubitow, 2017). As scholarship of black feminists (and scholarship that builds on this body of work) has shown, systems of social power that structure advantage and disadvantage based on race, class, gender, sexual orientation, and other factors interplay such that multiple forms of discrimination can compound one another in policies, institutions, and at the level of lived practice (Lorde, 1984; Crenshaw, 1989; Collins, 2002; Hopkins, 2019; Kendi, 2019). Intersectional difference can have a significant impact on how women and other feminized subjects are treated in public space, and as research has shown women of colour both experience more sexual violence than white women, and this violence is racialized (Buchanan and Ormerod, 2002; Nielsen, 2009). This pattern is bound up with historical legacies of slavery and colonialism in which women of colour have been subjected to institutionalized sexual violence (Hernandez, 2000; Collins, 2002; Woods et al, 2009). The ways that gender discrimination and racism can intertwine is suggested in the portmanteau *misogynoir* recently coined by Moya Bailey (Bailey, 2010; Kwakye and Ogunbiyi, 2019).

Building on this work, this chapter will synthesize current scholarship on sexual harassment and efforts to combat it through the lens of the three spatial contexts of: street-space; the night-time economy; and spaces of higher education. Through this discussion I argue that there is considerable scope for geographers to extend both scholarly and activist work in this field through employing conceptual lenses of embodiment, relationality, and everyday practice.[5] These three sites were chosen so as to echo the tripartite focus of the *Inquiry on Sexual Harassment of Women and Girls in Public Places* undertaken by the Women and Equalities committee of the UK Parliament in 2018.[6] These three (sometimes overlapping) sites were chosen for particular focus because together they constitute the spaces in which sexual harassment is most prevalent. While street-space and other spaces of public transport (marked by crowding and anonymity) have long been recognized as sites of sexual harassment; gender-based harassment and assault (especially in the form of groping) within spaces in the night-time economy is now considered 'the norm' in the UK according to parliamentary inquiries.[7] Finally, higher education was selected as the final site of analysis due to the rates of sexual and gender violence in these spaces, with over 60 per cent of all UK students reporting that they experience some form of gender violence while at university (NUS, 2014, Revolt Report, 2018). This chapter is not meant to be exhaustive but instead seeks to highlight key trends and conceptual innovations within this field. Finally, the chapter concludes by outlining an agenda for future research in this field, including a consideration of efforts to fight back against sexual harassment. I suggest geographers have an important role to play in both deepening understanding on this subject and, by working with activists and others outside the academy, change social practice on this issue.

Sexual harassment in relation to mobility and spaces of transport

With the 'mobilities turn' over the last ten years geographers have begun attending to the sensory, affective, embodied, and experiential aspects of movement and transport (Cresswell, 2010). In regards to experiences of moving through urban (and other kinds of) space the mobilities turn has generated a suite of work focusing on the poetic and artistic nature of walking (Solnit, 2001; Pinder, 2001; Wylie, 2005; Pile, 2005; Edensor, 2010). Drawing on Lefebevre's concept of rhythmanalysis, this work has led to heightened conceptual understanding of walking as a sensory experience that can function as a form of 'mobile belonging' (Edensor, 2010, p 70), including through collaborations with the more than human. Yet as a rejoinder to this Middleton cautions that 'the emancipatory potential and democratic possibilities of ... walking are far from straightforward and unproblematic as much of the literature on walking in the city is imbued with a degree of romanticism whereby walking is often considered, without question, as a positive urban practice' (Middleton, 2010, p 579).

As scholarship in feminist geography has shown, the possibility of experiencing walking as a poetic practice is fundamentally bound up with multiple, intersecting forms of social privilege, which are experienced through and read-off bodies in the public realm to produce spatial and other kinds of freedoms. As Simonsen observes, it is crucial to attend to the ways social positionality and intersecting power geometries of race, gender, class, and other factors shape everyday experiences of walking, embodiment, and public space (Simonsen, 2010; also see Cresswell, 2010). While certain kinds of social markers (whiteness, middle-classness, heterosexuality, maleness, and cis-gender identity) increase the likelihood of experiencing walking as an artistic practice, other kinds of social positions can lead to significantly different kinds of experiences.

Loukaitou-Sideris and Ehrenfeucht have called attention to the 'political importance of everyday acts and manners as mechanisms of resistance and subjugation' (Loukaitou-Sideris and Ehrenfeucht, 2009, p 87), focusing particularly on the role of sidewalks as a site of oppression and social control. As research has shown, sidewalks are important sites for making determinations about who 'belongs' in public space and reproducing social hierarchies; highlighting that the ability to pass without comment in public space is fundamental to feeling respected and establishing a sense of belonging (Ryan, 1992; Fyfe, 2006; Loukaitou-Sideris and Ehrenfeucht, 2009). These conscious and unconscious determinations about 'who belongs where' can be shaped by tenacious spatial imaginaries which code public space as 'male', leading to the tolerance of harassment and victim-blaming in cases of sexual violence (Rendell et al, 2000; Sweet and Ortiz Escalante, 2015).

As feminist theorist Sara Ahmed's observes, in addition to being bound up with gender, the ability to pass without notice or comment in a given space is also bound up with race and white privilege, such that people of colour can be made to feel that their very presence disrupts the 'public comfort' or is viewed as a challenge within white space (Ahmed, 2010, p 548). As scholar-activist Ore Ogunbiyi noted about her experience as a student in a UK university: 'as a black woman in a white dominated space, I discovered my very existence was an act of resistance' (Kwakye and Ogunbiyi, 2019, p 225). Being continually marked and othered in public space can lead to feelings of alienation and social isolation (Browne, 2004; Ahmed, 2010). For people of colour this can take a heavy toll in terms of mental health with, for example, the experience of continually being treated as a potential source of danger to which many black and brown men (including young men) are subject; and the experience of being sexually objectified which many black and brown women (including young women) are subject can be a source of trauma and suffering throughout life (Hernandez, 2000; Kendi, 2019).

Following on from this, scholarship on minoritized subjects' experiences of public space suggest, on the whole, significantly less pleasurable and less liberatory experiences of walking than the invocations of walking as poetry or a form of artistic practice noted earlier. Street harassment has been shown to be a common feature of (especially young) women's (including trans-women's), and non-binary peoples' experiences of movement in urban space across a range of cultural contexts (Macmillan et al, 2000; West, 2002; Fairchild and Rudman, 2008; Fileborn, 2014; Dhillon, 2014; Logan, 2015).

As noted, research also shows that women of colour face higher levels of harassment and violence than white women, and that, owing to broader racialized patterns of economic inequality and sexualized stereotypes, racism and sexism are often combined within these encounters (Nielsen, 2009; Buchanan and Ormerod, 2002). Though little work has examined experiences of harassment by gay and bisexual men, what work that has been done in this area show 90 per cent of gay and bi men to experience street harassment (McNeil, 2012).

While variegated by race, sexual orientation and other factors, street harassment is also a global phenomenon (Senthillingam, 2017; Sen et al, 2018), in which police campaigns often reinforce the view that certain kinds of streets, at certain times, are unsafe for women (Loukaitou-Sideris and Ehrenfeucht, 2009, p 92). Work from 2008 suggests that 70 per cent of US women in their late teens and early 20s experience some form of gender-based street harassment at least once a month, with 30 per cent experiencing harassment every few days and over 25 per cent experiencing groping or grabbing about once a month (Fairchild and Rudman, 2008). Similarly, over 90 per cent of women in Afghanistan (WCLRF, 2015) and just under 90 per cent of women in Australia (Fileborn, 2014; Johnson and Bennett, 2015) report experiencing gender-based harassment in public at some point in their lives; while women in India report experiencing harassment between half and all the time they go out in public (Dhillon and Bhakya, 2014). However it is important to note that these figures exist within very different levels of overall gender discrimination, meaning that the nature and intensity of harassment, how it is perceived socially and whether legal remedies exist to challenge it all vary significantly by cultural context. A systematic country by country review of sexual harassment in global context is beyond the scope of this chapter. However research on broad global trends has noted the broad-scale normalization of male control of public space in many parts of Asia, South-Asia, and Latin America, together with the potential for shame and fear of retribution on the part of victims in some Middle Eastern and North African contexts to be powerful factors shaping the prevalence and intensity harassment and whether it is reported (Senthillingam, 2017).

Street harassment often happens in broad daylight, and victims can fear retaliation if they confront harassers. Such fears can be especially strong in cultural contexts in which there have been high-profile cases of violent retaliation from confronted harassers (such as India in the form of acid attacks) (Dhillon and Bhakya, 2014). Scholarship further shows that harassment can lead to a range of negative feelings including depression, anger, distrust, fear, and increased body surveillance (Logan, 2015). The combination of repetitively experiencing harassment and limited legal recourse to address it can be experienced as dehumanizing (Fileborn and Vera-Gray, 2017), and traumatic (Buchanan and Ormerod, 2002), and can lead those experiencing harassment to feel unsafe and anxious, have poor sleep, and limit their mobility outside the home (Dhillon and Bhakya, 2014; Logan, 2015). Harassment can also lead to long-term emotional problems including feeling haunted by a particular incident for years, while experiences of sexual harassment in public as a young person can lead to the feeling of having had one's childhood taken away (Fileborn and Vera-Gray, 2017). As this scholarship amply shows, while some experience the street as a space of belonging, others patently do not.

In addition to sidewalks, spaces associated with other forms of mobilities can be problematic as well. As Dunckel Graglia's work on sexual violence within Mexico City's public transit system shows, for example, 9 out of 10 women are sexually assaulted on the city's buses, metro, or taxi system at least once in their lifetimes (Dunckel Graglia, 2016). Based on interviews with survivors of encounters ranging from leering and rude comments to groping and being assaulted, this work argues that women's sense of possibly and confidence can be bound up with their freedom of movement, and that experiences of sexual harassment and other forms of gender violence can erode this. This work situates harassment within the broader spatial politics of gender violence, showing how 'transport is an institution through which hegemonic masculinity is maintained' (Dunckel Graglia, 2016, p 625). Similarly, framed by the shocking gang rape of a 23-year-old student on a bus in Delhi in 2012, Bhattacharyya's work has charted the pervasiveness of sexual harassment and assault of women in India in public spaces of roads and lanes, within markets and in spaces of public transport, together with the connections between gender violence in public and other forms of violence, including partner violence (Bhattacharyya, 2015).

Meanwhile, in the global north, Lubitow et al have explored experiences of harassment (including rude or threatening remarks and 'weird looks') on the part of transgender and gender diverse public transit riders in Portland, Oregon (Lubitow et al, 2017). Building on the work of Doan (2010), Johnson (2016), Nash (2010), and Browne, Nash, and Hines (2010) which has expanded understanding of the lived experiences of transgender and gender diverse individuals, Lubitow et al found high levels of harassment among trans and gender diverse riders, especially among trans people of colour. Usefully, this work shows how, in addition to occurring in ways that are clearly recognizable, harassment can also occur in more subtle, 'below the radar' (including non-verbal) registers. Following Deleuze and Guattari's observation that 'affects transpierce the body like arrows' (Deleuze and Guattari, 1988, p 356), non-verbal signals such as 'weird looks' can send a powerful message about who does and does not belong in public space. Through this work we see how harassment in public transport works through affective and material environments to exert a range of different kinds of domination: including sexism, racism, heterosexism, and cissexism, as well as transphobia and trans-misogyny.

That said, even high-cost, relatively privileged spaces of transport are not immune to harassment. As Adiv (2017) has highlighted in her work on being, in one instance, groped on airplane and, in another instance, stared at the duration of the flight, the shock of these events is bound up in complicated ways with the cultural value placed on 'not making a fuss' in public (alongside concerns about not being believed and violence escalation). Like the previous example of being subject to 'weird looks', through the example of prolonged staring (and the profound sense of discomfort it can produce) we see again how harassment is bound up with affect as much as embodiment (as revealed in feelings of violation in the absence of any physical contact); as well as powerful proscriptions against disrupting 'smooth' relations with others in public, after Ahmed.

At the same time, it is also important to note the various efforts to challenge street harassment (and in other spaces of transport) that have emerged in recent years. Laura Bates' *Everyday Sexism* project, which began life as an online forum to share experiences of sexual harassment and other forms of gender violence and which has since turned into a book, has created an outlet for sharing troubling or traumatic events while creating a document of collective testimony, raising popular awareness of the range and extent of this problem (Bates, 2014). In a similar vein the online *Hollaback* project which began in 2005 and is designed to identify street harassers, likewise constitutes a site of informal or alternative justice and space of support (Fileborn, 2014; Fileborn and Vera-Gray, 2017). Documentary film has been another means of drawing attention to the issue of street harassment, such as the film Cairo 678 (Logan, 2015, p 200). Scholars and activists have also called for the need for stronger policies and laws as well as better reporting mechanisms (Bhattacharyya, 2015; Dunckel Graglia, 2016) and the need for targeted training for those who work in public transport (Lubitow et al, 2017). In the UK, public action group *Our Streets Now* has been working on challenging street harassment through community-directed awareness-raising campaigns, school-based education work, and endeavouring to make street harassment a crime (OurStreetsNow.Org).

This section has considered some of the ways scholars have explored how intersectional difference shapes experiences of harassment in the context of spaces of mobility and transport; highlighting the ongoing need to attend to this call (Mollett and Faria, 2018). It has shown how sidewalks function as a space of social control in the maintenance of gender orders (Ryan, 1992; Loukaitou-Sideris and Ehrenfeucht, 2009), highlighting the cost of everyday embodied racist and sexist micro-aggressions when considered in aggregate. This work reveals how certain citizens are objectified, assaulted and otherwise degraded within spaces of transport and mobility through words, gestures and even staring and other non-verbal actions that create threatening atmospheres for those on the receiving end of harassment. As such this scholarship reveals how harassment is bound up with affect as much as embodiment, as well as proscriptions against disrupting 'public comfort' (Ahmed, 2010). Having considered harassment in spaces of transport and mobility let us now turn to consider harassment in the night-time city.

The night-time city

As scholarship has shown, night-time space (and particularly night-time cities) is marked both by a sense of risk as well as a sense of excitement (Jayne et al, 2010). In recent years work in and beyond geography has begun to explore some of the different kinds of identity- and body-work that take place in the night-time city, particularly in the context of alcohol-drinking on 'nights out' (Leyshon, 2008; Jayne et al, 2010; Waitt et al, 2011; Brands and Schwanen, 2014; Nicholls, 2017). This work has shown the role of nights out in female sociability and bonding including through shared and collective bodily display (Waitt et al, 2011); and explored bodily self-presentation as a means to celebrate or alternatively disguise one's sexuality or gender identity (Nichols, 2017), or as a means of deflecting unwanted sexual attention (Leyshon, 2008; Nicholls, 2017). Other work has focused on alcohol as a means to achieve the 'carefree' body (Brands and Schwanen, 2014), including through enhanced confidence and reduced bodily inhibition (Waitt et al, 2011).

In a similar vein, Jayne, Valentine, and Holloway (2010) have explored the forms of community and belonging that can emerge in the night-time city in the context of drinking alcohol and walking between venues. They point out how these spaces can be both playful and create a sense of heightened sexual desire, and argue that this can be liberating (Jayne et al, 2010, p 547). They cast: 'consuming alcohol as a project of experimentation, of allowing venturesome couplings, of being creative and "letting go"' (Jayne et al, 2010, p 548); further arguing that 'alcohol consumption combined with the time spent in public spaces and commercial venues (facilitates) "ethical" interactions of belonging and sociability' (Jayne et al, 2010, p 550). This experience of 'liberation through drinking' is expressed by one young male study participant thus:

> I don't get much time to see my mates, I work hard and I'm often tired but on a Friday you get a buzz there's nothing like that feeling that you've the whole weekend ahead of you to do what you want ... you don't have to get up to work so you can go out and get pissed ... drink what you want, do what you want, go where you want ... mess

around ... you feel the places you go are aimed at you and the way you want to live. After a hard week at work it's exactly what I need. (Jayne et al, 2010, p 548)

Jayne, Valentine, and Holloway go on to argue that even 'bad behaviour' can play a positive role in night-time social-scapes, providing opportunities for 'remembering, forgiving and forgetting' among friend groups (2010, p 550). While Jayne, Valentine, and Holloway do note some participants mentioning hearing sexist comments during their nights out, these are not explored, and instead the text paints what is an overall very rosy picture of alcohol-fuelled night-time sociability. In this rendering the night-time economy is marked by ethical encounters, camaraderie, and general bonhomie. Indeed, even 'bad behaviour' appears as a force for good, providing a means of collective remembering (and then forgetting) of particular actions, enabling friend groups to strengthen the bonds between them.

We don't know the actions or intentions of the participants in this particular study. That said, it is worth flagging up the fact that 'harmless fun' for some night-time revellers might be understood very differently by others. As research has shown, sexual harassment is typically understood by perpetrators as simply part of 'normal gendered interactions' (Quinn, 2002, p 386, quoted in Logan, 2015, p 203), while Benard and Schlaffer have shown that most men view sexual harassment as harmless fun, which confers a 'feeling of youthful camaraderie' when done with friends (Benard and Schlaffer, 1984, p 71 in Logan, 2015, pp 203–4). Wesselmann and Kelly (2010) have likewise found male social bonding to be a key motivating factor in harassment (Wesselmann and Kelly, 2010, in Logan 2015, p 204).

As this research suggests, interactions within crowded, dark spaces of lowered inhibitions and heightened sexual desire among drunken revellers are not experienced as equally fun by all. Without doubt some actions understood as 'harmless fun' by some are experienced as threatening by others. And, the way actions are interpreted is framed by social positionality and intersectional differences between revellers, with those in positions of greater social power (by race, gender, sexual orientation, and gender identity) most likely being able to 'go where they want and do what they want', and others less so. Again, this highlights the need to bring the role of embodied difference and how it shapes experiences of everyday space and patterns of spatial privilege back into the frame.

While some have focused on the creative and liberatory aspects of the night-time economy others have instead investigated how night-time space is experienced by those who do not possess the kind of social and spatial entitlements suggested in the last quote. Alongside excitement, these experiences are also likely to be marked by feelings of risk and concern about personal safety. As research within and beyond geography has shown, verbal and physical harassment is ever-common within spaces of the night-time economy; and women and LGBTQ people commonly employ a range of tactics in order to both feel safer and try to decrease the amount and kind of harassment they receive (Wattis et al, 2011; Kavanaugh, 2013; Fileborn, 2016; Nicholls, 2017).

Recalling Valentine (1992) these tactics can include limiting where they go (Fileborn, 2016); going out in groups and looking after one another while out (Waitt et al, 2011; Fileborn, 2016); dressing to downplay one's sexuality as read within the framework of heteronormativity (Leyshon, 2008; Nicholls, 2017); and using one's phone as a means to stay connected to friends while travelling home (Brands and Schwanen, 2014). As Brands and Schwanen argue (2014), these tactics illustrate some of the ways in which safety is subjective, relational, and subjectively constituted (Brands and Schwanen, 2014). In addition to constituting an example of the classic neoliberal subject who is expected to be responsible for their own well-being and safety (Walklate, 1997; Rose, 1999), Fileborn argues that the cultivation of these forms of vigilance and personal preparedness in order to produce feelings of safety can also be understood as a form of gender work (Fileborn, 2016).

In addition to constituting a means of symbolically reinforcing patriarchal power (Valentine, 1992), as recent scholarship has shown sexual harassment in spaces of the night-time economy also functions to reinforce compulsory heterosexuality and the gender binary (Waitt et al, 2011; Kavanaugh, 2013; Nicholls, 2016; Nicholls, 2017). Within such spaces women are expected to conform to often highly stylized expressions of hyper-feminine forms of bodily self-presentation that echo celebrity culture as disseminated by social media (Kavanaugh, 2013; Nicholls, 2016). Indeed as recent work argues the night-time economy can even be viewed as 'pornified' space (Griffin, 2013) in which expectations of female bodily self-presentation border on caricature. Within this context sexual harassment functions as part of a continuum of violence in which smaller acts of sexual violence are trivialized, symbolically legitimating more serious forms of sexual violence (Kavanaugh, 2013). Thus, while the night-time economy serves as a space for different kinds of sociability and gender and identity work, it also functions as a disciplinary space reinforcing hetero-patriarchy through the control and regulation of a whole range of bodily practices.

Yet as with daytime street harassment, those on the receiving end of harassment are not simply passive victims, and research has outlined both collective and individual forms of resistance to harassment within spaces of the night-time economy. While events such as *Take Back the Night* marches have long constituted a means of resisting harassment and gender violence in night-time space as well as providing a means for people to develop activist identities (Logan, 2015, p 200; Lewis and Marine, 2018, p 137), more contemporary activist initiatives such as slut walks emphasize the message that no form of bodily self-presentation equates to sexual consent (Logan, 2015, pp 199–200). Meanwhile in the UK young women have mobilized with bands to stop groping at gigs and music festivals (Garvan, 2015), and we also see city-level campaigns emerging (such as the 'Bristol Nights' campaign) offering anti-harassment training to NTE workers and public awareness-raising campaigns (Bristolnights.co.uk). In addition to these more formalized types of activism, research has also detailed some of the many 'everyday' resistances that take place in night-time space in which individuals let harassers know their words or actions are not appropriate (Phipps and Young, 2015, p 13). Having explored key themes in scholarship on harassment in spaces of transport and the night-time economy (together with efforts to resist these), let us now turn to consider the issue of sexual harassment within spaces of higher education.

Spaces of higher education

In addition to street-spaces and spaces within the night-time economy, in recent years spaces of higher education have been increasingly recognized as particularly problematic sites for sexual harassment and other forms of gender violence (NUS, 2014; Dills et al, 2016; Batty et al, 2017; Busby, 2018; Reynolds, 2018; NUS, 2010).[8] Research from the UK has shown that over 60 per cent of all students experience some form of sexual violence while at university, with 40 per cent reporting experiencing sexual misconduct on the part of staff. Within this, people with disabilities and LGBTQ students experience the highest levels of violence (NUS, 2014; Revolt Report, 2018). Forty-eight per cent of female university students and 17 per cent of male university students in the UK report having experienced sexual assault while 46 per cent of non-binary students and 54 per cent of students with a disability report having experienced sexual assault while at university (Revolt Report, 2018). The most common form of assault is groping or unwanted touching and the spaces where assaults are most likely to take place are halls of residence, social events and university social spaces (Revolt Report, 2018).

Linking back to the argument about the continuum of sexual violence in which everyday micro-aggressions create an environment in which more serious violations are more likely to occur, research suggests that students at university in England and Wales are twice as likely to be raped than the general population; while environments in which sexual violence is normalized also take a toll on learning with a quarter of students reporting that they have skipped lectures or seminars or dropped out of a module in order to avoid a perpetrator (Revolt Report, 2018). Scholarship also shows these trends to resonate across a wide range of cultural contexts. Research from the US suggests over 60 per cent of female university students experience sexual harassment (Cantor et al, 2015) while research from India reveals 45 per cent of women to be affected by sexual harassment at university (Dhillon and Bhakaya, 2014, p 2). Scholarship likewise shows sexual harassment and other forms of gender violence in educational spaces to be an issue in South Korea (Park et al, 2013); Jordan (Takash et al, 2013); Chile (Lehrer et al, 2013); Germany, Italy, Poland, and Spain (Feltes et al, 2009).

Scholarship has focused on two factors in explaining this problem. The first is reticence on the part of universities to acknowledge issues of sexual violence out of fear of reputational damage within fiercely competitive higher education marketplaces (Heldman and Brown, 2104; Jackson and Sundaram, 2015; Anitha and Lewis, 2018). The argument here is that the widespread failure to track, investigate, or prosecute sexual harassment and violence on the one hand, or implement rigorous prevention programs on the other is not simply a matter of institutional negligence but instead an intentional strategy to downplay this issue in order to allow institutions to save face and preserve reputations. Sexual harassment and other forms of misconduct occurs both among students and between students and staff. The invisibilization, silencing, and historical acceptance of sexual misconduct on the part of (typically male, often senior) academic staff is compounded by the tremendous power (including over marks and career prospects) perpetrators wield over victims (typically female students and junior academic staff). This problematic was recently brought into sharp relief in the UK when social theorist Sara Ahmed resigned her post at Goldsmiths University out of protest to her institution's failure/unwillingness to address issues of sexual harassment (Ahmed, 2016). Within geography, Mansfield et al (2019) have called for the need to confront the magnitude and severity of sexual misconduct on the part of senior males in our own discipline, highlighting how harassment constitutes a message of non-belonging which can (and does) cause gifted individuals to leave academia.

The second explanatory factor has been the prevalence of lad culture/rape culture (Heldman and Brown, 2014) in shaping atmospheres on university campuses. In broad outline lad culture refers to male social cultures of heavy drinking, shared participation in sport, sexist and homophobic banter (and sometimes actions), and (hetero)sexual prowess/promiscuity (Phipps and Young, 2015). In the pack mentalities (and practices) of some male sports and other kinds of elite clubs, through practices of heavy drinking, performative, and competitive displays of (hyper) masculinity and initiation rituals drawing on elements of domination, and bodily and often sexual degradation (Phipps and Young, 2015; Phipps, 2018). This strand of laddism is bound up with proscriptions about bodily comportment in which women are expected to present themselves in a sexualized manner in night-time social settings, expected to always be 'up' for sex and may be shamed and mocked if they are not (Griffin et al, 2013; Phipps and Young, 2015). Shaped by soft-porn 'lad mags' of the 1990s and easily accessible hard-core pornography online in current times, this strand of middle-class misogyny is further marked by a thoroughly male-focused understanding of sexual pleasure, in which women are expected to be almost entirely passive during sex (Phipps and Young, 2015; Bates, 2019). It is likewise associated with the perpetuation of rape myths, victim-blaming and victim non-believing, reinforced through social media (Bates, 2019).

This strand of laddism is closely linked to the feminist backlash, and is fundamentally bound up with the prevalence and normalization of everyday sexual harassment (NUS, 2010; Phipps, 2017; Anitha and Lewis, 2018; Phipps et al, 2018). While such impulses are evident within the broader culture, within the relatively isolated micro-cultures of university life lad culture can have a disproportionate sway in tone-setting, making higher education a toxic and unsafe space for many (Phipps et al, 2018). At the same time, echoing activism against sexual harassment in other settings, a range of different forms of activism and educational programming have emerged in recent years to resist sexual harassment in spaces of higher education. Research has shown education-based prevention programs which explore gender socialization and challenge rape myths to have success in changing sexist attitudes which are linked to the incidence of sexual violence (Day, 1995; Vladutiu et al, 2011). In the US and the UK, intervention programs seeking to achieve these goals have gained traction in recent years, with sessions featuring emotional engagement and which seek to develop empathy such as through role play reporting some of the best results in terms of attitude change (Fenton and Mott, 2018).

And finally, at the same time as university campuses can be challenging spaces they can also be supportive environments for feminist activism, including by providing physical space on campus as well as ICT and other kinds of infrastructure to support community-building activities (Lewis and Marine, 2018; Lewis et al, 2018). As Ruth Lewis and Susan Marine's work on feminist activism on university campuses has shown, in addition to the many negative emotions harassment and other forms of sexual violence can generate, these experiences can also be galvanizing, and serve as a motivation for collective action and resistance (Lewis and Marine, 2018). Building communities with other feminist-identified students can be empowering and create a shared sense of belonging. Feminist societies can serve as a space to process experiences of everyday sexism and in which to build confidence (Lewis and Marine, 2018). Members often become change-agents on campus, calling out instances of sexist behaviour and actions on the part of students and staff, while also challenging sexual violence collectively through performative, artistic, and other means (Lewis and Marine, 2018). These activities can also include men and the cultivation of allyship, for example through the Scottish National Union of Students' campaign #I'mNotThatLad aimed at challenging lad culture (Phipps and Young, 2015). However, it is also worth noting the broader power relations structuring whose voices tend to be heard within higher education spaces and whose do not. Reflecting UK higher education as a whole, feminist activist spaces can sometimes be dominated by white women, and as scholar-activists Chelsea Kwakye and Ore Ogunbiyi note, work still needs to be done to ensure issues of white privilege and racism can be raised and discussed openly within these spaces (as well as beyond them) (Kwakye and Ogunbiyi, 2019, pp 255–6).

Conclusion

This chapter has explored key themes in current scholarship on sexual harassment within and beyond geography through the three spatial frames of street-space, the night-time economy and spaces of higher education, arguing that through day-to-day interactions in public space bodies become territoralized within heteropatriarchal relations of power. I argue that this conceptual framework can help feminist geographers and others in the work of combatting gender-based violence.

I have highlighted how, after Ahmed, the pressure to maintain public comfort can shape how harassment is experienced, the extent to which it is (or is not) discussed or reported, and the impact that everyday exchanges between strangers in public can have on nurturing – or foreclosing – one's sense of belonging in a given space. Through this work we can see the corrosive and cumulative effect such interactions can have on one's mental health, sense of self and sense of one's place in the world. We can see how harassment is tied up with the feminist backlash, racism and homo/transphobia, and how harassment may relate to feelings of 'fragility' among subjects who occupy positions of historical (and contemporary) social dominance based on whiteness, class-privilege, heterosexuality, masculinity, and traditional binary gender identity when confronted with their privilege (DiAngelo, 2018).

Such a review is needed at this time in order to both shape an agenda for future research and inform the work of policy makers and activists seeking to end harassment culture. Geographers have both an opportunity and a responsibility to contribute to this discussion. There is work to be done in terms of understanding the extent of harassment and how it is experienced both across different cultural contexts and across axis of social difference, especially by race and ethnicity, sexual orientation, gender identity, and disability. Geographers might also fruitfully extend understanding about sexual harassment as an embodied experience by exploring how such micro-aggressions operate in and through material, discursive and affective practices of spatial dominance. I suggest that theoretical lenses of relationality, embodiment and affect could prove particularly useful in this regard. Especially in light of Colls' argument about the potential of the more than representational to advancing feminist theory (and practice) within and beyond geography (Colls, 2012), one can see the value of the more than discursive in approaching this issue. This might include the exploration of how affective atmospheres are shaped in and through harassment, and/or the role of the non-verbal in constructing feelings of belonging and non-belonging in interactions between strangers in different kinds of space, in addition to other approaches.

In addition to the need to extend our understanding about both the magnitude of sexual harassment and how it is experienced, more work is needed to understand efforts to combat it, in order that the 'right to everyday life' (Beebeejaun, 2017) may be experienced by all. Building on the remit of activist feminist geographies, one way geographers could extend knowledge in this area is by working collaboratively with activists seeking to challenge the interlocking forms of societal privilege that currently structure the potential for having a sense of 'mobile belonging' (Edensor, 2010) in public space, thus building on the strong tradition of scholar activism in our discipline (Gilmore, 2007; Wright, 2009; Chatterton and Pickerill, 2010; Routledge and Derickson, 2015). The *#MeToo* movement has led to a massive increase in awareness about harassment and the need for both policy and cultural change on this issue. In turn this has led to a range of initiatives directly or indirectly aimed at reducing harassment across different cultural contexts. However, little as yet is known about many such initiatives.

To give two examples from the UK, in 2020 relationships and sex education became mandatory for all secondary school students in England, thus creating the potential to roll out a version of 'consent workshops' across the population as a whole. While near-peer relationships and sex education has been shown to be an effective means of promoting more positive, informed, and respectful attitudes about gender relations and power within romantic and sexual relationships (Han et al, 2018), we don't yet know much about the effects of such programming rolled out at the population level, or in a curricular format that meets 2020 guidelines that such education must be explicitly LGBTQI+ inclusive. This ambitious move constitutes a potentially rich field of research for exploring what is needed to effect wide-scale culture change regarding understandings of gender, race, embodiment and rights to space including through the cultivation of understanding, empathy and allyship. Meanwhile over 2021 and 2022, in collaboration with advocates, educators, and others a number of UK city councils have instituted a range of innovative programs aimed at combatting sexual harassment and other forms of gender violence in public, including through education and awareness-raising campaigns. While awareness-raising campaigns have been shown to be effective in changing behaviour relating to sexual harassment in spaces of transport (Gekoski et al, 2015), little is known about interventions on the part of the local state to reduce gender violence, or within public space of the city generally. I suggest this offers a further potentially rich field for research.

Finally, after Mansfield et al (2019) I suggest we also look to our *own* workplaces and institutions to consider what is going on in our own metaphorical backyards. It behoves us to take account of the role we play – and might play – as educators, leaders, and community members in settings where harassment is an increasingly recognized problem. We might do this by raising awareness about this issue within our own departments; setting out clear behavioural expectations relating to gender and sexual conduct for both students and staff (together with the consequences for breaching these); making sure systems are in place for students to report misconduct (and ensuring students are aware of these); collaborating with students and staff already engaged in the work of combatting sexual misconduct in order to share best practices; and providing consent and/or bystander training to ensure community expectations are understood, recognizing that a large body of literature now snows such interventions to be effective in changing both attitudes and behaviours relating to sexual misconduct (Mujal et al, 2021). Indeed, many universities are already engaged in this work. In the UK context, for example, according to the 2019 Universities UK sector-wide report on tacking sexual misconduct in UK higher education, over half of the 95 Institutions of Higher Learning surveyed had made major revisions to their student codes of conduct in recent years, and were providing either consent or bystander training to their students; while over 80 per cent had recently updated their disciplinary procedures in this area. Each of these initiatives represent potential articulations of activist feminist geography in that they represent efforts to not just document but *change* unjust power structures relating to gender and sexuality and enable more equitable access to and experiences of space and place. As such, they warrant our critical attention, time, and energy.

Notes

1. It is noted that the AAG has initiated work groups to combat sexual harassment at annual conferences.
2. Although this inquiry nominatively focused on 'Sexual Harassment of Women and Girls in Public Places' it is important to stress that people of any gender can experience sexual harassment, and that LGBTQ+ individuals can experience significantly higher levels of harassment than cis-gender and heterosexual individuals.
3. Gender violence can be understood as threatening or hurtful words or actions toward someone 'because of their [perceived] gender or sexuality' (Anitha and Lewis, 2018: 1).

4   This chapter does not consider sexual harassment in the workplace for two reasons. First, while sharing some features with the more common phenomenon of stranger sexual harassment (Fairchild and Rudman, 2008), unlike stranger harassment sexual harassment in the workplace occurs within the context of existing social relations and power relations. Second, sexual harassment in the workplace occurs within the context of myriad distinct policy and legal contexts that both differ from sexual harassment in public and are beyond the scope of this chapter to examine properly.
5   https://publications.parliament.uk/pa/cm201719/cmselect/cmwomeq/701/70102.htm [Accessed 17/11/2020].
6   https://publications.parliament.uk/pa/cm201719/cmselect/cmwomeq/701/70102.htm [Accessed 17/11/2020].
7   'Report on Sexual Violence at University Revolt Sexual Assault', The Student Room, 2018. https://web.unican.es/unidades/igualdad/SiteAssets/guia-derecursos/acoso/NUS_staff-student_misconduct_report.pdf [Accessed 17 November 2020]. This report was based on responses from 4,500 students at 153 institutions.
8   'Power in the Academy: Staff Sexual Misconduct in UK Higher Education, National Union of Students, 2018'. www.nusconnect.org.uk/resources/nus-staff-student-sexual-misconduct-report [Accessed 18 November 2020].

Acknowledgements

This chapter is a modified version of the open access article: Boyer, K. (2022). 'Sexual Harassment and the Right to Everyday Life'. *Progress in Human Geography* 46(2): 398–415, https://doi.org/10.1177/03091325211024340

References

Adiv, N. (2017). 'On Being Groped and Staying Quiet. Or, What Kind of Place an Airplane Can Be'. *Gender, Place and Culture* 24(5): 621–27.

Ahmed, S. (2010). 'Killing Joy: Feminism and the History of Happiness'. *Signs* 3 (35): 571–94.

Ahmed, S. (2016). 'Resignation Is a Feminist Issue'. Available from: http://genderinstitute.anu.edu.au/news/sara-ahmed-resignation-feminist-issue [Accessed 5 May 2020].

Anderson, B. (2009). 'Affective Atmospheres'. *Emotion, Space and Society* 2(2): 77–81.

Anitha, S. and Lewis, R. (2018) 'Introduction: Some Reflections in These Promising and Challenging Times', in S. Anitha and R. Lewis (eds) *Gender Based Violence in University Communities: Policy, Prevention and Educational Initiatives*. Bristol: Policy Press.

Bailey, M. (2010). 'They Aren't Talking about Me'. *Crunk Feminist Collective* 14.

Bates, L. (2014). *Everyday Sexism: The Project That Inspired a Worldwide Movement*. London: Simon and Schuster.

Bates, L. (2019). 'Teenage Boys Are Not Inherently Misygynistic: They Are Being Fed Lies'. *The Sunday Times Magazine* 17(2): 8–13.

Batty, D., Weale, S., and Bannock, C. (2017). 'Sexual Harassment "at Epidemic Levels" in UK Universities'. *The Guardian*. Available from: www.theguardian.com/education/2017/mar/05/students-staff-uk-universitiessexual- harassment-epidemic [Accessed 2 January 2019].

Beebeejaun, Y. (2017). 'Gender, Urban Space, and the Right to Everyday Life'. *Journal of Urban Affairs* 39(3): 323–34.

Benard, C. and Schlaffer, E. (1984). 'The Man in the Street: Why He Harasses', in A.M. Jagger and P.S. Rothenberg (eds) *Feminist Frameworks: Alternative Theoretical Accounts of the Relations between Women and Men*, 3rd ed. New York: McGraw Hill, pp 70–2.

Bhattacharyya, R. (2015). 'Understanding the Spatialities of Sexual Assault Against Indian Women in India'. *Gender, Place & Culture* 22(9): 1340–56.

Brands, J. and Schwanen, T. (2014). 'Experiencing and Governing Safety in the Night-time Economy: Nurturing the State of Being Carefree'. *Emotion, Space and Society* 11: 67–78.

Brickell, K. and Cuomo, D. (2020). 'Geographies of Violence: Feminist Geopolitical Approaches', in A. Datta, P. Hopkins, L. Johnston, E. Olsen and J.M. Silva (eds) *Routledge Handbook of Gender and Feminist Geographies*. New York: Routledge, pp 297–307.

Brickell, K. and Maddrell, A. (2016). 'Geographical Frontiers of Gendered Violence'. *Dialogues in Human Geography* 6(2): 170–72.

Browne, K. (2004). 'Genderism and the Bathroom Problem: (Re) Materialising Sexed Sites, (Re) Creating Sexed Bodies'. *Gender, Place and Culture* 11(3): 331–46.

Browne, K., Nash, C., and Hines, S. (2010). 'Introduction: Towards Trans Geographies'. *Gender, Place and Culture* 17(5): 573–77.

Buchanan, T. and Ormerod, A. (2002). 'Racialized Sexual Harassment in the Lives of African American Women', in C. West (ed) *Violence in the Lives of Black Women: Battered, Black, and Blue*. New York: Haworth Press, pp 107–24.

Busby, E. (2018). 'Three in Five Students Sexually Assaulted or Harassed at University, Survey Finds'. *The Independent*. Available from: www.independent.co.uk/news/education/education-news/university-studentssexual-assault-harassment-experiences-revolt-student-room-survey-a8234741.html [Accessed 10 December 2018].

Cantor, D., Fisher, B., Chibnall, S., Townsend, R., Lee, H., Thomas, G., Bruce, C., and Westat, Inc. (2015). 'Report on the AAU Campus Climate Survey on Sexual Assault and Sexual Misconduct'. Available from: www.aau.edu/sites/default/files/%40%20Files/Climate%20Survey/AAU_Campus_Climate_Survey_12_14_15.pdf [Accessed 12 May 2020].

Chatterton, P. and Pickerill, J. (2010). 'Everyday Activism and Transitions Towards Post-Capitalist Worlds'. *Transactions of the institute of British Geographers* 35(4): 475–90.

Collins, P.H. (2002). *Black Feminist Thought: Knowledge, Consciousness, and the Politics of Empowerment*. New York: Routledge.

Colls, R. (2012). 'Feminism, Bodily Difference and Non-Representational Geographies'. *Transactions of the Institute of British Geographers* 37(3): 430–45.

Crenshaw, K. (1989). 'Demarginalizing the Intersection of Race and Sex: A Black Feminist Critique of Antidiscrimination Doctrine, Feminist Theory and Antiracist Politics'. *University of Chicago Legal Forum* 140(1): 139–67.

Cresswell T (2010). 'Towards a Politics of Mobility'. *Environment and Planning D: Society and Space* (28): 17–31.

Day, K. (1995). 'Assault Prevention as Social Control: Women and Sexual Assault Prevention on Urban College Campuses'. *Journal of Environmental Psychology* 15(4): 261–81.

Deleuze, G. and Guattari, F. (1988). *A Thousand Plateaus*. London: Bloomsbury.

Dhillon, M. and Bakaya, S. (2014). 'Street Harassment: A Qualitative Study of the Experiences of Young Women in Delhi'. *Sage Open* 4(3): 1–11.

DiAngelo, R. (2018). *White Fragility: Why It's So Hard for White People to Talk About Racism*. Boston: Beacon Press.

Dills, J., Fowler, D., and Payne, G. (2016). 'Sexual Violence on Campus: Strategies for Prevention, Division of Violence Prevention'. National Center for Injury Prevention and Control Centers for Disease Control and Prevention. Available from: www.cdc.gov/violenceprevention/pdf/campussvprevention.pdf [Accessed 3 March 2018].

Doan, P. (2010). 'The Tyranny of Gendered Spaces: Reflections from Beyond the Gender Dichotomy'. *Gender, Place and Culture* 17(5): 635–54.

Duff, C. (2010). 'On the Role of Affect and Practice in the Production of Place'. *Environment and Planning D: Society and Space* 28(5): 881.

Dunckel Graglia, A. (2016). 'Finding Mobility: Women Negotiating Fear and Violence in Mexico City's Public Transit System'. *Gender, Place and Culture* 23(5): 624–40.

Edensor, T. (2010). 'Walking in Rhythms: Place, Regulation, Style and the Flow of Experience'. *Visual Studies* 25(1): 69–79.

Fairchild, K. and Rudman, L. (2008). 'Everyday Stranger Harassment and Women's Objectification'. *Social Justice Research* 21(3): 338–39.

Feltes, T., Balloni, A., Czapska, J., Bodelón, E., and Stenning, P. (2009). 'Gender-based violence, stalking and fear of crime'. *European Commission Country Report*.

Fenster, T. (2005). 'The Right to the Gendered City: Different Formations of Belonging in Everyday Life'. *Journal of Gender Studies* 14(3): 217–31.

Fenton, R. and Mott, H. (2018). 'The *Intervention Initiative*: Theoretical Underpinnings, Development and implementation', in S. Anitha and R. Lewis (eds) *Gender Based Violence in University Communities: Policy, Prevention and Educational Initiatives*. Bristol: Policy Press, pp 169–88.

Fileborn, B. (2014). 'Online Activism and Street Harassment: Digital Justice or Shouting into the Ether?'. *Griffith Journal of Law & Human Dignity* 2(1): 43–51.

Fileborn, B. (2016). 'Doing Gender, Doing Safety? Young Adults' Production of Safety on a Night Out'. *Gender, Place & Culture* 23(8): 1107–20.

Fileborn, B. and Vera-Gray, F. (2017). '"I Want to Be Able to Walk the Street without Fear": Transforming Justice for Street Harassment'. *Feminist Legal Studies* 25(2): 203–27.

Fyfe, N. (2006). *Images of the Street: Planning, Identity and Control in Public Space*. New York: Routledge.

Garvan, S. (2015). 'These Young Women Are Fighting against Groping at Gigs'. BBC News. Available from: www.bbc.co.uk/newsbeat/article/34921 372/these-young-women-are-fightingagainst- groping-at-gigs [Accessed 6 May 2020].

Gekoski, A., Gray, J.M., Horvath, M.A., Edwards, S., Emirali, A. and Adler, J.R. (2015). 'What Works in Reducing Sexual Harassment and Sexual Offences on Public Transport Nationally and Internationally: A Rapid Evidence Assessment'. London: Project Report, Department for Transport.

Gilmore, R. (2007). *Golden Gulag: Prisons, Surplus, Crisis, and Opposition in Globalizing California*. Berkeley: University of California Press.

Griffin, C., Szmigin, I., Bengry-Howell, A., Hackley, C., and Mistral, W. (2013). 'Inhabiting the Contradictions: Hypersexual Femininity and the Culture of Intoxication among Young Women in the UK'. *Feminism and Psychology* 23(2): 184–206.

Han, S., Miu, H., Wong, C., Tucker, J., and Wong, W. (2018). 'Assessing Participation and Effectiveness of the Peer-led Approach in Youth Sexual Health Education: Systematic Review and Meta-analysis in More Developed Countries'. *The Journal of Sex Research* 55(1): 31–44.

Heldman, C. and Brown, B. (2014). 'Why Colleges Won't (really) Address Rape Culture'. *Ms Magazine*, 8 October. Available from: http://msm agazine.com/blog/2014/10/08/why colleges-wont-really-address-rape-culture/ [Accessed 12 May 2020].

Hernandez, T.K. (2000). 'Sexual Harassment and Racial Disparity: The Mutual Construction of Gender and Race'. *Journal of Gender, Race & Justice* 4: 183–216.

Hopkins, P. (2019). 'Social Geography I: Intersectionality'. *Progress in Human Geography* 43(5): 937–47.

Jackson, C. and Sundaram, V. (2015). 'Is "Lad Culture" a Problem in Higher Education? Exploring the Perspectives of Staff Working in UK Universities'. *Final report, Society for Research into Higher Education*. Available from: www.srhe.ac.uk/downloads/JacksonSundaramLadCulture.pdf [Accessed 17 March 2023].

Jayne, M., Valentine, G., and Holloway, S. (2010). 'Emotional, Embodied and Affective Geographies of Alcohol, Drinking and Drunkenness'. *Transactions of the Institute of British Geographers* 35(4): 540–54.

Johnston, L. (2016). 'Gender and Sexuality I: Genderqueer Geographies?'. *Progress in Human Geography* 40(5): 668–78.

Johnston, L. (2017). 'Gender and sexuality II: Activism'. *Progress in Human Geography* 41(5): 648–56.

Johnson, M. and Bennett, E. (2015). *Everyday Sexism: Australian Women's Experiences of Street Harassment*. Melbourne: The Australia Institute.

Kavanaugh, P. (2013). 'The Continuum of Sexual Violence: Women's Accounts of Victimization in Urban Nightlife'. *Feminist Criminology* 8(1): 20–39.

Kelly, L. (1988). *Surviving Sexual Violence*. Minneapolis: University of Minnesota Press.

Kendi, I.X. (2019). *How to Be an Antiracist*. London: Vintage.

Kwakye, C. and Ogunbiyi, O. (2019). *Taking up Space: The Black Girl's Manifesto for Change*. London: #Merky Books.

Lehrer, J., Lehrer, E. and Koss, M. (2013). 'Sexual and Dating Violence among Adolescents and Young Adults in Chile: A Review of Findings from a Survey of University Students'. *Culture, Health and Sexuality* 1(1): 1–14.

Lewis, R. and Marine, S. (2018). 'Student Feminist Activism to Challenge Gender Based Violence', in S. Anitha and R. Lewis (eds) *Gender Based Violence in University Communities: Policy, Prevention and Educational Initiatives*. Bristol: Policy Press, 129–48.

Lewis, R., Marine, S., and Kenney, K. (2018). '"I Get Together with My Friends and Try to Change It". Young Feminist Students Resist "Laddism", "Rape Culture" and "Everyday Sexism"'. *Journal of Gender Studies* 27(1): 56–72.

Leyshon, M. (2008). '"We're Stuck in the Corner": Young Women, Embodiment and Drinking in the Countryside'. *Drugs: Education, Prevention, and Policy* 15(3): 267–89.

Logan, S. (2015). 'Street Harassment: Current and Promising Avenues for Researchers and Activists'. *Sociology Compass* 9(3): 196–211.

Lorde, A. (1984). 'The Master's Tools Will Never Dismantle the Master's House', in A. Lorde, *Sister Outsider: Essays and Speeches*. Trumansburg: Crossing Press, pp 10–14.

Loukaitou-Sideris, A. and Ehrenfeucht, R. (2009) *Sidewalks: Conflict and Negotiation Over Public Space*. Cambridge, MA: MIT Press.

Lubitow, A., Carathers, J., Kelly, M., and Abelson, M. (2017) 'Transmobilities: Mobility, Harassment, and Violence Experienced by Transgender and Gender Nonconforming Public Transit Riders in Portland, Oregon'. *Gender, Place & Culture* 24(10): 1398–418.

Macmillan, R., Nierobisz, A., and Welsh, S. (2000). 'Experiencing the Streets: Harassment and Perceptions of Safety Among Women'. *Journal of Research in Crime and Delinquency* 37(3): 306–7.

Mansfield, B., Lave, R., McSweeney, K., Bonds, A., Cockburn, J., Domosh, M., Hamilton, T., Hawkins, R., Hessl, A., Munroe, D. and Ojeda, D. (2019). 'It's Time to Recognize How Men's Careers Benefit from Sexually Harassing Women in Academia'. *Human Geography* 12(1): 82–7.

McNeil, P. (2012). 'Harassing Men on the Street'. Guest blog post, *Feministe*. Available from: https://feministe.us/blog/?p=21492 [Accessed 6 May 2020].

Middleton, J. (2010). 'Sense and the City: Exploring the Embodied Geographies of Urban Walking'. *Social & Cultural Geography* 11(6): 575–96.

Mollett, S. and Faria, C. (2018). 'The Spatialities of Intersectional Thinking: Fashioning Feminist Geographic Futures'. *Gender, Place and Culture* 25(4): 565–77.

Mountz, A. (2018). 'Political Geography III: Bodies'. *Progress in Human Geography*, 42(5): 759–69.

Mujal, G.N., Taylor, M.E., Fry, J.L., Gochez-Kerr, T.H., and Weaver, N.L. (2021). 'A Systematic Review of Bystander Interventions for the Prevention of Sexual Violence'. *Trauma, Violence, & Abuse* 22(2): 381–96.

Nash, C. (2010). 'Trans Geographies, Embodiment and Experience'. *Gender, Place and Culture* 17(5): 579–95.

National Union of Students (2014). 'Hidden Marks: A Study of Women Students' Experiences of Harassment, Stalking, Violence and Sexual Assault'. Available from: www.nus.org.uk/Global/NUS_hidden_marks_report_2nd_edition_web.pdf [Accessed 13 May 2020].

Nicholls, E. (2016). '"What On Earth Is *She* Drinking?" Doing Femininity through Drink Choice on the Girls' Night Out'. *Journal of International Women's Studies* 17(2): 77–91.

Nicholls, E. (2017). '"Dulling it Down a Bit": Managing Visibility, Sexualities and Risk in the Night Time Economy in Newcastle, UK'. *Gender, Place & Culture* 24(2): 260–73.

Nielsen, L. (2009). *License to Harass: Law, Hierarchy, and Offensive Public Speech*. Princeton: Princeton University Press.

Pain, R. (2014). 'Everyday Terrorism: Connecting Domestic Violence and Global Terrorism'. *Progress in Human Geography* 38(4): 531–50.

Park, Y., Park, S., Lee, Y., and Moon, J. (2013). 'Sexual Harassment in Korean College Classrooms: How Self-construal and Gender Affect Students' Reporting Behavior'. *Gender, Place and Culture* 20(4): 432–50.

Phipps, A. (2017). '(Re)Theorising Laddish Masculinities in Higher Education'. *Gender and Education* 29(7): 815–30.

Phipps, A. and Young, I. (2015). '"Lad Culture" in Higher Education: Agency in the Sexualization Debates'. *Sexualities* 18(4): 459–79.

Phipps, A., Ringrose, J., Renold, E., and Jackson, C. (2018). 'Rape Culture, Lad Culture and Everyday Sexism: Researching, Conceptualizing and Politicizing New Mediations of Gender and Sexual Violence'. *Journal of Gender Studies* 27(1): 1–8.

Pile, S. (2005). *Real Cities: Modernity, Space and the Phantasmagorias of City Life*. London: Sage.

Pinder, D. (2001). 'Ghostly Footsteps: Voices, Memories and Walks in the City'. *Ecumene* 8(1): 1–19.

Quinn, B. (2002). 'Sexual Harassment and Masculinity: The Power and Meaning of "Girl Watching"'. *Gender & Society* 16: 386–402.

Rendell, J., Penner, B., and Borden, I. (eds) (2000). *Gender Space Architecture: An Interdisciplinary Introduction*. London, Routledge.

Revolt Report (2018). 'Report on Sexual Violence at University Revolt Sexual Assault'. The Student Room. Available from: https://web.unican.es/unidades/igualdad/SiteAssets/guia-derecursos/acoso/NUS_staff-studen t_misconduct_report.pdf [Accessed 17 November 2020].

Reynolds, E. (2018). 'Universities Are Home to a Rape Epidemic. Here's What They Can Do'. *The Guardian*. Available from: www.theguardian.com/commentisfree/2018/mar/02/universities-rapeepidemic- sexual-assault-students [Accessed 5 October 2018].

Rose, N. (1999). *Powers of Freedom: Reframing Political Thought*. Cambridge: Cambridge University Press.

Routledge, P. and Derickson, K. (2015). 'Situated Solidarities and the Practice of Scholar-activism'. *Environment and Planning D: Society and Space* 33(3): 391–407.

Ryan, M. (1992). *Women in Public: Between Banners and Ballots, 1825–1880* (Vol. 16). Baltimore: John Hopkins University Press.

Sen, P., Borges, E., Guallar, E., and Cochran, J. (2018). 'Towards an End to Sexual Harassment: The Urgency and Nature of Change in the Era of #MeToo'. United Nations, UN Women. Available from: www.unwo men.org/en/digital-library/publications/2018/11/towards-an-end-to-sex ual-harassment [Accessed 3 February 2021].

Senthillingam, M. (2017). 'Sexual Harassment: How It Stands around the Globe'. CNN. Available from: https://edition.cnn.com/2017/11/25/hea lth/sexual-harassment-violence-abuse-global-levels/index.html [Accessed 3 February 2021].

Simonsen, K. (2010). 'Encountering O/other bodies: Practice, Emotion and Ethics', in B. Anderson (ed) *Taking-Place: Non-Representational Theories and Geography*. London: Routledge, pp 221–39.

Stewart, K. (2011). 'Atmospheric Attunements'. *Environment and Planning D: Society and Space* 29(3): 445–53.

Sweet, E.L. and Ortiz Escalante, S. (2015). 'Bringing Bodies into Planning: Visceral Methods, Fear and Gender Violence'. *Urban Studies* 52(10): 1826–45.

Takash, H., Ghaith, S., and Hammouri, H. (2013). 'Irrational Beliefs about Family Violence: A Pilot Study within Jordanian University Students'. *Journal of Family Violence* 28(6): 595–601.

Valentine, G. (1992). 'Images of Danger: Women's Sources of Information about the Spatial Distribution of Male Violence'. *Area* 24(1): 22–9.

Vladutiu, J., Martin, L., and Macy, J. (2011). 'College or University-based Sexual Assault Prevention Programs: A Review of Program Outcomes, Characteristics, and Recommendations'. *Trauma, Violence, & Abuse* 12(2): 67–86.

Waitt, G., Jessop, L., and Gorman-Murray, A. (2011). '"The Guys in There Just Expect to Be Laid": Embodied and Gendered Socio-spatial Practices of a "Night Out" in Wollongong, Australia'. *Gender, Place and Culture* 18(2): 255–75.

Walklate, S. (1997). 'Risk and Criminal Victimisation: A Modernist Dilemma?'. *British Journal of Criminology* 37(1): 35–45.

Wattis, L., Green, E., and Radford, J. (2011). 'Women Students' Perceptions of Crime and Safety: Negotiating Fear and Risk in an English Post-industrial Landscape'. *Gender, Place and Culture* 18(6): 749–67.

WCLRF (2015). 'Research on Sexual Harassment against Women in Public Places, Workplace and Educational Institutions of Afghanistan'. Kabul: Women and Children Legal Research Foundation. Available from: www.wclrf.org.af/wp-content/uploads/fifinal%20EN.pdf [Accessed 13 May 2020].

Wesslemann, E. and Kelly, J. (2010). 'Cat-Calls and Culpability: Investigating the Frequency and Functions of Stranger Harassment'. *Sex Roles* 63: 451–62.

West, C. (2002). *Violence in the Lives of Black Women: Battered, Black, and Blue*. New York: Haworth Press.

Woods, K.C., Buchanan, N.T., and Settles, I.H. (2009). 'Sexual Harassment across the Color Line: Experiences and Outcomes of Cross Versus Intraracial Sexual Harassment among Black Women'. *Cultural Diversity and Ethnic Minority Psychology* 15(1): 67.

Wright, M. (2009). 'Gender and Geography: Knowledge and Activism Across the Intimately Global'. *Progress in Human Geography* 33(3): 379–86.

Wylie, J. (2005). 'A Single Day's Walking: Narrating Self and Landscape on the South West Coast Path'. *Transactions of the institute of British Geographers* 30(2): 234–47.

7

Giving Birth in a 'Hostile Environment'

Maria Fannin

In 2012, the UK government's Home Office, under the leadership of then Conservative party and Home Office Secretary Theresa May, outlined a series of policies aimed, in May's words, at creating a 'really hostile environment for illegal migration' (Kirkup and Winnett, 2012). Formalized in subsequent pieces of legislation on immigration in 2014 and 2016, these policies sought to implement a range of practices aimed at reducing the number of migrants living in the UK who had not been granted legal right to remain. The policy also created new procedures aimed at identifying those without legal right to remain. Measures were put in place to restrict migrants' ability to access education, rental accommodation, driving licenses, bank accounts, and healthcare. These measures became known as the 'Hostile Environment' policies and have been roundly criticized by activists, religious leaders, and academics as profoundly cruel, with the UK human rights organization Liberty stating that 'It's impossible to have a hostile environment which doesn't result in human rights abuses' (Liberty, 2020).

This chapter explores one aspect of the broader set of hostile environment policies: those that affect access to maternity care for pregnant migrants. Although healthcare during pregnancy is defined by the UK government as 'immediately necessary' and therefore should never be withheld even if a woman has no means of payment, the fear of being asked for payment upfront has meant women without a legal right to remain in the UK may delay or avoid accessing needed healthcare. This chapter situates 'accompaniment' as a central part of activist responses to hostile environment policies for pregnant and birthing people as local projects aimed at resisting the Hostile Environment policy and the vulnerability faced by pregnant and birthing women seek to support women navigating 'hostile healthcare' in the UK.

These projects also demonstrate how natural, alternative, or home birth movements – movements often associated with white, middle-class women's efforts to 'choose' place of birth and birth attendant – are linking birth politics to the concerns articulated by reproductive justice activists, in what Oparah with Black Women Birthing Justice (2015) call struggles for 'birth justice'. Connecting the disciplining of pregnant bodies to broader anxieties over migration and citizenship, this chapter considers how the work of midwives, doulas, birth companions, and activists involved in birth justice projects draw on the theological and radical social movement roots of accompaniment as political practice.

This chapter begins with a discussion of the UK's Hostile Environment policy and then moves to discuss its impact on pregnant people trying to access maternity care. I then discuss two activist responses to the Hostile Environment policy and the role of accompaniment in each. Accompaniment, in these projects, is imagined as a form of material and affective – and thus deeply political – response to the effects of the Hostile Environment policy and the wider public sentiments of animosity and racism directed at migrants on care for pregnancy and birth in the UK. In doing so, the chapter demonstrates how accompaniment, with its roots in liberation theology and religious practices of witnessing, has found a place in contemporary cultures of childbirth (Fannin and Perrier, 2019). It also seeks to link the telling of birth stories to feminist praxis, a connection elaborated through discussion of the uses of testimonial theatre and the ambiguities and contingencies of performance (Pratt and Johnston, 2017). The emergence of doula practice in the UK and elsewhere as a non-medical form of companionship through transformative life events is a resource for thinking about relationships and practices of solidarity in new ways. While not expressly or only articulated as feminist practices of solidarity, accompaniment suggests that the relational and affective dimensions of being with another can be profoundly transformative. The work of activists in the UK to accompany birthgiving for women and pregnant people seeking sanctuary in the UK is part of broader shift in the work of doulas and midwives from 'birth reform' centred on enhancing women's choices around pregnancy and birth, to reproductive justice, a movement that makes central the efforts to eliminate systemic inequalities that affect marginalized women's lives (Basile, 2012; Oparah and Bonaparte, 2015).

The Hostile Environment policy

In the UK context, 'right to remain' or 'leave to remain' is the permission granted by the state to migrants that establishes their rights to live and work in the country. The Hostile Environment policy created new procedures aimed at identifying those who might be living in the UK without such a legal right to remain. This could include refused asylum seekers, people arriving without documentation attesting to their sponsorship by an employer, individuals trafficked into the UK, and those overstaying tourist or educational visas. The measures put in place by the Home Office as part of the Hostile Environment policies were designed to affect almost all aspects of the life of a person in these conditions and sought to restrict the ability of migrants to access education, rental accommodation, driving licenses, bank accounts, and healthcare. Restrictions on accessing rental property, on accessing any form of social support or health care provided by the National Health Service, opening bank accounts and acquiring driving licenses were intended to make life as unbearable as possible for people in the country without documentation.

The Hostile Environment policy was developed in the wake of anti-immigration anxieties encouraged by conservative and nationalist political parties in the UK, whose rhetoric targeted the UK's membership in the European Union that permitted the unrestricted movement of EU citizens between EU countries. While undocumented migrants made up (and continue to make up) an extremely small proportion of the number of migrants (EU and non-EU) moving to the UK, the unrestricted movement of EU citizens and the targeting of migrants as racially and ethnically other were conflated in the discourse surrounding the country's need to 'control' migration, a rhetoric that strongly informed political and media coverage of parliamentary elections and the lead-up to the national vote on EU membership and the subsequent exit of the UK from the EU. Some of the most grievous effects of the application of the Hostile Environment policy involved the children and grandchildren of the 'Windrush' generation, whose parents and grandparents were recruited from the Caribbean as labourers in the post-WWII era but who were much later unable to provide documentation attesting to their legal right to remain in the UK. In some cases, people were forcibly deported to the Caribbean, places where many had never lived or had lived only for a short period when they were young children.

The Hostile Environment policies also introduced a whole set of controversial measures around document checking and data sharing between the Home Office and its immigration enforcement arm and other institutions such as schools and the National Health Service. The Hostile Environment policy's application at the interface with health care services, and the anecdotal evidence that clinicians themselves are unaware of the details of NHS charging policy, or of its exceptions, has moved the border into the hospital. As one lawyer working for the advocacy group, Maternity Action (Adiseshiah, 2017), stated:

> I now wonder how much longer I can maintain that the hospital is 'separate' from immigration control. After all, as I explained to [a

client], the hospital would contact the Home Office to find out her immigration status and to report any unpaid debt, thereby alerting the Home Office to her overstaying and her location.

Such data sharing agreements ended when a new Conservative government, and a new Home Secretary, Sajid Javid, attempted to rename the Hostile Environment policy the 'Compliant Environment' policy in 2018, although many of its other elements remain unchanged. The view that migration needed to be controlled and that migrants need to adopt a compliant view towards measures aimed at making their lives as difficult as possible were, and remain, a central feature of the Conservative government's policies on immigration.

Hostile Environment policies and care for pregnancy and birth

The Hostile Environment policy on accessing health services introduced a series of significant changes to the way the National Health Service operates. Immigration checks became the responsibility of health services. However, the Hostile Environment policy is part of a longer history, across both Conservative and Labour governments, of singling out migrants as a 'cost burden' on public services, or as Jean McHale and Elizabeth Speakman (2020, 573) write: 'long before the era of an explicit Government policy of hostile environment, the development of NHS overseas visitor charging regulations often proceeded in tandem with immigration controls'. The rhetoric couches anti-immigrant sentiment in a broader discourse on the need to ensure rational and efficient use of public resources (Shahvisi, 2019). In 2004, charges were introduced for non-citizens and those without leave to remain for health care (those deemed 'not ordinarily resident') for secondary health care provided by the National Health Service. Regulations since then have broadened the scope of charging for secondary and community health services, but not primary health care. In 2017, NHS hospitals were tasked with billing patients in advance for services based on estimated cost, and for including in a patient's medical record whether they are 'chargeable' or exempt.

Historically and since its inception, accessing health care that is free at the point of service has been one of the underpinning tenets of the NHS. The Hostile Environment Policy and its successive legislative changes turned the 'Cost Recovery' practices of the NHS, which had been in place since 2004 to ensure that non-residents cover the costs of care provided within the service, into a central feature of the state's anti-immigrant architecture. The charges for health services apply to anyone who migrates from outside of Europe and effectively put in place measures that allow the NHS to check the immigration status of patients and their eligibility for free or no payment access to health care. It also put in place the possibility for the NHS to request payment upfront for certain services.

Reflecting on the effects of this policy, Liberty, a human rights charity in the UK, argued: 'if you seem visibly foreign, these policies have created a kind of legitimacy and a mandate for racial discrimination against you', for asking you for your immigration status, for you to prove that you are part of this country (Liberty, nd). Racial discrimination and ill treatment by health care professionals is cited as one of the reasons for the disproportionately high maternal mortality and morbidity rates for black, mixed race, and Asian women in the UK. The most recent analysis of maternal mortality in the UK demonstrates that 'black women are five times more likely; mixed-ethnicity women are three times more likely; Asian women are twice as likely to die in pregnancy then white women (Knight et al, 2019). Moreover, black women are up to twice as likely to have a stillbirth at all gestational ages (Muglu et al, 2019)' (Khan, 2021, 100). These inequalities have been documented and known for at least two decades, but no demonstrable progress has been made to reduce them, or to better understand the reasons why such disparities exist. Black and minority ethnic women in the UK are more likely to face educational, housing, employment and income disadvantage, and the stress of disadvantage and racial discrimination affects health.

In this context, the Hostile Environment policy exacerbated the anxieties about accessing healthcare for undocumented women and introduced new ambiguities around the policy of charging for NHS services. Professional associations such as the Royal College of Midwives publicly voiced their opposition to the Hostile Environment policy, stating,

> midwives resent being made part of Cost Recovery architecture, finding it an anathema to the professional ethics of midwifery ... There is scant evidence that Cost Recovery actually helps the NHS. We need to recognise that vulnerable migrant women are not responsible for pressures in maternity services or the NHS generally; the government has a duty to give the NHS the resources it needs and should not be using NHS clinicians, including midwives, to patrol our borders and demonise some service users. (Walton, 2019)

Despite these criticisms, the policies continue to be enforced in hospitals, where the majority of midwives practice. The effects on maternity care have become clearer as they have been taken up and rolled out across the NHS. In 2019, a report analysing the cases of mothers who died in a two-year period cited that at least three maternal deaths could be linked to the impact of immigration status on women's access to healthcare and concerns over the cost of care (Knight et al, 2019). These were instances in which women had not accessed antenatal or prenatal care during their pregnancies due to concerns over being reported to the Home Office or Immigration enforcement, or over being unable to pay for care: 'exorbitant NHS charges for maternity care increase the likelihood that chargeable women (as well as other migrant or minority ethnic women who do not know whether they are chargeable) will book [antenatal appointments] late, if at all, or fail to attend necessary appointments' (Feldman et al, 2020). Despite how this policy is interpreted by pregnant people seeking care, the government's own Department of Health and Social Care states that in its guidance on NHS charging that 'all maternity services, including routine antenatal treatment, must be treated as being immediately necessary. No woman must ever be denied, or have delayed, maternity services' (Section 8.6, 'Guidance on implementing the overseas visitor charging regulations'). This includes routine antenatal appointments that should never be denied because of one's inability to pay. It is very clear from evidence gathered, however, that some maternity services are asking pregnant people for evidence of eligibility for free care (for example passport documenting their residency) or for payment in advance of care. In some cases, women being refused appointments with GPs who would then provide referrals to midwifery care, despite GP services being exempt from charging. What is clear from women's accounts (see Feldman, 2021) is that being asked to pay in advance works as a disincentive to women to seek care. This is even though maternity service is 'the only service explicitly classed as "immediately necessary" in the regulations, meaning it cannot be withheld even if a woman has no means to pay' (Knight et al, 2019).

While the practice of asking for payment in advance flouts both the spirit and indeed the letter of the law, the biopolitical context of what Natalie Fixmer-Oraiz (2019) calls 'homeland maternity' offers an analytical framing of the practices that surround the hostile birthing environment of the UK. In Fixmer-Oraiz's analysis, maternity care becomes a locus for defending the nation and the maternal body a site of political contestation. At points of crisis, the concentration of discipline and surveillance that accompanies pregnancy and birth are intensified. In this reading, control over the maternal body is not extraneous and supplemental to the apparatus of securitizing the nation in the early 21st century 'security state', but intrinsic to it. Fixmer-Oraiz's work centres on the juncture of the US politics of security culture, aimed both at enshrining the protection of the 'homeland' as a maternal duty and extending the protection of citizens of the nation to the 'uterine environment'. The intensification of political and legal efforts to limit access to abortion and the prosecution of pregnant people for violation of 'unborn child protection' laws situates the maternal body as simultaneously a danger and a service to the nation. Fixmer-Oraiz's (2019, p 4) concept of 'homeland maternity' points to the contemporary framing of 'how national security is tethered to securing the domestic and reproductive body'.

In the UK context, the securitizing of the reproductive body is framed through the practices of recouping the costs to the nation of care for migrant women or, indeed, any women deemed 'chargeable', replacing the hospitality of the social welfare system with hostility. While the legal right to care is enshrined in regulations that acknowledge the life-saving necessity of maternity care, the calculus of who must pay and who need not recalls the moral stratification of earlier laws stratifying the deserving from the undeserving poor. Fixmer-Oraiz situates US 'homeland maternity' as the nexus of postfeminist and governmental sensibilities that entangle motherhood with personal choice, risk, and individual responsibility and that enshrine whiteness and heteronormative family forms as the national ideal. In the UK, the maternity care charging schemes target women viewed as 'visibly' non-British and operate under the guise of financial accountability to the state's economic commitment to reduce the supposed drain of scarce national resources by migrants.

Countering these forms of biopolitical suppression of the birthing body and violence done to it has long been the cause of reproductive justice activists and theorists, for whom the rights of people to become pregnant (and to safely stay pregnant and give birth) or to avoid pregnancy is one part of a broader struggle for the economic, social, and political support for reproductive health. Fixmer-Oraiz's articulation of the myriad imagined forms of resistance to homeland maternity include a rethinking of the ability of struggles waged in the name of the 'maternal' to directly address questions of reproductive justice. She notes the many successful articulations of maternity and motherhood to *other* struggles, from protests against state violence to support for environmental struggles, and yet 'reproductive rights and justice seem to be the locus where maternal appeals are most silenced' (2019, p 154). Envisioning new ways to resist both pronatalism and ideologies of intensive mothering requires creative re-imaginings of family and kinship, and, importantly, new forms of accompaniment through pregnancy and birth.

In the terrain of the compliant environment for migrants and the hostile environment for birth, resistance to the enforced alienation, separation, loneliness, fear, and bewilderment that such policies seek to induce in those seeking maternity care takes many forms. This next section focuses on two projects, the first reflecting the national network of urban-based projects of welcome through the City of Sanctuary, which describes itself as 'simultaneously an organisation, a movement and a network' dedicated to welcoming refugees (Gill, 2018; see also City of Sanctuary, 2022).

The second draws on Sanctuary's language of solidarity, welcome, and community, but is independent of formal ties to the City of Sanctuary network. Based in Bristol, UK, Project Mama is a network of doulas, midwives, and other professionals trained to accompany pregnant people in need of support. As a project serviced by volunteer midwives, doulas, and other 'birth workers', Project Mama offers doula support and other forms of care to pregnant and birthing people who are experiencing vulnerability in some way during their pregnancies and births: refugees, asylum seekers, those with failed asylum applications, those who have been in abusive relationships or who have been trafficked or anticipate being alone and unsupported during their pregnancies and births.

Maternity Stream of Sanctuary

The Maternity Stream of the City of Sanctuary movement began in 2011 from the efforts of a group of women volunteering as 'Health Befrienders' at the Refugee Council in Leeds, UK. The Refugee Council is a charity organized to support refugees and people seeking asylum in the UK; the Health Befriending Network ran from 2011–2014 to advocate for refugees and people seeking asylum in the healthcare system through a peer support service. Befrienders were refugees or people seeking asylum who met regularly to support the work of the charity. Funding for the Health Befriender network could not be sustained beyond 2014, but by that time, the network had provided a platform for women involved to speak publicly about their experiences of maternity care, of pregnancy and birth, and of their experiences of seeking asylum in the UK (Haith-Cooper and McCarthy, 2015).

These activities developed into a network of asylum-seeking and refugee women, midwives, researchers, and activists who founded the 'Maternity Stream' in the City of Sanctuary UK charity. The City of Sanctuary UK seeks to create a 'movement' and a 'network' of welcome for those seeking sanctuary (https://cityofsanctuary.org). Within it, 'Streams' focus on a particular area or topic and bring networks together within and across cities. They 'encourage professionals or practitioners within a sector to come together and collaborate with other interested parties including people seeking sanctuary' (City of Sanctuary, 2022, p 12). The Maternity Stream of Sanctuary is now active in five cites in the UK: Leeds, Hull, Bradford, Manchester, and Swansea.

The role of the Maternity Stream of Sanctuary is to continue the work of training and support for refugee and asylum-seeking women to speak about their experiences of maternity care, and to tell their stories of pregnancy and birth alongside their experiences of seeking asylum. The Maternity Stream of Sanctuary also brings together a research network and seeks to publish data and evidence on the experiences of migrant, refugee and asylum-seeking pregnant and birthing women, documenting their experiences at the 'border' in the antenatal clinic and birthing suite, where women experience hostility, questioning of their right to healthcare, and interrogation over their ability to pay for maternal healthcare services.

The Maternity Stream of Sanctuary began from the principle that telling stories of one's own experiences could be an empowering and even therapeutic practice for women seeking asylum. These principles underpin the Maternity Stream of Sanctuary's role as a story-telling vehicle for exposing the stresses and difficulties faced by refugee and asylum-seeking women during their pregnancies and births in the UK. Resources provided by the Stream aimed at health care providers and local authorities draw on testimonies and accounts of experiences with the healthcare system in the UK by refugee and asylum-seeking women to recount the complex dynamics, histories, and social and cultural contexts that shape their experiences of maternity care. These stories are presented alongside information about the UK immigration system and the complexities that migrants must navigate to access healthcare, housing and other services. For example, definitions of a migrant's status may be little understood by healthcare providers who have never personally interacted with the UK's immigration system, for example, the differences between economic migrant, asylum seeker, and 'No Recourse to Public Funds' status, which prohibits a person from seeking help with housing or receiving other public benefits. Professionals are urged to consider how ambiguities over the status of a migrant seeking healthcare are shaped by the broader public discourses surrounding immigration:

> The media in the UK often uses these terms synonymously. This can confuse the audience as to who is an economic migrant and who is a person seeking sanctuary. It is important for people promoting inclusion and welcome to understand the difference between individuals seeking sanctuary and individuals moving across borders for other reasons. (City of Sanctuary, 2022b, p 7)

Resources aimed at health care professionals also seek to raise awareness about the specificities of how people seeking sanctuary might experience pregnancy, birth, and labour 'as traumatic for a whole host of reasons that may not be related to maternity services' (2022b, p 4). Prolonged residence in a refugee camp may have affected women's mental and physical health and increased their risk of experiencing sexual and other forms of violence, and women may want to choose a caesarean or refuse vaginal examinations to avoid retraumatization. Practices such as co-sleeping, circumcision of male infants, and postnatal confinement may be expected by women and their families but are not generally supported or offered by the National Health Service.

In highlighting the differences between medico-cultural practices surrounding pregnancy, labour, and birth in the UK and elsewhere, the Maternity Stream of Sanctuary project seeks to both individualize women as bringing their own desires, expectations, and wishes for their pregnancies, births, and relationships with their children and their families as well as prompt caregivers' own personal and collective reflections on how 'stereotypes might influence the care you give' (p 54). Producing resources that centre the testimonies of women seeking sanctuary thus foregrounds the role of the Maternity Stream in making space for 'witnessing' and making visible and public another's suffering. Like other projects of witnessing the experiences of migrants (see Pratt et al, 2020), the Maternity Stream of Sanctuary seeks to raise awareness of the complex experiences of women before and after their arrival in the UK and to generate more complicated responses, reflections, and relations of empathy.

Project Mama and 'radical nurturing'

Project Mama is a Bristol-based charity, established in 2018 by a 'hive of midwives, activists, doulas and birth companions who form a peer network of skills, support and solidarity for women and their children' (https://projectmama.org/our-story/). The Project's aim is to support pregnant people who are migrant to the UK and are experiencing or have experienced mental health issues, are survivors of violence or abuse, or who may have been trafficked to the UK, and may not be supported by a birth partner. 'Mother companions' provide support and accompaniment beginning at any stage of pregnancy, birth, and the first eight weeks of infancy. Support is both emotional and physical (especially during labour, for example massage, breathing and relaxation techniques) and also includes helping navigate NHS care and entitlements during pregnancy and after birth. Mother companions work in groups of three and are either trained doulas or midwives or have comparable experiences with pregnancy and birth. The role of the Mother Companion is a voluntary one, and the services provided by Project Mama also included, prior to the COVID-19 pandemic, a drop-in space ('MAMAhub') that offers yoga sessions, a home-cooked meal, and a place to socialize and pick up nappies and baby clothing. The services provided by the charity are free to access.

Reflecting on the identification of "women" as their primary clients, Project Mama articulated its support for trans and non-binary people experiencing pregnancy and birth, preferring the 'gender-additive' language of both women and people to describe the charity's clients ('Why "mama"?', 2022). In the last two years, the charity supported 63 mothers who gave birth to 47 babies. Of those, nearly half (30) were seeking asylum at the time of their pregnancies and births. This reflects the precarious circumstances under which asylum seekers must live in the UK, where the law prohibits paid work for up to 12 months while awaiting a decision on an asylum claim (in comparison to the EU, which gives asylum seekers the right to seek work after nine months waiting for a decision on their claim, the US [after a six-month wait], or Canada, where claimants can seek work immediately). In 2020–2021, the Project supported women from 24 different countries of origin, with nearly half (15) from countries in East Africa (Eritrea, Somalia, Kenya, and Sudan).

While operating outside the formal health care structure provided by the NHS, Project Mama is integrated into the referral system for refugee support in the city of Bristol and in the welfare and health services that are provided by the city or by other charitable organizations to support maternal and migrant/refugee health. In this way, the organization is both an 'outsider' to the formal provision of NHS maternity health services and is networked into the state and non-state support structures with other advocacy organizations or services that put women in touch with the Project. And although Project Mama does not explicitly identify as a feminist political project, its expression of solidarity and support to confront the hostile environment for pregnancy and birth speaks directly to the articulation of both the reproductive justice and birth reform movements.

The relationship between birth activism and feminist movements has been complex and often fraught, especially where such sought to de-essentialize motherhood and to elaborate a critical perspective on feminine subjectivity and its relationship to the maternal. Project Mama's mission resonates with the women-centred alternative health and birth movements that identify pregnancy and birth as under-supported by conventional medical care. Of its five guiding principles – 'Solidarity', 'Radical Nurturing', 'Reinforcing Resilience', 'Cultivating Community' and 'Championing Cultural Safety', Radical Nurturing articulates this vision:

> Our trauma-informed practice is built on the fundamental belief that all pregnant people need compassion, support, care, and space leading up to the birth of their children. It is our belief that women have the right to be supported through their pregnancy and beyond in order to harness their power and to give birth safely, in spite of political barriers. (https://projectmama.org/our-guiding-principles/, accessed March 2022)

At the same time, the work of the 'radical doula' centres on a notion of nurturing as a right which all birthing people should enjoy. The doula's work of accompaniment through pregnancy and birth began, as Monica Basile writes of the US context, through efforts to de-medicalize childbirth in the 1970s and 1980s. In the 1990s, the number of birth workers identifying as doulas and articulating an increasingly professional identity for the work of emotional and non-medical accompaniment began to grow significantly.

This emergence involved, as it does now in the 'mainstreaming' of doula services in some hospitals in the US, for example, concerns over the co-optation of the radical potential of the birth companion to advocate for a mother's wishes, choices, and concerns. Despite these concerns, doula work began to align with calls for recognizing the limitations of a reproductive rights approach to fertility, pregnancy, and birth and for the greater recognition of LGBT rights, prisoners' rights, and of the inextricability of struggles for reproductive, economic, and racial justice. The practice of accompaniment expanded out of the spaces of pregnancy and birth into other domains. There are doulas supporting individuals undergoing fertility treatment, doulas accompanying women to terminate their pregnancies and through miscarriage. In addition to support during pregnancy and birth, doulas may also specialize in supporting lactation and breastfeeding, especially in the early critical period after birth when many struggle to breastfeed despite their desires to continue. Doulas are also working to support gender transition. The work of the end-of-life or 'death doula' also focuses on accompanying an individual through the last stages of their life.

Working as mother companions, doulas or other trained birth workers involved in Project Mama might accompany women to antenatal appointments, to their births, and to their homes for visits after birth. They may talk to them about their desires, as well as their fears, for their pregnancies and births. They may provide information about women's options, plans and choices for birth, but they are also, importantly, co-present, talking, sharing, and *being with* the women they support. As testimonials gathered by Project Mama (2021, p 7) attest, this support can involve sharing information about moving through the NHS and its procedures and systems. One client commented: 'Before I just came to Bristol and I didn't know how to book any appointments, now that they have supported me and explained I am more used to it and understand the processes.' Mother companions were also involved in explaining the kinds of choices women could make about their births in the context of midwife-led care that is the norm for most births in the UK: 'It's hard to explain, but they tell me details, they tell me the options I can have, such as water delivery or natural delivery and explain very well the pain relief. ... They tell me everything about positions to help me, like yoga ball, they tell me everything' (2021, p 7). And, finally, mother companions also offer to listen, to provide the support that women might not feel they can seek from midwives working in time-pressured maternity services, and importantly, to accompany women through their pregnancies and births:

> I don't have anyone how to speak my opinion wasn't confident to talk to people. Project MAMA like my mother and my sister, I feel like I speak to them freely. I talk to them like my family. They really support me. At the time I was alone and really appreciate Project MAMA. Many people don't have this support. Really appreciate. If

you concerned about baby or pregnancy they go with you help you and go to appointment. (Project Mama, 2021, p 7)

Accompaniment and a feminist politics of solidarity

Reflecting on the significance of accompaniment as a feminist practice of solidarity recalls the significant work of UK feminist movements to provide safe shelter and access to healthcare, in recognition that state provision of housing and of healthcare services did not adequately recognize the paternalism and violence faced by women (see Bowstead, 2019; Olszynko-Gryn, 2019), a paternalism that looms large in accounts of the politics of the UK women's liberation movement. The fraying of the state's paternalism during the neoliberal years of Thatcher's premiership and the anti-immigrant sentiment that has become part of conservative political discourse have made the pregnant and birthing bodies of migrants into targets for state intervention and control.

Efforts like those of the Maternity City of Sanctuary and Project Mama seek to create forms of protection and support *beyond* the state but without abandoning or rejecting the universalist ethos of a National Health Service that should provide 'care for all'. Confronting racial and anti-immigrant discrimination and hostility in the healthcare system situates these projects as new forms of 'birth justice' that view the efforts of women's health activists to expand access to choice in maternity services as limited if not completely irrelevant to the material concerns of poor and minority ethnic women. Birth justice projects draw on the perspectives and praxis of the reproductive justice movement and its critique of the 'multiple ways in which women of color and poor women are denied reproductive freedom' (Oparah with Black Women Birthing Justice 2015, p 6).

What lessons might accompaniment have for broader feminist politics of solidarity? On the one hand, pregnancy and birth are events of dramatic bodily transformation, hormonal fluctuation, biophysical change, and emotional and affective intensity. They could be defined, therefore, as moments of great vulnerability. The language of the vulnerable pregnant person, and the vulnerability of the birth giver, certainly underscores how the work of the Maternity City of Sanctuary and Project Mama imagine the pregnant and birthgiving person as defined by their need: for care, for shelter, for advocacy, and for welcome. The vulnerability created by the Hostile Environment policy also exacerbates what may be some pregnant and birthing people's vulnerabilities as migrants without documentation, whose immigration status may have changed, or who may be vulnerable because of the ways their migration to the UK puts them in positions of dependence on others (Feldman, 2021). Reflecting on the discriminatory way in which charging for NHS maternity services affects women who may be in the UK without documentation or as visitors without long-term leave to remain, Rayah Feldman (2021, p 462) remarks: 'The individual billing of NHS patients is particularly inappropriate in the case of maternity care, where women's partners are involved in creating the need for such care, but are entirely absolved from responsibility for contributing to it financially.'

This is compounded by the way that immigration services and the discourses surrounding medical tourism and the 'burden' of overseas visitors on NHS services has tended to 'regard women migrants solely in terms of their presumed reproductive intentions' (p 462). And yet, the doula as dialogical partner, guide, translator, advocate, and support speaks to how the transformations wrought by pregnancy and birth offer a way to theorize accompaniment as a form of feminist solidarity, and recentres birth justice – the bringing together of reproductive justice and birth activism – as central to feminist practices of solidarity. As Jennifer Hyndman and Johanna Reynolds (2020) write, these practices also point to more embodied and affective notions of 'security' for migrants. Solidarity in accompaniment speaks to Hyndman and Reynold's concept of an embodied notion of *ontological security*, a notion of 'feeling safe' that is, in their view, self-authorized, local, urban. What might not self-evidently be viewed as a feminist practice, given the complexity with which feminism and feminists confront the maternal (and by no means is the maternal inherently feminist; it offers a possibility among many other biopolitical possibilities), is the ground from which feminist solidarity can spring and be shared.

References

Adiseshiah, K. (2017). 'Creating a hostile environment in maternity care #RefugeeWeek2017'. *Maternity Action*, blog, 21 June. Available from: https://maternityaction.org.uk/2017/06/creating-a-hostile-environment-in-maternity-care/ [Accessed 23 March 2023].

Basile, M.R. (2012). *Reproductive Justice and Childbirth Reform: Doulas as Agents of Social Change*. PhD thesis, University of Iowa. Available from: https://iro.uiowa.edu/esploro/outputs/doctoral/Reproductive-justice-and-childbirth-reform-doulas/9983776600802771?institution=01IOWA_INST [Accessed 23 March 2023].

Bowstead, J.C. (2019). 'Spaces of Safety and More-than-safety in Women's Refuges in England'. *Gender, Place & Culture* 26(1): 75–90.

City of Sanctuary (2022a). 'City of Sanctuary Charter 2022–2025'. Available from: https://cityofsanctuary.org/2022/02/02/charter/ [Accessed 14 April 2022].

City of Sanctuary (2022b). *Maternity Stream of Sanctuary Resource Pack*. Available from: https://maternity.cityofsanctuary.org/resources [Accessed 24 April 2022].

Fannin, M. and Perrier, M. (2019). '"Birth work" Accompaniment and PhD Supervision: An Alternative Feminist Pedagogy for the Neoliberal University'. *Gender and Education* 31(1): 136–52.

Feldman, R. (2021). 'NHS Charging for Maternity Care in England: Its Impact on Migrant Women'. *Critical Social Policy* 41(3): 447–67.

Feldman, R, Bewley, S. Bragg, R. and Beeks, M. (2020). 'Hostile Environment Prevents Women from Accessing Maternal Care'. *British Medical Journal* 368(8238): m968.

Fixmer-Oraiz, N. (2019). *Homeland Maternity: US Security Culture and the New Reproductive Regime*. Urbana: University of Illinois Press.

Gill, N. (2018). 'The Suppression of Welcome'. *FENNIA* 196(1): 88–98.

Haith-Cooper, M. and McCarthy, R. (2015). 'Striving for Excellence in Maternity Care: The Maternity Stream of the City of Sanctuary'. *British Journal of Midwifery* 23(9): 648–52.

Hyndman, J. and Reynolds, J. (2020). 'Beyond the Global Compacts: Re-imagining Protection'. *Refuge* 36(1): 66–74.

Khan, Z. (2021). 'Ethnic Health Inequalities in the UK's Maternity Services: A Systematic Literature Review'. *British Journal of Midwifery* 29(2): 100–7.

Kirkup, J. and Winnett, R. (2012). 'Theresa May interview: "We're going to give illegal migrants a really hostile reception"'. *The Telegraph*, 25 May.

Knight, M., Bunch, K., Tuffnell, D., Shakespeare, J., Kotnis, R., Kenyon, S. and Kurinczuk, J.J. (eds) (2019). *Saving Lives, Improving Mothers' Care – Lessons Learned to Inform Maternity Care from the UK and Ireland: Confidential Enquiries into Maternal Deaths and Morbidity 2015–17*. Oxford: National Perinatal Epidemiology Unit, University of Oxford.

Liberty (2020). 'Liberty Calls for End to Hostile Environment as Immigration Bill Returns'. Available from: w.ww.libertyhumanrights.org.uk/issue/liberty-calls-for-end-to-hostile-environment-as-immigration-bill-returns/ [Accessed 20 April 2022].

Liberty (nd) 'Hostile Environment'. Available from: www.libertyhumanrights.org.uk/fundamental/hostile-environment/ [Accessed 20 April 2022].

McHale, J.V. and Speakman, E.M. (2020). 'Charging "Overseas Visitors" for NHS treatment, from Bevan to Windrush and Beyond'. *Legal Studies* 40: 565–88.

Muglu, J., Rather, H., Arroyo-Manzano, D., Bhattacharya, S., Balchin, I., Khalil, A. et al (2019). 'Risks of Stillbirth and Neonatal Death with Advancing Gestation at Term: A Systematic Review and Meta-Analysis of Cohort Studies of 15 Million Pregnancies'. *PLOS Medicine* 16(7): e1002838.

Olszynko-Gryn, J. (2019). 'The Feminist Appropriation of Pregnancy Testing in 1970s Britain'. *Women's History Review* 28(6): 869–94.

Oparah, J.C. with Black Women Birthing Justice. (2015). 'Beyond Coercion and Malign Neglect: Black Women and the Struggle for Birth Justice', in J.C. Oparah and A.D. Bonaparte (eds) *Birthing Justice: Black Women, Pregnancy and Childbirth*. New York: Routledge.

Oparah, J.C. and Bonaparte, A.D. (eds) (2015). *Birthing Justice: Black Women, Pregnancy and Childbirth*. New York: Routledge.

Pratt, G. and Johnston, C. (2017). 'Crossing Oceans: Testimonial theatre, Filipina Migrant Labor, Empathy, and Engagement'. *GeoHumanities* 3(2): 279–91.

Pratt, G., Zell, S., Johnston, C. and Venzon, H. (2020). 'Performing Nanay in Winnipeg: Filipino Labour Migration to Canada (Creative Intervention)'. *Studies in Social Justice* 14: 55–66.

Project Mama (2021). *Annual Report*. Project Mama: Bristol.

Shahvisi, A. (2019). 'Austerity or Xenophobia? The Causes and Costs of the "Hostile Environment" in the NHS'. *Health Care Analysis* 27: 202–19.

Walton, G. (2019). 'Duty of Care? The Impact on Midwives of NHS Charging for Maternity Care'. Maternity Action. Available from: www.maternityaction.org.uk/wp-content/uploads/DUTY-OF-CARE-with-cover-for-upload.pdf [Accessed 6 June 2023].

8

Respectful Relationalities: Researching with Those Who Contest or Have Concerns about Changes in Sexual and Gender Legislation and Cultures

Kath Browne and Catherine Nash

Introduction

Feminist and queer methodologies emphasize the creation of research through relational spaces of betweenness, particularly between researchers and those who participate (Haraway, 1988; Stanley and Wise, 1993; Rose, 1995; Collins, 1990/2000; Nash, 2010). These spaces are negotiated through not only research practices and processes created by the researcher/s, but also by the ways in which interactions play out in research spaces (Rose, 1993, 1995). Attending to this relationality foregrounds the complexity of power relations in the research process; where positionalities and their effects are taken seriously but where assumptions about hierarchical power relations are continually troubled. Power is then seen as diffuse, circulatory, and productive of effects, rather than as something straightforwardly held by some in a hierarchical relationship with others (Bondi, 1990; Browne and Nash, 2010; Kelly and Gurr, 2019). Research participants can be in positions of disproportionate social, cultural, or economic power and privilege in relation to the researcher, and this can influence the research process and outcomes in important ways (for example see feminist research with 'elites': Puwar, 2001; Glass and Cook, 2020). This conceptualization of the nature of research spaces emphasizes practices and relationalities with the caution that research spaces should be understood as *interactional and negotiated* spaces, or in other words, as relational. They are formed via the research priorities and processes created by the researcher/s with imagined audiences, and through the interactions that play out across the lifetime of a research project. Relationality is operationalized in undertaking geographical research in order that we might ask questions about the possibilities and limitations of communicating or empathizing across difference and engaging the 'other' (Nash, 2010; Rose, 1993, 1995; 1997).

In the contemporary moment, heteroactivism associated anti-gender ideologies are increasing in many parts of the world (Correa et al, 2018; Nash and Browne, 2017, 2020). It is therefore vital for feminist and queer geographers to interrogate how hard-won sexual and gender rights, including same-sex marriage, abortion, and trans rights, are being challenged and contested across different geographical contexts (Browne et al, 2018; Browne and Nash, 2019; Nash and Browne, 2020). In this chapter, we focus on research that engages with those who see the heterosexual family as the pinnacle of society and who believe that marriage should only occur between biological men and women and/or that families should be based on a heterosexual union. Whether this research can be considered 'activist' is contentious, as activism can seek particular forms of social change, and yet in seeking to work with difference differently, this research promotes another (and different) interrogation of (and the development of potential approaches to) social cohesion and power. Our research also engages with those who are concerned about the legalization of abortion and/or people who disagree with, or question, transgender inclusion policies. We are interested in how such individuals and groups experience what have been termed new sexual and gendered landscapes (Browne and Nash, 2017), that is, the resulting geographies arising from the extensive legal, social, and political changes in the praxis of sexual and gender rights in some places in the early 21st century. This enables an exploration of the broader sexual and gender landscapes that shape everyday worlds, as well as how the circulation of power produces effects that are often unexpected, and unanticipated, as well as those that contest hard-won changes in sexual and gender legislations and cultures. Thus, while activism is often conceptualized as working with those you agree to fight the 'the other side', establishing communication across difference could also be conceptualized as a radical act, where presumptions of 'echo chambers' and 'polarization' are apparent.

Relationality in the research process needs further consideration when researching those who might object to, have concerns about, or actively reject the values of the researcher. Relationalities are grounded in positionalities that we create and that are created for us. This research was created and is led by Kath Browne with Catherine J. Nash who, for over two decades, have undertaken LGBT and queer geographical work that seeks to empower

LGBTQ people and others to work for those marginalized by gender or sexual hierarchies. This, along with information available on all the researchers, particularly but not only Browne/Nash, through the internet, can pose a 'credibility' problem for the project (along with other risks to researchers) for those we seek to engage with as they distrust our motivations given our past work. As this chapter shows, we are not seen as 'on their side' and therefore are understood as dangerous and the research as not to be trusted. Awareness of these perceptions and how our imagined participants might engage with us, drove us to create a clear ethos to guide the research project from the outset, grounded in what we call 'respectful relationalities'. This research is different to other work we have undertaken, yet grounded in it, including our deep personal and professional understandings of how (dis)comfort/alienation in space is experienced.

This chapter will explore some of how the project works/ed to create respectful research spaces with those who contest or continue to be concerned about sexual and gender equalities. Respect is thus understood through what we do, or do not do, through our relationalities, rather than something that can be easily defined or delineated. It has various effects, only some of which we can explore here. We begin this chapter by examining why we think it is important to engage with those who remain, variously opposed to, and/ or at odds with contemporary sexual and gender transformation. We then explore the creation of a research project that employs what we call respectful relationalities to aid us in working across differences and the problematics of labels and groupings in bounding research. Following this, we consider how we envisage writing up this research, recognizing that this will be formed within the ethos of the project and cannot be predicted in advance. The final section will outline some of the emerging considerations of the affects/ effects of this research on the researchers, recognizing that the negotiations of power relations are not neutral experiences and that negotiations in this arena can be difficult. Overall, this chapter contends that the relational power relations that constitute research are continually being negotiated, and require a flexible approach to research design, implementation, and write up. These processes have effects on all involved.

Why look 'beyond opposition'?

This chapter draws on the project Beyond Opposition,[1] a research project originating in the work that the authors undertook/began in 2012 on heteroactivism, that is, activism that seeks to oppose LGBT rights by reiterating the place and importance of heteronormative legislative and policy regulation together with related social and cultural practices (Nash and Browne, 2020). Heteroactivism conceptualizes the move away from the vilification of certain forms of gender and sexualities, towards discourses that argue for the 'best for society and best for children' in opposition to sexual and gender issues (Browne and Nash, 2014; Nash and Browne, 2015). This also led to a recognition of the emergence of seemingly more tangential discourses about 'parental rights' and 'freedom of speech' that surfaced in public debates (Nash and Browne, 2020). At the time, we were examining what we understood to be 'fringe' groups contesting issues such as teaching about same-sex families in Ontario or opposing same-sex marriage in the UK (Browne and Nash, 2014; Nash and Browne, 2015). However, it became apparent over the course of our research that these groups/organizations were increasingly well-organized, mobilized, and were discussing issues and building alliances transnationally (Nash and Browne, 2020). Their activism often rested on stories and experiences about the impact of LGBT equalities and rights on the lives of 'ordinary people', when, for example, individuals lost jobs for expressing their opinions in the workplace or found themselves (or their young children) accused of bullying in school settings for questioning other trans/genderqueer students. It was clear that these experiences were unexpected and unwelcome and that these negative experiences were deployed by specific groups as a reason to target LGBT rights and equalities in the courts and in the media for their own protection (Browne and Nash, 2018; Nash and Browne, 2019). The Beyond Opposition research project is focused on understanding these experiences and on how these experiences are represented and understood by groups and organizations in their activities online and in conference spaces.

In contrast to the extensive literature on the limitations of legislation in addressing the exclusions of queers and others marginalized because of their sexual and gender identities, lives, and expressions (for example, Browne and Bakshi, 2013; Duggan, 2003), there is little work on the experiences of those who perhaps find themselves on 'the wrong side' of contemporary political, social, and legislative changes around sexualities and genders. The Beyond Opposition project is, at the time of writing (in 2021), seeking to explore these experiences in the hopes of offering a fuller picture of the effects of sexual and gender legislative and cultural changes for those who encounter them in negative ways or who do not agree with such changes. The focus is on those who seek to reinstate some version of heteronormativities, those who are pro-life and those who are opposed to/concerned about inclusions that contest their understandings of sex and/or who should have access to women's spaces. In seeking understanding, we are attempting to move beyond the binary (and oppositional) framing of marginalization/privilege, to conceptualize the complexities of, for example, occupying both heterosexual positionalities while also finding oneself subject to state/workplace sanctions or to potential state intervention and surveillance of your family because of your deeply held views/family values. The research begins from the assumption that how contestations over gender and sexualities play out in everyday life is complex and that the people engaged in these contestations occupy multiple, and sometimes seemingly contradictory, positions. The project therefore seeks to think differently about binaries and boundaries, without negating the material effects that such binary categorizations and boundary-making can have. This means paying attention to experiences where certain forms of privilege, such as occupying a heterosexual positionality, does not offer protection from other forms of marginalization, such as being subject to state surveillance.

A key purpose of this research is to understand how these experiences are contributing to, and perpetuating, the myriad social divisions that make up contemporary social and cultural life. The latter part of the project, which is not discussed in this chapter, will experiment in engaging across difference using workshops focusing on issues of social polarization and cohesion. By engaging in this high-risk project, the Beyond Opposition team is exploring the possibilities of 'unpredictable discoveries and potentially new modes of interaction with others' (Keating, 2013, p 19). It is investigating the potentialities associated with working beyond binaries to create new social, cultural, and political possibilities of engaging difference differently. The Beyond Opposition project hopes to offer a different (scholarly and practical) approach to social division and polarization, one that poses the question, how can we relate to each other when 'hearts and minds' are not altered in relation to their opinions on sexual and gender rights despite extensive legal/social/cultural changes/debates/education initiatives? What other ways might we engage with differences? We began this journey by developing the notion of respectful relationalities as a means of engaging and conducting research between researchers such as ourselves with our previous intellectual commitments, and participants whose political and social positioning would suggest that we are at odds with each other.

Respectful relationalities: creating space for researching across difference

Relationalities are always about where we are positioned, and while Beyond Opposition seeks to consider more than 'sides', these 'sides' are nonetheless manifest through the research process. We are placed in particular positions and on specific 'sides', namely pro-LGBT and trans rights, especially given our previous writing and associated work. This requires a specific engagement with the relationalities of the data collection process, and naming aspects that might otherwise be assumed if we positioned ourselves as 'on the same side'. Our research design is a fluid process that adapts over the course of the project and partly in response to participant engagements. This is particularly important in a project such as this where trust and confidence are an issue. Where we are seen as 'the other', methodological and practice changes can show listening, awareness, and engagement, that can enable a project such as this to collect data.

Our desire to institute respectful relationalities as central to the research design began by considering our potential participants. The information to draw on was limited given our previous research has been desk-based or covert (Maguire et al, 2019; Nash and Browne, 2020). We thus drew on what we could know to consider how they could read us. This created a clear sense of how we would ask people to be involved, how we would engage with them and what they could expect from the project. We decided to develop a public-facing ethos statement for the project that detailed (alongside a privacy document and ethics forms) how this project would be undertaken and what participants could expect from the research, the researchers, and the project overall. This is located on our website (https://beyondopposition.org/about-the-project/#AboutTheEthos) and guides our practice in recruitment, interviews, questionnaire design, and will also inform analysis and write up. In this section, we explore how we sought to engage potential participants through a respectful relational approach to difference, specifically focusing on how respect was manifest in the ethos of the project.

As with all feminist and queer research, and indeed other research that explores listening to those who are seen/read as 'other' to the author/researcher (Horchschild, 2016), the research starts with affording respect to participants and giving them space to tell their stories. This is perhaps what all researchers who work ethically begin with, however, when researching the groups in our research, it is not a given where the aims and purposes of the research differ from ours. Before recruiting participants,[2] we designed the ethos to be explicit about this. The ethos on the website reads: 'We are academics who believe in respecting people's lives and experiences and reporting them as they tell us.'

After starting with a statement of the research aims, this part of the ethos seeks to establish our grounding in respect, namely the respect for people's lives and their experiences. This 'as they tell us' means that we will report their experiences without seeking to distort or interpret them in ways that seek to belittle or undermine them or their experiences. Respect here moves from the telling to the reporting, and back to encourage engagement with the research. This means that the linearity of the research (recruitment, data collection, write up) is disrupted, iterative, and mutually informative, which we will explore next when we examine recruitment, and the research spaces that are created.

In contrast to our expectations, some who considered participating read our academic positioning through the lens of 'unbiased' researchers. However, more often potential participants have also cited our backgrounds, research work, and political practices as evidence of 'bias' and that the research and the write-up will not engage them fairly or accurately represent their views. While the Beyond Opposition research recruitment via email contacts, social media advertising, and attending events is undertaken by the postdoctoral researchers, all the research team can be assessed, evaluated, and implicated in the decision about whether a participant takes part. Who we are can be researched through our webpage which names the project team, and a quick internet search often places us on a particular 'side' in the eyes of those we seek to involve. However, this 'side' can move from 'leftist professor' to 'far right hate group'.

Similar to queer thinking around identities, while theoretically sides are problematic and easily deconstructed, Beyond Opposition and its researchers can be or are defined as being on a particular 'side'. Second, our stated goal of engaging with other's 'experiences' was read as a 'set up' or a trojan horse to gain information to be used against those concerned about sexual and gendered changes. This can lead to a disengagement with outright condemnation of the project or result in curious (and cautious) and tentative engagement questions about our intentions via email and social media messages/comments. Because of this, and our limited networks within key arenas, our recruitment process was initially slow and iterative. Starting with key organizations, we sought in the first year of the project to reach new audiences, by building trust and a relationship with those who have engaged with us. Their experiences of interviews and questionnaires which we hope are positive, we thought would be crucial, particularly where conferences and other events cannot be attended in-person because of COVID restrictions to develop trust and rapport about the integrity of the project. However, targeted social media adverts, particularly on Facebook proved more effective in engaging and involving participants. It brought more people in to respond to questionnaires and to contact the team for interviews. In social media spaces, such 'sides' can be even more pronounced, and demands to declare, place oneself and denounce the 'other' were apparent in the adverts. The polarization of sides can also make recruitment problematic, but not impossible. Our experience is that participants critique us before, during, and after interviews and yet still consent to the data being used as part of the project.

Respectful relationalities across difference require trust, such that the process of encountering and re-encountering the research is necessary. In this research we needed to be patient and create opportunities to approach us with curiosity, to go away and come back, and to gain an understanding of the project through that back and forth. This process is also often visible when people fill out the online questionnaire. There are many incomplete attempts – checking us and the questionnaire out before it is complete. Similarly, interviews can take some time to set up with numerous email exchanges and telephone conversations. This coming and going and returning characterizes much of the participant engagement and their process of getting to know us in order for them to participate in the research.

We also seek to create respectful relationalities in the interview setting where participants are asked to discuss their everyday spaces. The focus on their experiences of space centralizes geography as the key framing for the project but is also critical for enacting respectful relationalities. Given the researchers background, participants often come to an interview anticipating a 'fight' around diverse ideologies/views/opinions and can be surprised to find the focus is on their experiences of everyday spaces – where they go or do not go, and how they feel in these places. In exploring how their views affect how they experience space, the purpose of the data-gathering process is not to criticize their views, instead it is to understand their geographies. Those of us who are queer/geographers deeply understand how experiences in space can be troubling as well as central to our experience of our identities and our relations with others. Thus, for the purposes of this project, respectful relationalities are not about creating spaces to debate, but instead we are engaging in ways that develop our understandings of their experiences of space through their stories and narratives. Yet, participants do want to tell us their views, and understanding them can help us to place and engage their experiences. This means we do listen to their opinions, without questioning them, even where they are very different to our own, and can be upsetting. More than this, it can feel as though, and we are accused by other activists, of being 'complicit'. This charge is not inaccurate and reflects the compromises of thinking and working in ways that seek to work across polarized differences, rather than towards specific forms of social justice.

It is clear that as we seek to create research spaces with participants, they are also creating space for their participation in the project – an engagement which feels very difficult. This requires trust and iterative engagements that can work across difference in ways that enable, as well as constrain research. Only some will be involved, and while all research is partial and the purpose was not to get a 'representative sample', it is important to acknowledge that this research is created through those who are willing to participate and have developed some trust in us and the research process. For those who recognize 'sides' and yet are still willing to engage, they offer valuable understandings of their lives, and also make space for creating research across difference.

Difference and research flexibilities

Learning and adapting is a key aspect of respectful relationalities, as well as a key part of broader research design and practice. Overtly showing consideration and transformation can support research recruitment, as well as indicate important attributes about the people who are part of the research. To date, in the Beyond Opposition research, a key learning aspect has been around categorization, labels, and homogenization of participants, in ways that reflect queer arguments regarding power, limitations, and contestations.

The creation of labels, the grouping together of individuals and organizations and the use of pre-existing identities for recruitment was found to be both problematic and pragmatic (Browne and Nash, 2010). From the outset, we worked to carefully design the website and project materials to recognize and respect a diverse range of audiences, including those who would be supportive of contemporary sexual and gender changes as well as those who are concerned about these changes. However, this was a learning process and required us to be flexible and adaptive, rather than sticking closely with our initial definitions and grounding labels, informing not only our data collection but the data itself.

When Beyond Opposition was initially envisaged, the term that we used to categorize or describe our possible participants was those individuals or groups 'opposed to sexual and gender rights and equalities'. However, it became clear early on that we were also interested in those who were 'concerned about' (as well as opposed to) these issues. Second, we used the phrase 'rights and equalities' to encompasses a range of topics such as abortion and reproductive rights, changes to sex and relationships education in schools, changes to gender recognition and identities, and changes to same-sex marriage and LGBT parenting. This was also problematic for participants, where they understood themselves as supporting 'rights and equalities', including the 'rights of the unborn child' and 'women's equalities'.

Some key issues also emerged in deploying these categorization and groupings that appeared to create homogenizations. Beyond Opposition participants argued that the people we are including are a diverse and complex grouping, that refuse easy categorization or delineation. For some participants, finding themselves grouped or associated with others that they would oppose in other circumstances was troubling. Participants who supported certain issues (for example, abortion or same-sex marriage) may not support, or have concerns about other issues such as trans rights. This can mean that they do not see themselves as similar to those who are pro-life or those who believe that a woman's place is in the home. As one participant stated: "It's beyond opposition – that's a good name for your project. I've always been pro-choice and pro-LGBT but now that I've experienced the radical activism that's behind the trans-rights social justice movement, it's truly scary".

This participant notes the need to move beyond sides, that 'opposition' exists even within the groups we seek to speak to/with and some participants rejected being 'lumped in' with certain others (including far-right groups, Nash and Browne, 2020). In both interviews and questionnaire responses, potential participants and groups do not use the same language or have the same understanding of key terms. Participants do not all share language, identities, politics, or worldviews. Yet, their experiences of being concerned about, or opposed to, legislative, political, cultural, and social changes in relation to sexualities and gender/sex, tell us that the effects and implications of these changes are nuanced and complex, refusing any homogeneity or overarching attribution or narrative.

The term 'rights and equalities' that we used at the outset of the project was also challenged, particularly by those who understand themselves as gender critical. They asserted their support for abortion rights and same-sex marriage, and they argued they also supported 'sex-based' women's rights. Indeed, we were told that the use of the term 'rights and equalities' was seen as 'antagonizing' the very people we sought to speak to. Similarly, the term 'sexual and gender' does not encompass the concerns of those who understand themselves as 'pro-life' in seeking rights and equalities for what they perceive as babies.

In considering who we are seeking to recruit, we are interested in those who have concerns about and/or are opposed to sexualities and/or gender legislation and related social/cultural changes occurring in Canada, the UK and Ireland. In Spring 2021, we revised the research project to reflect what we had learned and to use terms that do not focus on only those who 'oppose' 'equalities and rights', instead we speak of those who are 'concerned about or opposed to legislative, political or social changes in relation to sexualities and sex/gender in the 21st century in Ireland, Canada, and the UK'. A flexible and iterative methodological approach, which is common to many projects, is a key part of the respectful relationalities that we are trying to create. This means that further reconsiderations and adjustments may be needed over the course of the project.

From the outset, we sought to carefully consider the language we used, its various potential interpretations, and the politics of how we deployed certain terms. Respectful relationalities inform not only how we recruit participants, but also what and how we learn about and understand the key issues at hand. In other words, these processes of engagement and discussion about who we are speaking to indicates how people understand their place in the broader sexual and gendered political landscapes, and what it might mean to address social divisions in those landscapes.

Writing respectful relationalities: representing social divisions

Respectful relationalities established throughout the data collection process will also need to be extended to writing up the research (as well as inform the ethos surrounding the establishment of workshops to consider how we might engage difference differently in the latter stages of the project). Relationalities are mutually formative, iterative, and cyclical rather than linear, such that how we will write about them, informs participants' decisions about whether they will be involved in the research to begin with. We decided that because of the fears potential participants communicated to us around how they might be represented, we would report some of our early findings through an initial report released in October 2020 (https://beyondopposition.org/blog/). The initial findings focused on the challenges and complexities associated with speaking to a wide range of people concerned about sexual and gender social changes. The report was written to reflect a key strand of the project ethos around respectful relationalities which emphasizes:

> A key goal is to understand how societal changes are experienced from as diverse a set of perspectives as possible. We work to ensure that we collect people's experiences in as professional an environment as possible. We seek to cultivate respectful engagement across diverse opinions so we can gain a greater understanding of how sexual and gender issues play out in everyday life. ...
>
> We will take time to analyse the data and will look across a range of people to gain an understanding of these experiences and similarities and differences between them. At times, we will use participant's own words to explain our findings and to show how people spoke about their experiences. We may also show how people understand or do things differently. We will not stereotype or demean.

In writing up Beyond Opposition, we will ensure that these are not used to undermine or 'catch out' participants. The project does not seek to 'educate' people to take up a specific position, nor does it intend to change participants minds about their fundamental values on issues of sex, sexualities, and gender. Instead, we seek a way of engaging with difference, differently to address social divisions. As we have seen, this requires new lexicons and respectful modes of engagement in working across difference and with people who are opposed to or concerned about changes in sexualities and genders. It is also not fixed, and how and what we will write, while adhering to the ethos of the project, cannot be anticipated in advance. We will seek ways of reporting and representing participant's experiences of space that do not focus on their positions and ideologies as other work has done, but also understands that these ideologies, views, and opinions are key to how people experience space. In this, we draw on another important aspect of the project ethos: "[participants'] views, values or beliefs are not the focus of the study. Instead, we are interested in everyday experiences; in other words, what happens when people are going about their lives and find that they are confronted with people or situations that challenge their values."

Beyond Opposition does not seek to gather data on ideologies, views, and opinions to create counter arguments, find flaws, or seek to demean participants' stories. The research conceptualizes respectful relationalities as drawing on feminist methods and values that emphasizes story-telling, and participants' narratives as valuable forms of insight created through respectful interactions. The focus on their experiences of space centralizes geography as key framing for the project but geography is also critical for enacting this ethos. Beyond Opposition is exploring how spatial experience has changed because of certain legal/social changes and is seeking to understand participants' spatialities to work out or think through how to engage with difference differently in ways that might address social divisions. This focus on spatialities shifts the emphasis from ideologies, views, and opinions, to understanding how these might be implicated in the uses and experiences of space. Writing on this enables explorations of difference, in part through experiences of alienation and comfort, moving beyond marginalization/privilege binaries.

However, we cannot predict the outcomes of the research or how these discussions will develop. We acknowledge that a valid viewpoint is that this research is, and will always be, inherently problematic. The people who we are speaking to are considered by some to be 'oppressors' and as only enacting their privilege as seen through their ideologies, politics, views, and opinions. This has potential implications for how others reuse our data and findings, even where they do not have access to our raw data, in ways that are beyond the researchers' control and potentially outside of the respectful relationalities we are seeking to create. This, of course, does not mean that others might not use the data they can access to identify and critique those who they view as 'oppressors'. As has long been recognized, readers are relational actors in the creation of texts. This points to the limits of respectful relationalities, that cannot be known or controlled by the team. This is made clear to the participants in the ethos document: 'The research seeks to respectfully investigate difference and we will report the findings carefully. However, we recognise that we cannot control how other people take up our findings and use them. We will work to correct any inaccuracies and present the ethos of respectful engagement with difference.'

This research has, and will be, critiqued for offering a platform to those who work against legislative and cultural changes that affect sexual and gender others. Our ethos of 'respectful engagement with difference' is different to how others seek to engage with these politics and oppositions. Its grounding within geographies and spatialities offers a different focus that is relational, both asking about difficult experiences of space, and also creating a different form of relational space in interview settings.

Seeing research as relational and constituted through power is based in longstanding feminist geographical work (Rose, 1995). We are working with our participants to generate information about their experiences and this power shift is fluid, we need them to be part of the research for the research to 'succeed' in a particular form. As with all research, after a point we control the data, this trust that they have given us means that we need to 'live up' to the ethos of respectful relationalities in all our activities. This is not easy or straightforward work and we will continue to reflect and adapt as the research progresses.

'Does not grant safe passage': doing respectful relationalities[3]

As others who have researched anti-gender and anti-LGBTQ movements have found (Maguire et al, 2019), it is emotionally, politically and ethically difficult work to research those who, at any other point in time, might oppose one's own livelihood, relationships, family, or beliefs. This is perhaps even more difficult when one is asked to engage respectfully without exposing their misunderstandings or identifying flaws in their values, opinions, and ideologies. While as researchers who engage with feminist and queer thinking, we might understand the construction of self-other as the basis of opposition as an illusion of a stable separation/opposition, putting this into practice is difficult (Bhattacharya, 2015). Conducting research in this space and under such conditions requires constant negotiation of ethical issues and personal and political boundaries.

In reconsidering social divisions and engaging with difference differently through respectful relationalities, there are ongoing risks and concerns that require continual engagement. The risks of doing this research are part of our reflexive practices, learned from our training and experiences within feminist research. Feminist research asks us to be cognisant of our positionalities and how they are constructed relationally as the data is being constituted (Rose, 1995). In addition, Beyond Opposition was designed with funded support in mind. The project has funding to support the researchers undertaking the data collection in terms of individual counselling (monthly or as needed), group counselling (twice annually), and it also offers direct supervisory support for the postdoctoral fellows undertaking the research. Yet, this can only ever partially address the ongoing personal challenges of doing this research.

Beyond Opposition, to cite Anzaldúa, 'moves us into unfamiliar territory and does not grant safe passage' (2002, p 3). Our use of respectful relationalities questions personal boundaries (including that of self/other) through reconsidering not only understandings of those who are other to us because they hold very different values and worldviews and who have/do engage in activisms that we experience as oppressive, and our relationships to/with them. In research where the aim is to help those who are marginalized through hetero/homonormative power relations, respectful relationalities can be deeply rewarding in ways that are very different from this research. Those who we speak to can both indicate viewpoints that we would disagree with, and show that they are marginalized in unexpected and upsetting ways. This means that conducting this research is difficult and unsettling as it plays at the edges of the self when it asks both participants and researchers to engage with the other in potentially unfamiliar ways. It asks for both to trust those with whom they might fundamentally disagree and asks researchers to be respectful when encountering people who have views that might oppose their very existence. Moments of connection can be felt as disorientating, confusing, and playing at the boundaries of the self that can 'know' good/bad, 'right/wrong'. The ethos of the research asks the researchers not to deny their political and personal viewpoints, but it does ask the researchers to engage with participants in ways that are not about opposing or debating their views and that are respectful of their stories and narratives. This may be very different to other professional and activist work that we have done and continue to engage in. It operates in contrast to contemporary oppositional politics, social networks, and political affiliations, in asking us to engage with, call out and critique those who we identify/are identified as wrong/dangerous. It is not easy work.

Yet we simultaneously hope that listening to the stories and experiences of 'the other' can also inform how we understand and engage 'the other', to produce less divisive futures. This approach has already led to important intellectual and political insights which contest 'sides' and the notion of radically oppositional 'others' in the field of gender and sexualities. Indeed, as we (Browne and Nash, 2020) have shown, these personal stories have weight, value, and political expediency that need consideration as we interrogate the assumed 'progress' of sexual and gender legislation and wider social changes. In our discussions with those working in community dialogue, those in transitional justice and other forms of engagements between opposing factions, we see resonances and potentials for the Beyond Opposition project that offer exciting directions into the future (Bland, 2002; Turner, 2016; O'Tuama, nd). We are working through how this project may engage with areas such as conflict resolution, community dialogue, and transitional justice (Turner, 2016). This is a significant field where feminist practices and thinking are well developed; this is less the case in terms of using these tools to explore conflicts within feminisms, and around sexual and gender politics (particularly beyond the USA). In the future, we hope to use and further develop tools and methodologies to explore these potentials that might be released in ways that create less polarized worlds. Whether these can be considered feminist activism requires further engagement and consideration, which we welcome.

Conclusions: Queer feminist methodologies of respectful relationalities

In previous research on heteroactivism, we have discussed some of the implications of undertaking research 'on' those who not only occupy different positionalities, but whose activism and ideologies are opposed to our lives, families and relationships (Maguire et al, 2019). Through the Beyond Opposition project, we are operationalizing key feminist research principles by recognizing the relational creation of knowledge, valuing experiential knowledge and participants' narratives in the constitution of that knowledge, and queer contestations of binaries. However, we are doing so by engaging overtly with those who may feel the effects of legislation and social/cultural changes in ways that mean that they do not support it. This requires us to overtly consider relationalities that might in another context be embedded into considerations of power in feminist, queer and ethical research focused on those who are marginalized. Creating an overt ethos of respectful relationalities was needed from the outset of Beyond Opposition to encounter the obvious issue of who the researchers conducting the research 'are' in relation to LGBTQ politics, and those we hoped would participate. This ethos allowed the project to have integrity and participants to have some assurance that the purpose was not to stereotype, degrade, or demean them.

Respectful relationalities names iterative, fluid, and respectful engagements with potential participants who see us, as queer researchers with specific forms of research/politics, as other and potentially dangerous to them. It asks for openness to change and to adapt in relation to what we hear and learn about 'the other'. Our discussions of respectful relationalities drew on our feminist and queer geographies and expanded and contested them. Thus, respectful relationalities are formed in and through feminist engagements with narratives and that respect these as data and recognize their value and import. They are also created through queer methodologies that see binaries and 'sides' are incongruous, fluid, and continually redefined. Our use of respectful relationalities is grounded in geographies where our focus on everyday spatialities that are informed by ideologies, opinions, and views is the object of study. Engagements with working beyond opposition require further considerations in terms of the feminist activist possibilities that seek to work with contemporary social divisions.

Notes

[1] It seeks to move 'Beyond Opposition' in the face of increasing social polarization in the UK, Canada, and Ireland. It considers how recent social and legal changes to sexual and gender legislation and cultures impact different people within these countries. The project initially focused on the experiences of individuals or groups who do not support or are concerned about these changes. For further information on the broader project see www.beyondopposition.org

[2] Participants were initially recruited through contacting key organizations and groups, and the idea was to attend events. However, due to COVID restrictions, the majority of our recruitment has been online and through social media. A full discussion of this is beyond the scope of this chapter, suffice to note that many of the oppositional relations, and movements beyond opposition have played out in these spaces.

[3] Anzaldúa (2002, p 3).

Acknowledgements

This project has received funding from the European Research Council (ERC) under the European Union's Horizon 2020 research and innovation program (grant agreement no 817897). The authors are grateful for the research assistance provides by Dr Laine Zisman Newman and Dr Elizabeth Ablett and the work of Ann-Kathrin Zielger and Sarah Foudy and the project support from Aoife Grant.

References

Abu-Lughod, L. (1990). 'Can There Be a Feminist Ethnography?'. *Women & Performance: A Journal of Feminist Theory* 5(1): 7–27.

Anzaldúa, G. and Keating, A.L. (2002). *This Bridge We Call Home: Radical Visions for Transformation*. London: Routledge.

Bhattacharya, G. (2015). 'Racialized Consciousness and Class Mobilizations'. *Ethnic and Racial Studies* 38(13): 244–50.

Bland, B.L. (2002). 'A tale of Interesting Conversations: Exploring Reconciliation in Northern Ireland'. *Conflict Resolution Quarterly* 19: 321–43.

Bondi, L. (1990). 'Feminism, Postmodernism, and Geography: Space for Women?'. *Antipode* 22: 156–67.

Browne, K. and Bakshi, L. (2013). *Ordinary in Brighton? LGBT, Activisms and the City*. Abingdon: Routledge.

Browne, K. and Nash, C.J. (eds) (2010). *Queer Methods and Methodologies: Intersecting Queer Theories and Social Science Research*. London: Ashgate Publishing.

Browne, K. and Nash, C.J. (2014). 'Resisting LGBT Rights Where "We Have Won": Canada and Great Britain'. *Journal of Human Rights* 13(3): 322–36.

Browne, K. and Nash, C.J. (2017). 'Heteroactivism: Beyond Anti-Gay'. *ACME: An International Journal for Critical Geographies* 16(4): 643–52.

Browne, K., Nash, C.J. and Gorman-Murray, A. (2018). 'Geographies of Heteroactivism: Resisting Sexual Rights in the Reconstitution of Irish Nationhood'. *Transactions of the Institute of British Geographers* 43(4): 526–39.

Collins, P.H. (1990/2000). *Black Feminist Thought: Knowledge, Consciousness, and the Politics of Empowerment*. London: Routledge.

Correa, S., Paternotte, D. and Kuhar, R. (2018). 'The Globalization of Anti-gender Campaigns'. *International Politics and Society*. Available from: www.ips-journal.eu/topics/human-rights/article/show/the-globalisation-of-anti-gender-campaigns-2761/ [Accessed 17 March 2023].

Duggan, L. (2003). *The Twilight of Equality: Neoliberalism, Cultural Politics, and the Attack on Democracy*. New York: Beacon Press.

Glass, C. and Cook, A. (2020). 'Performative Contortions: How White Women and People of Colour Navigate Elite Leadership Roles'. *Gender Work Organ* 27: 1232–52.

Haraway, D. (1988). 'Situated Knowledges: The Science Question in Feminism and the Privilege of Partial Perspective'. *Feminist Studies* 14(3): 575–99.

Keating, A.L. (2013). *Transformation Now! Toward a Post-Oppositional Politics of Change*. Champaign: University of Illinois Press.

Kelly, M. and Gurr, B. (2019). *Feminist Research in Practice: A Primer*. Lanham: Rowman & Littlefield.

Hochschild, A.R. (2016). *Strangers in Their Own Land: Anger and Mourning on the American Right*. New York: New Press.

Maguire, H., McCartan, A., Nash, C.J. and Browne, K. (2019). 'The Enduring Field: Exploring Researcher Emotions in Covert Research with Antagonistic Organisations'. *Area* 51: 299–306.

Nash, C.J. (2010). 'Queer Conversations: Old Time Lesbians, Transmens and the Politics of Queer Research', in K. Browne and C.J. Nash (eds) *Queer Methods and Methodologies: Intersecting Queer Theories and Social Science Research*. London: Ashgate Publishing, pp 129–42.

Nash, C.J. and Browne, K. (2015). 'Best for Society? Transnational Opposition to Sexual and Gender Equalities in Canada and Great Britain'. *Gender, Place & Culture* 22(4): 561–77.

Nash, C.J. and Browne, K. (2019). 'Resisting the Mainstreaming of LGBT Equalities in Canadian and British Schools: Sex Education and Trans School Friends'. *Environment and Planning C* 39(1): 74–93.

Nash, C.J. and Browne, K. (2020) *Heteroactivism: Resisting Lesbian, Gay, Bisexual and Trans Rights and Equalities*. London: Zed Books.

Paternotte, D. and Kuhar, R. (2018). 'Disentangling and Locating the "Global Right": Anti-gender Campaigns in Europe'. *Politics and Governance* 6(3): 6–19.

Puwar, N. (2001). 'The Racialised Somatic Norm and the Senior Civil Service'. *Sociology* 35(3): 651–70.

Rose, G. (1993). *Feminism and Geography: The Limits to Geographical Knowledge*. Cambridge: Polity Press.

Rose, G. (1995). 'Distance, Surface, Elsewhere: A Feminist Critique of the Space of Phallocentric Self/Knowledge'. *Environment and Planning D: Society and Space* 13: 761–81.

Rose, G. (1997). 'Situating Knowledges: Positionality, Reflexivities and Other Tactics'. *Progress in Human Geography* 21(3): 305–20.

Stanley, L. and Wise, S. (1993). *Breaking Out Again Feminist Ontology and Epistemology*. London: Routledge.

Turner, C. (2016). *Violence, Law and the Impossibility of Transitional Justice*. London: Routledge.

Conclusion

Kate Boyer, LaToya E. Eaves, and Jennifer Fluri

Activism is part of feminist geography's foundational mission. As Melissa Wright has noted, a commitment to activism weaves through the sub-discipline, constituting a unifying theme and approach to practice (Wright, 2008). As the authors of this volume have shown, this orientation continues to open new dialogues between academics, practitioners, and activists across different cultural contexts, and topical foci in ways that advance both scholarly work and real-world efforts to fight injustice and re-make the world as a fairer, more equitable and more accepting place. While GeoBrujas' open discussion on the entwined projects of theory and method production in feminist collective spaces toward addressing problems of dispossession and violence, Zaragocin traces out how feminist geography has become part of larger critical praxis in Latin American focusing on decolonialization.

Fluri's chapter reflects on the difficulties of navigating between the production of knowledge and the prodigious task of disseminating knowledge that counters prevailing political discourses in the context of Afghanistan, connecting with Eaves' chapter, which describes Black women's everyday resistance in the United States South over two centuries of movement work. Boyer's chapter mapped the background to understanding efforts to fight back against sexual harassment and other forms of gender violence in the UK, while Fannin's work highlighted the ruthlessness of the state in implementing anti-immigrant policies through the restriction of services to pregnant people, also highlighting the power and potential of *maternal activism* in the form of witnessing and accompaniment of pregnant people to help them get the services they need in hostile environments.

Through his detailed study of the unfolding of the LGBTQI+ rights movement through the 20th and 21st centuries in Czechia, Pitoňák's work reveals the complexities and challenges in this struggle. Finally, Browne and Nash's work challenges feminist geographers and others working for LGBTQI+ rights to 'reach across the aisle' to engage in radical listening with hetero-activists challenging the dialogue-ending tendencies intensified by social media and cancel-culture.

Looking back, the period from when this project began to when it finished was one beset by many challenges. The project got underway more or less at the same time as the COVID-19 pandemic began. This moment has served as a grim backdrop to the work, at times impelling us to dig deep in order to muster the reserves to keep this project going amid the significant challenges a global pandemic has thrown – and continues to throw – at us. In addition, more than one of our authorial team were personally affected by environmental disasters in different parts of the world that have become more commonplace under climate change, and others have been personally affected by humanitarian crises caused by legacies of US and other military interventions. Clearly these are challenges that have touched many lives indeed, and we recognize our relative privilege regarding the resources at our disposal for coping with them.

At the same time, this period has been one bristling with activism, bearing witness to some of the most wide-scale protests in history. Protests against police brutality and systemic racism were held in over 50 countries in response to the murder of George Floyd in Minneapolis (USA) in 2020, demonstrating the global reach and significance of the Black Lives Matter movement and the struggle against anti-Blackness, linking in to Eaves' work. In turn, 2021 saw protests against the restriction of LGBTQI+ rights in Poland (tying in to Pitoňák's work), as well as the coming-together of indigenous women from Canada, Latin America, and beyond to protest for political action on climate justice at the Cop26 meeting and elsewhere, linking into issues covered in the chapters by the GeoBrujas and Zaragocin. Meanwhile the rape and murder of Sarah Everhard by an English Police Officer and murder of London school teacher Sabina Nessa (both in 2021) set off a wave of vigils and protests against the many different kinds of systemic misogyny and violence against women in the UK, ranging from street harassment to entrenched sexism from sport-culture to domestic violence, linking in to Boyer's chapter. Then in 2022, the removal of a constitutional right to abortion access in the US signalled a flurry of activism globally as rights to bodily autonomy and reproductive justice, which links to work by Eaves, Pitoňák, and Browne and Nash. It is a testament to the (global) thirst for gender, racial, environmental, social, and economic justice the extent to which activism has continued and even flourished through COVID times and the many ongoing challenges it has brought.

Clearly, this volume has been necessarily selective. While the research presented here represents an important component of feminist geography's ongoing engagement with activism it is of course only a small part of the story. Given nearly every country on the planet now has some expression of feminist activism, there is no shortage of directions for further work. To give some indicative examples of some of the many types of feminist activisms taking place globally, in Africa such groups as the Pan-African

Human Rights Defenders Network, The Reseau des Femmes Leaders pour le Developpment, Voix des Femmes, the African Women's Development Fund,[1] and others are working collaboratively and from the grassroots level to end gender inequalities and discrimination, and advance women's rights and political representation including ending female genital mutilation (FGM) and gender-based violence across Africa. Meanwhile, in Brazil in recent years collective anger about the retrenchment of women's rights, abortion rights, and society-wide issues of gender-based violence and femicide led to protests so wide-scale they were collectively termed the 'Women's Spring'.[2] Relatedly, protests against Brazilian president Jair Bolsonaro organized under the banner #EleNao/ #NotHim have unfolded in Brazil and beyond in response to his consistently misogynistic and homophobic statements and actions;[3] while, claiming digital and city space, Brazilian feminist activists Juliana de Faria and Panmela Castro have initiated campaigns to end sexual harassment including through the feminist blog OLGA,[4] and used street muralling as means to raise awareness of domestic violence and champion women's empowerment respectively.[5] Additionally in the fall of 2022, the women-led revolution, 'Women, Life, Freedom' in Iran began in response to the murder of Jina Masha Amini in police custody after being arrested by the morality police or allegedly wearing her hijab improperly. While these diverse actions give a taste of range of work being done, they represent just a small fraction of the vast amount of feminist activist work currently taking place.

Before concluding, we would like to trace out how we see the essays herein extend current conceptual work in feminist geography.

Relations between 'bodies' and 'territories'

Building on scholarship in feminist geography on the body as politicized space, these chapters deepen our understanding about how state power is lived through the body in different ways (Fannin, GeoBrujas, Eaves, Zaragocin, Fluri, Pitoňák). They explore how state violence, patriarchy, homophobia, racism, colonialism, extractivism, and other forms of oppression – which the GeoBrujas employ as the useful metaphor of weaving to conceptualize the relations between – manifest at the level of (especially) women's bodies such that, as Eaves puts it, 'the body is a geographic location of struggle' (p 112). In turn, they shine a light on creative strategies for *resisting* state power and dispossession across cultural contexts from Afghanistan, the US, the UK, Central America, and Eastern Europe. Zaragocin's and the GeoBrujas' work did this by describing collaborative work with migrants in Central America in an effort to 'figure out how to legalize themselves' (to paraphrase a participant in Zaragocin's work (p 92)), through strategies of art and popular education workshops; while Eaves' chapter explores how African American women activists have employed literacy programs as a way to empower disenfranchised women of colour in the American South.

In turn, both Pitoňák's and Eaves' chapters highlight how bodies and territories can come together figuratively to resist power by claiming representational space in the city through the form of billboards and parades (in cultural contexts from Czechia and the American South) in efforts to promote causes of LGBTQI+ rights and reproductive justice. Meanwhile both Pitoňák's and Brown and Nash's chapters seek to deepen our understanding of efforts to restrict or retract hard-won rights for those whose sexual or gender identities position them outside the cis-gender heterosexual hegemony. These chapters shine light on some of the drives and tactics of movements seeking to retain (or restore) historical systems of gender power and oppression in relation to homophobia (Pitoňák) and heteroactivism (Browne and Nash), including through international networking with like-minded others across different cultural contexts through social media. Building on this, Brown and Nash's chapter extends understanding about how forging connections across radically different ideological and ethical positions (in this case with those who are effectively 'on the other side' of much feminist and LGBTQI+ activism) can inform practices of community dialogue, transitional justice, and conflict resolution.

We suggest that each of these chapters represents new expressions of foundational feminist work exploring how the personal is political and highlight the importance of making connections in feminist struggles across different geographic (and ideological) territories. They offer useful examples of how to foreground concerns and knowledges of subjects outside global centres of power while putting these concerns in dialogue with those positioned within (different) academic contexts, highlighting how, as Zaragocin puts it: 'knowledge is multidimensional and travels through transcultural subjects' (p 77).

Relations between mobility, security and insecurity

A second set of themes connecting virtually every chapter herein are those of security and precarity (on the move or otherwise); the importance of feeling secure in one's life and fighting for the conditions necessary to live. These concerns come together differently in different chapters: from the importance of feeling safe in a given space, be it from sexual harassment (Boyer), or from punitive state policies (Fannin; GeoBrujas, Zaragocin, Fluri). In this way the edition extends understanding about the politics of gendered movement and violence against women who move, be that in the form of migration or nomadism, or moving around in their daily lives in the city (including workspaces, universities and leisure spaces); as well as efforts to keep women immobile (Boyer, GeoBrujas, Fannin) through different mechanisms of state, symbolic, and bodily control.

At the same time these works also explore these themes in completely different ways. One instance of this is through the purposeful creation of spaces which have a high likelihood of creating feelings of *insecurity* for the researchers in cultivating dialogue with people who disapprove of the researchers' core values (and even their very identities), with the goal of creating bridges across big ideological divides, as in Brown and Nash's chapter. Meanwhile Pitoňák explores the choice on the part of LGBTQI+ individuals to *not* leave a cultural context which denies them certain rights.

Relations between activism, emotions, and care

These chapters also extend understanding about the emotional labour involved in activist research. All of the issues explored herein are ones in which the authors themselves are personally invested (in most cases deeply so). As Fluri rightly notes, the emotional ties and feelings of connection to a particular issue or community provide a powerful motivation for this work. Sometimes this was an explicit part of the narrative, and other times (such as Boyer's motivation to study sexual harassment stemming from years of hearing undergraduate students speak about it) it was tacit. In these chapters we see the result of the feeling of responsibility to use our voices and platforms as academics (such as they are) to try to address these issues and, where possible, make things better for marginalized communities.

Together these narratives explore some of the different relations of care that flow from these emotional ties and sense of responsibility, including between researchers and the communities or groups they research/research with. We see them in Fannin's exploration of the embodied care practice of accompanying refugees to antenatal appoints and births; and in the honouring of Black feminist fore-mothers such as Septima Clark and Anna Julia Cooper as a means of re-casting understandings of the American South in Eaves' work. We see them in the 'mobile caring' practices of migrants taking care of each other on their journeys (GeoBrujas), and through healing practices of collective touch. Meanwhile Browne and Nash push our understandings of radical empathy in feminist geographic practice as a means to resist (increasing) ideological polarization. The emotional investment in Fluri's harrowing narrative of her efforts to help research associates and their families escape Afghanistan is palpable, and explains both the lengths to which she goes with these efforts and her related work of calling out the US government for how badly it has let the Afghan people down. These chapters help us reflect on the need for self-care as researchers in environments that can challenge one's sense of hope and optimism. Browne and Nash's work explicitly discusses the importance of creating structured time space to process research encounters that can be critical of one's own beliefs or identity, while Fluri's, Pitoňák's, the GeoBrujas', and Zaragocin's chapters all highlight the need for such processing – and self-care for ourselves as researchers – in the face of the exhaustion of battling for 'the right to life' in its broadest terms.

The issues that the researchers and activists discussed in these chapters are collectively battling are big and complex. As such, this work will inevitably carry with it its share of disappointments and frustration about what is not yet achieved, or what has been lost. However, we argue that it is precisely because of this that we need to pause and take stock of all that *has* been accomplished: to recognize and honour the collective achievements in order to give us strength to carry on. By way of conclusion, we invoke Amanda Gouw's 2007 reflection on the march that kicked off the 2005 Global Feminist Dialogues conference in 2005, in which she observed that: "While marching, (the) energy made me believe that other political options were indeed possible. The activism embodied in women's bodies and presence in a space that has become characteristic of resistance ... showed that solidarity across difference was possible" (Gouws, 2007, p 5). We hope that this volume helps advances the wide-ranging discussion and understanding of just this kind of energy, and that it might serve as a springboard for further work both within and beyond feminist geography.

Notes

[1] https://africandefenders.org/; https://rflgd.org/; https://www.voixdefemmes.bf/qui-sommes-nous/nos-valeurs/; https://awdf.org/ [Accessed 7 April 2022].
[2] https://www.aljazeera.com/features/2015/12/11/is-a-womens-spring-blossoming-in-brazil [Accessed 7 April 2022].
[3] https://www.reuters.com/article/us-brazil-election-protest/brazilian-women-lead-nationwide-protests-against-far-right-candidate-idUSKCN1M90E5 [Accessed 7 April 2022].
[4] https://www.as-coa.org/speakers/juliana-de-faria [Accessed 7 April 2022].
[5] https://awomensthing.org/blog/panmela-castro-graffiti-artist/ [Accessed 7 April 2022].

References

Gouws, A. (2007). 'Ways of Being: Feminist Activism and Theorizing at the Global Feminist Dialogues in Porte Alegre, Brazil, 2005'. *Journal of International Women's Studies* 8(3): 28–36.

Wright, M. (2008). 'Gender and Geography: Knowledge and Activism Across the Intimately Global'. *Progress in Human Geography* 33(3): 379–86.

Index

References to figures appear in *italic* type. References to endnotes
show both the page number and the note number (52n12).

A

abolition 85
abortion 83–5, 150, 170
accompaniment 145, 146, 156, 157–8
   see also doulas; mother companions
activism 1, 4, 162, 178
   emotional labour of 182–3
   in feminist geography scholarship 5–7, 179–80
   see also feminist activism; heteroactivism;
     LGBT+ activism
Adiv, N. 127
Afghanistan 15–16
   evacuation attempts from 23–7, 28
   gender-based harassment 125
   historical overview of conflict in 16–18
   media attention and academic activism 27–8
   research on gender, geopolitics, and
     economic development 18–23
Afghanistan Adjustment Act 27
Ahemd, S. 124, 132
alcohol 128–9
Altermiradas Viajeras 41–2
Álvarez, S. 58–9
American Rescue Plan of 2021 87
anticolonial thought 33–4
Anzaldúa, G. 173
Association of American Geographers 3
Association of Homosexual Citizens'
   Organisations in the Czech Republic
   (SOHO) 97–8, 99
Australia 125

B

Baker, E. 87, 89
Bártová, D. 97
Bates, L. 127
Belgrade Pride 103
Benard, C. 129
Benda, M. 102
Beyond Opposition 163–5
   diversity of research participants 168–70

   respectful relationalities 165–8
   difficulties of 173–4
   writing up research 170–93
Bhattacharyya, R. 126
Biden, J. 87
Bilić, B. 103
billboards 83–5
biopolitics 150–1
birth activism *see* Maternity Stream, City of
   Sanctuary; Project Mama
birth justice 146, 157
Black feminism 74
   see also women of colour
Black feminist activism 74–6, 82–7
Black feminist activist legacies 78–82, 89–90
Black feminist geographies 76–8
Black geographies 75
Black womanhood 87–9
   see also women of colour
bodily experience 35–6, 37
body mapping 39–40, 46–7
body politics (*corpolitica*) 45, 47, 52n12
body-territory (*cuerpo-territorio*) 57–8, 59, 68,
   69, 70n1, 180–1
   see also territorio-cuerpo-tierra
     (territory-body-earth)
Brands, J. 130
Budapest 102, 103
business corporatism 40

C

Calveiro, P. 44–5
capitalism 34, 36, 38, 49
care 182–3
Carruthers, C. 90
categorization 168–9
Charron, K.M. 73
Chipko movement 38
citizenship 62
Citizenship Schools Program 73–4
City of Sanctuary 152–4, 157
Clark, S. 73–4, 79, 81

INDEX

Cold War 96–102
collaboration 6
collective reflection 66–8, 69
Collins, P. 77
Colls, R. 135
coloniality 51n4
Combahee River Collective (CRC) 76–7, 78
consumption 39–40
Cooper, A.J. 79
corpolitica (body politics) 45, 47, 52n12
COVID-19 pandemic 32, 85, 179
Cracow Equality March 103
Critical Geography Collective of Ecuador 55–6
  feminist geography activist praxis 68–70
    feminization of migration 60–5
    Naporuna river territories 65–8
  feminist geography praxis and activism 56–60
Croatia 104
Crusade for Justice (Wells-Barnett) 81
cuerpo-territorio (body-territory) 57–8, 59, 68, 69, 70n1, 180–1
  see also *territorio-cuerpo-tierra* (territory-body-earth)
Czechia
  anti-gender ideology 106
  history of LGBT+ activism 95–102
  queer geography 111–14
  sexuality in 94–5

D

Daud, M. 16
Davis, A. 77
De Leeuw, S. 5
decolonization 5
Deleuze, G. 126
Diagnostic and Statistical Manual of Mental Disorders (DSM III) 96
dispossession 34
diversity 3–4
  of research participants 168–70
doulas 146, 151–2, 155–6, 158
Dunckel Graglia, A. 126

E

ecofeminism 38
Ecuador see Critical Geography Collective of Ecuador
education 81
  see also Citizenship Schools Program; freedmen's schools; higher education spaces, sexual harassment in
el Colectivo see Critical Geography Collective of Ecuador
embodied knowledges 61, 75, 77
embodiment 57–8
emotional labour 182–3
emotions 47, 60, 69
environmental issues/problems 33–40, 51n5
environmental racism 34

European Union (EU) 102, 104, 147
Evans-Winter, V.E. 74
Everyday Sexism project 127

F

Falanga, G. 59
Federal Writers' Project 78
Feldman, R. 158
femicide violence 43–4
feminism, inclusive and intersectional 3
  see also Black feminism; ecofeminism; translocal feminism
feminist activism 133–4
feminist collectives 57
feminist geography scholarship 1–2
  activism in 5–7, 179–80
  emotional labour in 182–3
feminist political ecology 34
feminization of migration 60–5
field-based research 6
Fileborn, B. 130
Fixmer-Oraiz, N. 150, 151
France 104
Freedmen's schools 80
Freund, K. 96

G

García-Ramón, D. 47
gender 5, 56, 83
gender diverse public 126
gender ideology 105–7
  and ontological (in)security 108–9
  scholarly responses, challenges and opportunities 109–11
  see also Beyond Opposition; heteroactivism
gender mainstreaming 106
gender studies 107
gender violence 41–8, 74
  see also patriarchal violence; sexual harassment; sexual violence
GeoBrujas Collective, Mexico 31–3
  environmental issues 33–40
  gender violence 41–8
  reflections 48–50
geographical imagination 45–6
geopolitics 47
Giddens, A. 109
Gilmore, R.W. 5
globalization 34
gold mining 66–8
Gouw, A. 183
Graff, A. 103, 104, 109
guardia indígenas (indigenous security forces) 66–8

H

Haebaert, R. 47
Haider-Markel, D.P. 107
Hamer, F.L. 77, 81
harassment see sexual harassment

Harvey, D. 45–6
Health Befriending Network 152
healthcare, Hostile Environment policies
    for 145–6, 147–52
    resistance to 152–8
Healthy and Free Tennessee 83–5
    #SMAy campaign 85, *86*
Hesová, Z. 105–6
heteroactivism 105, 162, 163–4
    see also Beyond Opposition
heterosexual adaptation therapies 97
higher education spaces, sexual harassment
    in 131–4, 136
HIV/AIDS pandemic 97, 98
Hollaback project 127
'homeland maternity' 150, 151
homosexuality 95, 96, 97
    see also LGBT+ activism
Hostile Environment policies 145–8
    for pregnancy and birth 148–52
    resistance to 152–8
Hromada, J. 98, 99
Human Machine exercise 43
humanistic geographies 35
Hungary 102, 103
Hyndman, J. 158

I

immigration, Hostile Environment policies
    on 145–8
    pregnancy and birth 148–52
    resistance to 152–8
inclusive and intersectional feminism 3
India 125, 126, 132
Indigenous peoples 65–6, 67–8
indigenous security forces (*guardia
    indígenas*) 66–8
Indigenous women 44, 46
insecurity 182
insider research 4
International Classification of Diseases (ICD) 96
International Security Assistance Force (ISAF) 22
intersectionality 4, 90
Italy 104

J

Javid, S. 148
Jayne, M. 128–9
Jsme Fér (We are fair) 100–1

K

Kaczynski, L. 103, 104
Kelly, A. 80
Kováts 105
Kuby, G. 106
Kwakye, C. 134

L

labels 168–9
lad culture 132–3, 134

Lee, B. 85
Lehr, R. 18, 19
Lewis, R. 133–4
LGBT+ activism
    and gender ideology 105–7
    history of Czech(oslovak) activism 95–102
    and morality politics 107–8
    and ontological (in)security 108–9
    scholarly challenges and
        opportunities 109–11
    transnational opposition to 102–5
    see also heteroactivism; queer geography
LGBTQ+ people 82–3, 130
    share of European populations with
        LGBTQ+ friends/family *115*
Liberty 145, 149
Lima, I. 47
Lincoln, Abraham 79
Loukaitou-Sideris, A. 124
Lubitow, A. 126

M

Mad'arová, Z. 106
Mansfield, B. 132
mapping 66–7
    see also body mapping
Massey, D. 58
maternal mortality 149
Maternity Action 147–8
maternity care *see* pregnancy care, Hostile
    Environment policies for
Maternity Stream, City of Sanctuary 152–4,
    157
Maxová, R. 100–1
May, T. 145
McCutcheon, P. 77
McHale, J. 148
McKittrick, K. 77, 87–9
McTighe 77
#Me Too 135
Meché, B. 77
media attention 27
Mexico *see* GeoBrujas Collective, Mexico
Mexico City 126
Middleton, J. 123
midwives 146, 151–2, 155–6, 158
Migrant Justice 61–5
migrant pedagogy 61
migrant women 60–5, 69
Migrante Universal 61–2
mining 66–8
mobility 123–8
morality politics 107–8
mother companions 154, 156
Mudde, C. 108

N

Nagar, R. 6–7
Naporuna river territories 65–8

INDEX

National Health Service (NHS) 148–9, 150, 153, 157–8
National Science Foundation (NSF) 24, 26
nativism 108
neoliberalism 34
night-time space 128–31
non-binary people 124, 131, 154

O

Ogunbiyi, O. 124
Okamura, T. 101
ontological security 108–9, 158
Oparah, J.C. 146
Ortega-Varcárcel, J. 48
Ortiz, A. 35
Osoria, L.B. 43
Our Streets Now 127

P

Pakistan 17
Participatory Action Research (PAR) 6
participatory mapping 66–7
Paternotte, D. 104, 106
patriarchal power 130
patriarchal violence 62
patriarchy 121, 180
People's Democratic Party of Afghanistan (PDPA) 16
photography 41, 42, 50
place-making 85
Poland 102, 103–4, 106, 108
political ecologies 33, 34
populism 107–8
positionality 3, 6, 77, 94–5, 111–12, 161
power relationships 33–4, 35, 45, 161
  see also patriarchal power
Poznan Equality March 104
Prague Pride 100
Prague Spring 97
precarity 181–2
pregnancy care, Hostile Environment policies for 145–6, 148–52
  resistance to 152–8
pride parades 98, 99, 100, 102–4
Project Mama 154–7
PROUD (Platform for Equality, Recognition and Diversity) 100
psychiatry 96
public transport 126–7

Q

queer geography 111–14
  see also LGBT+ activism
Queer Parade 99
Queer Pride 99

R

race 5, 34, 124
  see also Black feminism; women of colour

racial discrimination 149, 157
racialization 75
racism 40, 62, 122
  environmental 34
racism-sexism 79, 81
radical nurturing 154–7
radical vulnerability 7
Rainbow festival 98
Ransby, B. 89
rape 122, 131
rape culture 132–3
Red Clamor 61–2
Refugee Council 152
Registered Partnership Act, Czechia 98–9
relationalities 161–2, 162–3
  see also respectful relationalities
relationships and sex education 135
reproductive justice 83–5, 151
research spaces 161–2, 163
  respectful relationalities 165–8
researching across difference 165–8
resource extraction 66–8
respect 163
respectful relationalities 165–8
  difficulties of 173–4
  diversity of research participants 168–70
  writing up research 170–93
Revolutionary Association of the Women of Afghanistan (RAWA) 16, 18
Rice, C. 77
right to everyday life 120, 135
Roosevelt, F.D. 78
Royal College of Midwives 149

S

same-sex marriage 100–1, 104–5
same-sex partnerships 98–9
Santos, M. 35
schools see Citizenship Schools Program; freedmen's schools
security 181–2
  see also ontological security
security culture 150
Segato, R. 34, 45
sentipensamiento (thinking-feeling) 41
Serbia 102–3
sexism see racism-sexism
sexology 96, 97
sexual harassment 120–3
  future research 134–5
  in higher education spaces 131–4
  initiatives to combat 135–6
  in night-time space 128–31
  in street-space 123–8
sexual violence 131
  see also gender violence; sexual harassment
sexuality 94–5
  Cold War politics and 96–102

see also Beyond Opposition; gender ideology; LGBT+ activism; queer geography
Shiva, V. 38
sidewalks 124, 127
Simonsen, K. 123–4
situated solidarities 6–7
slave narratives 78–9
Slovakia 106
Slovenia 104
social divisions *see* Beyond Opposition
socio-environmental conflict 51n5
SOHO (Association of Homosexual Citizens' Organisations in the Czech Republic) 97–8, 99
Soja, E. 39, 40
Southern Movement Assembly (SMA) 85–7
The People's Fist 100 Days 87, *88*
Southerners on New Ground (SONG) 82–3
Soviet Union 16–17, 22–3
space 45–6, 52n13, 168
see also higher education spaces, sexual harassment in; night-time space; research spaces
spatial consciousness 45–6
spatial (in)justice 40
state violence 44–5, 180
story-telling 152–3
street harassment 123–8

T

Take Back the Night marches 130–1
Taliban 17, 22, 23
Teatro del Oprimido (Theatre of the Oppressed) 43, 51–2n11
Terra Earth Resources 67–8
territorio-cuerpo-tierra (territory-body-earth) 32, 36, 38
thinking-feeling (*sentipensamiento*) 41
Torres, R.M. 7
trans people 100, 126, 154
transgender public 126
translation 58–9
transloca 58
translocal feminism 59
translocalities 58–9
transnationalization 40
transport 126–7
Trump administration 22
Tuan, Y. 35
Turkey 106

U

Ulloa, A. 34
United Kingdom (UK)
Hostile Environment policies 145–8
for pregnancy and birth 148–52
resistance to 152–8

sexual harassment 120–1, 123, 127, 131, 132, 134, 135–6
United States Agency for International Development (USAID) 19, 20, 21
United States Institute for Peace (USIP) 19
United States (US)
Afghans seeking to resettle in 25, 27
Black feminist activism 74–6, 82–7
Black feminist activist legacies 78–82, 89–90
Black feminist geographies 76–8
Black womanhood 87–9
Citizenship Schools Program 73–4
homosexuality 96
involvement in Afghanistan 16–17, 17–18, 22–3
morality politics 107
security culture 150
sexual harassment 125, 132
universities *see* higher education spaces, sexual harassment in

V

Vary, K. 102
Velvet divorce 98
Velvet Revolution 97
violence 103
see also femicide violence; gender violence; patriarchal violence; sexual violence; state violence
Voice from the South, A (Cooper) 79
Výborný, M. 101

W

walking 123–4
Warsaw Equality Marches 102, 103
water basins 66–8
Wells-Barnett, I. 81
Wesselmann, E. 129
white privilege 124
Wilson, R. 85
Windrush generation 147
Wintr, J. 98
women of colour 83, 122, 124–5, 180
see also Black feminism; Black womanhood
Women With A Vision (WWAV) 77
Women's rights organizations,
Afghanistan 16, 17, 18
limitations 20–2
WPA Slave Narratives 78–9
Wright, M. 178

Y

Ysunza, V. 35, 45, 47, 52n12

Z

Zahradníková, Z. 101
Zaragocín, S. 58, 59

www.ingramcontent.com/pod-product-compliance
Lightning Source LLC
Chambersburg PA
CBHW051546020426

42333CB00016B/2124